D1564952

LIFE FOR DEATH

LIFE FOR DEATH

Michael Mewshaw

Doubleday & Company, Inc., Garden City, New York

Dedicated to
Robert and Barbara Kirby

January 7, 1961

It was one of those mild, windless mornings when the Chesapeake Bay gleams like taut silk and sailboats lie becalmed, their masts and shrouds reflected with barely a ripple on the water. That balmy Saturday broke a skein of raw, wet days and freezing nights which since mid-December had left the narrow roads of Anne Arundel County, Maryland, glazed with ice. Even now, in shady spots, there remained a few patches of dirty snow, but they were melting quickly, giving off a springlike scent of moist earth.

By 10 A.M. the community of Franklin Manor was drenched with sunlight, and the temperature had risen into the fifties. On the enclosed porch off their kitchen, Dallas and Lena Talbert were finishing a late breakfast and gazing out the side window at the bay. The view, changeable according to the season and hour of the day, was one which the Talberts never tired of.

Mornings like this, Dallas reflected that he had been right eleven years ago when he bought a vacation cottage on the waterfront, winterized and expanded it, and moved in to live year-round. At the Department of the Interior in Washington, D.C. where he worked as an industrial auditor, some people said he was crazy to commute eighty miles every day, but he believed it was worth the drive. Although he was only an occasional fisherman, Dallas loved living near the water and he thought his sons, Danny and Chris, were better off here than they would have been in the city. Southern High School was small, friendly, and well staffed, and both the Talbert boys were honor students and eager athletes. Just the night before, Dallas had driven to Upper Marlboro to watch Chris play basketball.

The community, like the school, was white, reasonably affluent, and safe. It wasn't until the 70s, when the roads improved, that bayfront developments like Franklin Manor became far-flung

suburbs of Washington, and the rigid social and political structure of the area started to bend. But in the early 60s much of
Maryland was still as rural—and sometimes as reactionary—as
Mississippi. Although it housed the state capital in Annapolis and
although it was by no means as hostile to change as certain precincts on the Eastern Shore, Anne Arundel County retained
something of the tempo and mentality of the Deep South. Washington was less than thirty miles to the west and Baltimore lay
approximately the same distance to the north, but in the 1964
and 1968 presidential primaries, most voters looked to George
Wallace for political leadership. And Spiro T. Agnew, sounding
considerably more liberal and tolerant than his Democratic oppo-
nent, won the 1966 gubernatorial race.

Franklin Manor, however, could claim with some justification
to be different from most of Anne Arundel County. For one
thing it was wealthier and populated largely by "outsiders, a better class of buyer," as a real estate agent expressed it. Among the
few full-time residents, the majority, like Dallas Talbert, worked
in Washington, Baltimore, or Annapolis. The other houses were
owned by families who moved in for the summer, or drove down
on weekends, so their kids could swim, boat, and fish in the bay.

In the next few days newspapers would refer to Franklin
Manor as "exclusive," "swank," "plush." But considering the horror which had prompted these articles, it is doubtful anybody who
owned property there felt much pride.

As Lena Talbert cleared off the table, Dallas stood up and
stared out the window. While his wife was short and had a pleasant, plump face framed by curls, he was tall, well over six feet,
and had the bearing of a military man. He had been commis-
sioned during World War II and seen action in the South
Pacific. Since then he had put on a few spare pounds around the
middle and his hair, slicked straight back, had thinned a bit, but
he still walked with his shoulders braced.

Yet, despite his often stern expression, he was a friendly man,
interested in all kids, not just his own. So it upset him to see Lee
Dresbach, a fourteen-year-old from the house two doors away,
come racing across the yard. Even at a distance Dallas could tell
something was wrong. Lee's eyes were closed to slits; his face was

twisted and wet with tears. When he reached the back door of the Talbert house, he was sobbing and screaming at the same time. It sounded as if he were saying, "Why'd you tell them? Why'd you tell my mother and father?"

Dallas thought Lee was talking about the watch. Yesterday the boy had been wearing his father's wristwatch and had absent-mindedly left it at the Talberts'. When Dallas found it, he had debated a good long time before calling to let Mr. Dresbach know the watch was safe. Well aware of the man's seismic temper, he suspected Lee's oversight had gotten him into trouble.

It was Lena who understood what Lee was actually saying. "Where's Wayne now?" she asked.

"I don't know. He took the car and drove off."

Suddenly Dallas felt the full weight of the boy's words sink in. Lee hadn't said, "Why'd you tell them?" He was crying, "Wayne killed them! Wayne killed them!"

While Lena took the boy in her arms and tried to calm him, Dallas asked, "Are you sure?"

"Yes, he shot them."

"I'll call the police."

"I already did," Lee said.

"You wait here. I'll go over and see what I can do."

"I'm coming, too," Lena said.

After calling their sons downstairs to stay with Lee, Dallas and Lena left the house and hurried down the gravel road that curved along the shore of the bay. The tide, a barely audible pulse, beat gently against the bulkhead, and the boards, baking in the sun, released the pungent scent of creosote.

The Talberts were moving too fast, were too agitated, to talk. Neither of them knew what to say anyway. They simply couldn't believe what they had heard. Wayne, Lee's fifteen-year-old brother, just couldn't have shot his parents. Of the two boys, he was the gentler, the more even-tempered, the more likable. Although often punished by his father, he retained his good humor, rolling with the punches—quite literally—and joking about his problems, of which he had more than his share.

Mr. Dresbach was an attorney, and the Talberts thought perhaps that explained his strange notions about discipline. Whenever he suspected the boys of misbehavior, he rigorously cross-examined them and, after overruling their excuses and finding them guilty, he laid down "sentences" far out of proportion to their supposed offenses. Frequently they were confined to the house "like prisoners," sometimes for so long they forgot what they were being punished for.

Going up the driveway, moving more slowly now, the Talberts stepped over a puddle of melted ice and passed Mr. Dresbach's pink-and-white Chrysler New Yorker. Mrs. Dresbach's white Chrysler Saratoga was missing. As they approached the door, Lena heard a pitiful moan, a whine of anguish and pain from somewhere inside the house.

Next morning, the Washington *Post* would call the Dresbach home a "showplace." While that description is a piece of journalistic exaggeration, the red brick house is spacious and bright and it has a handsome 180-degree view of the Chesapeake. A cluster of white wrought-iron furniture on the lawn suggested an informal, outdoor life of leisure, but nobody could remember seeing the Dresbachs sitting out front. They had a secluded patio around back.

Judging by the broad, plain facade, one couldn't imagine the curious arrangement of space inside. The house—especially on the second floor—is a warren of small rooms, narrow staircases, crannies, and crawlspaces.

There are two front doors: one opening directly into the south end of the living room; the other, next to the carport, leading into a hallway from which one can proceed into the kitchen or up a half-flight of stairs to Mr. Dresbach's office. The Talberts took the door next to the carport, turned toward the kitchen, and stopped dead. Lena's hand gripped Dallas' arm. He expected her to cry out, but she said nothing and did not turn away. She couldn't. She had never seen anything like this and would never forget it.

Sprawled on the tile floor in front of the stove, Harold Dresbach lay on his right side in a pool of blood. Wearing only a quilted long-sleeved undershirt, he was pathetically small and disheveled, like a rag doll that had been chewed up by a mad dog. He appeared to have been hit by more than a dozen bullets. His jaw was shattered; his chest was perforated in several places; his bare, sinewy shanks and lower back were pocked with bloody dime-size holes.

Unlike his wife, Dallas *had* seen something like this. He had seen it when he was with the Marines on Okinawa. Slipping away from Lena's grasp, he made himself move forward, crouch down, and feel for a heartbeat, a pulse, any vital sign. But Dresbach was cold, already rigid. Dallas wondered how long he had been dead.

When he heard the moan, he feared it was his wife fainting. But she was standing where he had left her, and she was looking toward the living room. Deeper in the house someone was whining, crying out incoherently. It was the same whine they had heard outside. Naturally, they believed—hoped—that Mrs. Dresbach was still alive.

Lena led the way through the dining area, past a potted philodendron speckled with blood, across a carpet splattered with still more blood. When the trail of red drops ended in the living room, they followed the wailing sound to the master bedroom.

Spraddle-legged and naked, Shirley Dresbach lay on her stomach between the closet and the bed, two neat punctures in her back. There was blood on her elbow, a few specks on the soles of her feet, and a gout of it covering her nose and mouth. Her body felt warm when Dallas put his hand to it, but there was no sign of life that he could detect.

The crying and whining came from one of the family dogs, a miniature dachshund named Dede, which kept sniffing at Shirley, skittering away, moaning, then creeping back on its belly.

This was not the first time Dallas had seen his neighbor in the nude and, stunned as he was now, the other occasion came immediately to mind. Once when he had stopped by the Dresbachs on an errand, Shirley had answered the door wearing only an inquisitive expression. This had shocked him so much he had never mentioned it to his wife; he doubted she would have believed him.

Lena didn't seem to believe what she was seeing now. Snatching a blanket off the bed, she covered Shirley, then scooped the dachshund up in her arms, went into the living room, and flopped down in a Barcalounger in front of the fireplace. She was hugging the dog to her chest, as if hoping that would stop her from shaking.

"You go back and see about Lee," she told her husband.

"Not without you."

"I'll stay here and wait for the ambulance."

"Honey, there's nothing you can do for them."

"Yes, there is. I can stay with them until somebody comes."

Lena was a strong, capable woman, not given to hysterics, and Dallas realized she just wanted to be alone. Touching her shoulder, he said, "I'll make sure Lee told the police how to get here."

By the time Dallas returned to his house, Lee had calmed down a bit. Later he began asking, "What's going to happen to me? What's going to happen to me?"

Dallas wished he knew. Danny, Chris, and he tried to reassure Lee and promised they would do all they could to help. But what would happen to Lee? And to Wayne? What had happened in the Dresbach house? And why?

2

Although there is no way of pinning down the time with absolute precision, it appears Wayne must have fled the house before 9 A.M. Shortly after that, Mrs. Jean Taylor, a client and old friend of the Dresbachs, telephoned long-distance from Washington, D.C. and spoke to one of the boys. As Mrs. Taylor told a reporter from the Washington *Post*, "I asked him if his father was in and he said 'no.' He said his mother was out, too . . . I asked when they would be back and he said 'around 10 A.M.'"

Jean Taylor admitted she wasn't sure which boy had answered. Later Wayne swore he talked to no one on the phone that morning and said the call must have come after he left. As he maintained, if he had spoken to Mrs. Taylor, he would have had no reason to deny it.

Approximately forty-five minutes after Mrs. Taylor's call and more than an hour after his parents had been shot, Lee placed a long distance, station to station call, to the home of Tommy and Mary Helen Dunn in East Riverdale, Maryland, a suburb of Washington, D.C. The Dunns' second-oldest son, Mike, a seventeen-year-old high school senior, answered it and simultaneously glanced at the clock on the kitchen wall. It was 9:50 A.M.

Lee asked for Mrs. Dunn, but Mike said she wasn't home.

When Lee then asked to speak to Karen, Mike explained that his mother and father, his sister, Karen, and his younger brother, Kris, had all gone to a junior high school basketball game in Hyattsville, and he had no idea when they would be back. Did Lee want to leave a message?

"No, never mind." Till that moment Lee had been calm, but suddenly there was a quaver in his voice. "I don't want to drag your parents into this."

"Into what?" Mike asked.

"It doesn't matter. It's not your worry."

"Tell me what's wrong."

Now Lee broke into sobs. "Wayne—he shot Mother and Father."

"You're joking."

"No. I swear."

"Are they dead?"

"I don't know."

"What about Wayne—where is he?"

"He took one of the cars and left."

"Call the police. Then get out of the house," Mike said, afraid that Wayne would return and shoot Lee. "Run to the Talberts. I'll get hold of Mom and Dad."

"I don't want to drag you into this," Lee repeated.

"Don't be silly. We'll . . . we'll do something. Just get out of the house."

Shocked as he was by what he had heard, Mike wasn't surprised that Lee had called his parents. The Dunns owned a summer place in Franklin Manor, a few blocks from the Dresbachs, and for almost a year Wayne and Lee had spent most of their spare time—too much time, in Mike's opinion—hanging around Karen. Although they came to flirt and show off, they liked Tommy and Mary Helen, too, and seemed to prefer the Dunns' small cottage to their own house.

With an older brother's proprietary concern for his only sister, Mike felt Karen was too young to date, and he was secretly jealous of the attention his parents paid to the Dresbach boys. Just last night, Tommy and Mary Helen had driven Karen to Upper Marlboro to watch Lee play basketball. Then they had given Lee a ride back to Franklin Manor and hadn't gotten home until after midnight.

But, of course, as he sped off to Hyattsville, Mike had no time to consider his petty resentments. He was too worried what this news would do to his mother and sister.

Tommy, Mary Helen, and Kris had gone to that morning's game less interested in who won than in watching Karen twirl and cartwheel across the glossy gym floor in her burgundy-and-gold uniform. Although somewhat embarrassed about it, she was a cheerleader and liked to have her family there to lend moral support. At thirteen she took things very seriously, had a heightened sense of responsibility, and wouldn't have dreamed of missing a practice or a game.

Quickly locating his parents in the crowd, Mike took Tommy aside first; then they both went back and told Mary Helen. With little or no discussion, they decided they should drive down to Franklin Manor to see what they could do. Only then did they tell Karen and Kris.

Karen, standing on the sideline, abruptly turned her back to the game, hunched her shoulders, and broke into tears. Her friends gathered around her, perplexed, and the coach called a time out. For an instant, the only sound in the gym was that of a young girl weeping. Then Karen dashed from the circle of people, out to the parking lot.

Once they were in the car, Mary Helen, too, started crying. She had a strong, angular face, with high cheekbones and hollows beneath them. But the severity of her features was softened somewhat by deep-set eyes that welled with emotion now, and a lower lip that trembled when she was sad.

"Look, it might not be as bad as it sounds," Tommy said.

"Maybe Lee was kidding," said Kris, who at eleven was the youngest in the family. "You know, just to get us to come down there so they can see Karen."

"Yeah," Tommy said. "Remember the time Wayne swiped my keys?" He repeated the story of a Sunday night when, just as the Dunns were about to leave the cottage, the car keys had disappeared. For hours they searched the house and it wasn't until Tommy went out into the yard with a flashlight to comb every inch of the property that Wayne, grinning, pulled the key ring from his pocket. When the Dunns got furious at him, he sheepishly explained that he had done it because he liked them so much and didn't want them to leave.

But Mary Helen broke in on her husband. "Just pray they're not dead. Pray they'll be all right." And silently she prayed that Mike had misunderstood Lee. If the Dresbachs had been shot—and in her heart Mary Helen had no doubt they had—she desperately hoped Wayne wasn't involved. Yet recalling an evening four months ago, she was filled with dread and regret and realized she should have told somebody what Wayne had said. Now, afraid it was too late, she felt the first faint and awful stirrings of a guilt which was never to leave her.

3

According to the records, Lee called the Edgewater Police Station at 9:58 A.M. The moment the message about the double homicide was relayed over the radio to all patrolling units, Private William Lindsey set out for Franklin Manor. He was driving a 1960 Chevrolet, a low-slung model with a mushy suspension system, and at high speed on the crowned roads of Anne Arundel County, the car had a tendency to pitch like a boat in choppy water. At every bump, the differential scraped sparks from the asphalt.

Although he kept the accelerator to the floor, Officer Lindsey wasn't sure he wanted to be the first one on the scene. He had been a policeman only nine months, had yet to see a dead body, and wondered how he would handle himself. He was relieved, then, when he reached the Dresbach house about 10:20 and saw that two squad cars and an ambulance were already there. Still, his first murder case made a deep impression on him. Unlike his fellow officers whose most vivid memories were of the size and lavishness of the Dresbach house, Lindsey had the clearest recall of details about the initial investigation.

Lena Talbert had let in Lieutenant Ashley Vick, along with several other officers, and when Lindsey arrived, the Seventh Rescue Squad was in the bedroom, futilely administering oxygen to Shirley Dresbach. Because the bullets had been small caliber, there wasn't as much blood as he had expected and the bodies weren't as torn up as he had feared. But he was surprised to find that Shirley was nude.

Harold Dresbach was still sprawled on the kitchen floor. The rescue squad had checked him first and found there was nothing they could do. Officer Lindsey noticed several paper bags leaning against a cabinet not far from the body. The bags were full of unopened liquor bottles. It looked as if somebody had been planning a big party.

Then Officer Owen Dove came in with his camera to photograph the bodies, the blood trail on the carpet, and the layout of the house. Lindsey was sent to fetch some chalk and when he got back, he outlined the bodies and circled some bullet holes in a closet door, the hall mirror, and down low, about six inches above the floor, on a lazy susan in the kitchen. He felt much steadier once he was working.

By now the house was crowded and bustling with noise and confusion. Dr. Wilbur Smith showed up, pronounced the Dresbachs dead, and went over to the Talberts to make sure Lee was all right. As Dr. Smith left, Captain Elmer Hagner arrived with Dr. Elmer Linhardt, the County Medical Examiner. After stating his opinion that the cause of death was multiple gunshot wounds, Dr. Linhardt ordered that both bodies be transported to the Baltimore City Morgue for autopsies.

Moving over the carpet in a ponderous crouch, Lieutenant Vick collected expended cartridges, several of which were scattered between a green armchair and the television set in the living room. He also picked up a shell in the kitchen, more than twenty feet from the television. Altogether he found five empty shells—which was strange since, judging by the Dresbachs' wounds, many more shots had been fired.

In the hallway outside the master bedroom, just off the living room, a table stood beneath the shattered mirror. On it Lieutenant Vick discovered a large bullet fragment beside a box of Polaroid film. After Owen Dove snapped a picture of the table, Ashley Vick put the bullet fragment into an envelope. He had no reason to think that the Polaroid film might be important.

Outside the Dresbach house there had developed what Officer Lindsey would describe as "the usual mob scene." Neighbors, kids,

newspaper and TV reporters, and even a few off-duty cops had
congregated on the front lawn. Some of them climbed up on
the wrought-iron chairs and tried to look in the picture windows.
The reporters were clamoring at the police, insisting they should
be allowed in before the bodies were brought out. But Captain
Hagner, "a real pro," in Lindsey's opinion, told them no and soon
had the situation thoroughly in hand. He would answer no
questions, he announced. He had come to investigate a crime, not
to hold a press conference.

Hagner was a man of considerable professional integrity, and
he had a talent for dealing with the public. Later he was elected
to the Maryland state legislature. But that afternoon he released a
statement about the killings before he had the results of the autopsies. As newspapers reported it, Mr. and Mrs. Dresbach had
both been shot in the back. Mr. Dresbach was said to have been
wearing pajamas. There was no mention of how Mrs. Dresbach
was dressed.

4

Maryland State Trooper Joseph Grzesiak, operating out of the
Annapolis post, was patrolling in his squad car when he got word
of the double homicide in Franklin Manor. The dispatcher advised him to head south and stay on the lookout for a white 1958
Chrysler.

As Grzesiak approached the intersection of Routes 4 and 2,
he spotted a car of this description parked at Thomas Moreland's
Sinclair station. Taking down the license number as he passed, he
contacted the post for a registration check, and when the tags
turned up under Shirley Dresbach's name, the trooper circled
back and stopped a short distance from the station.

There was no one in the Chrysler, no one outside around the
gas pumps. It was the sort of situation which, though full of risks,
demanded a quick decision. The suspect was believed to be
armed. For all Grzesiak knew, Wayne Dresbach was in there robbing the owner. Or worse. Yet if he rushed into the store to make
the arrest, the boy might panic and a lot of people could be hurt.
Grzesiak decided to wait.

A minute went by. Then another. It occurred to Grzesiak that the Chrysler might have been abandoned—in which case he was wasting time. But then the door to the store opened and three boys stepped out.

The trooper strained forward. He had no information about possible accomplices, and these kids didn't look like killers. One of them, the smallest fellow, had short hair full of cowlicks and didn't appear to be older than twelve or thirteen.

Swigging at bottles of soda pop and chewing bubble gum, the boys crossed the parking lot. They could have passed the Chrysler and sauntered on up the road toward Southern High School. But one kid slid behind the steering wheel, while the other two went around to the passenger side and climbed into the front seat with him.

Grzesiak notified the post that he was going to pick them up.

The instant the Chrysler started, Grzesiak swerved around in front of it and scrambled out of the squad car with his revolver drawn. Yanking open the door of the Chrysler, he grabbed the driver.

"Are you Wayne Dresbach?"

"No. Him." Frightened, the fellow could barely speak. He pointed to the small baby-faced kid with the spiky crewcut.

"Everybody freeze right where you are. Put your hands up on the dashboard." As he shouted orders, Grzesiak eased his way around the car, aiming over the hood at the trio in the front seat who were nervously jawing at their gum. He opened the other door and told Wayne to get out.

"Now grab the roof and spread 'em," Grzesiak demanded.

"What?"

The trooper turned him toward the Chrysler. "Lean your hands on the side there. Now spread your legs." As he patted Wayne down, he kept an eye on the other boys.

"What have you been doing this morning?" Grzesiak asked.

Immediately Wayne admitted, "I shot my parents." There was no expression on his face, no emotion in his voice.

"Where'd these guys come from?"

"They're friends. I saw them up at school and gave them a ride."

The boys, Denny Zang and Cub Scotten, quickly confirmed this and claimed they knew nothing about the murders.

"Okay, climb in the squad car," Grzesiak told Wayne. Once they were in it, he was unnerved as much by the boy's apparent indifference as by the enormity of his crime. "Why'd you do it?"

"Well, they were hollering at me."

"What did you use?"

"A twenty-two."

"Where's it at?"

"In the Chrysler. Under the front seat."

Grzesiak got the rifle, opened the bolt wide enough to see it was loaded, then put it into the trunk of his car. After ordering the two boys to follow him in the Chrysler, he set off for the Edgewater Station, calling ahead that he had apprehended the suspect and was bringing him in.

5

By the time the Dunns reached Franklin Manor, Mary Helen and Karen had been crying for more than an hour and the news that the Dresbachs were dead stunned them into silence, numbed them. There was nothing to do now except trudge up the gravel road to the Talberts' house, try to console Lee, and learn what had happened.

The Talberts had managed to piece together a sketchy outline of the story. Apparently Wayne had come home from last night's basketball game long after Lee. When his parents reprimanded him for being late, he tried to explain, but they wouldn't listen to his excuse. Then this morning he waited for them to wake up and shot them as they stepped out of the bedroom.

"The awful thing is," Dallas Talbert said, "I saw Wayne at the game. But I never thought to ask if he needed a ride. That way he wouldn't have been late."

"We did ask him," wailed Mary Helen. "We were bringing Lee home, and there was plenty of room for him. But he said he'd rather take the bus."

When word came that Wayne had been captured, the Dunns and the Talberts agreed that someone should hurry to Edgewater and stand by the boy. The Dunns volunteered to go. As Mary Helen saw it, much as they were concerned about Lee, he had the Talberts to look after him. She felt Wayne should have somebody—some friend—with him, too. No matter what he had done —and at that point they weren't sure of anything—they figured he must have been going through hell.

Edgewater is a police substation, located near South River on a road that leads to several Chesapeake Bay resorts. Built of discolored bricks, it resembles a once-successful business establishment—a discount furniture outlet, perhaps—that has fallen on hard times.

When the Dunns arrived around noon, they left their children in the car, and Tommy and Mary Helen went in and asked to see Wayne.

"Who are you?" the duty officer at the front desk wanted to know.

Tommy told him their names.

"I mean, what are you to the boy?"

"Neighbors. Close friends."

"Sorry. He can't see anybody except his family."

"His parents are . . . dead," Mary Helen said.

"I know that, ma'am."

"Well, he doesn't have anybody else except a younger brother."

"That's the rule. Any relatives ask to see him, we'll let them in."

"They're somewhere out west. Kansas, I think."

"Sorry."

"They may not get here for days. You can't just hold him in isolation," Mary Helen said, growing angry.

"He's not in isolation."

"Then where is he?"

"I imagine right now he's being questioned."

"Does he have a lawyer?"

"Ma'am, like I said, unless he's some kin to you, I can't give out any information."

"We'd like to speak to your superior," Tommy said, trying to keep his voice level, polite.

Glad to get this problem and these two people off his hands, the man called a higher-ranking officer who repeated to the Dunns what they had just been told. Unless they were relatives, he couldn't let them see Wayne. As for a lawyer, the boy could have one whenever he wanted; he had been advised of his rights.

"But he's a baby," Mary Helen said. "He doesn't know enough to ask for a lawyer. You're taking advantage of a kid."

"He's old enough to have killed two people this morning."

"You don't know that!" Tommy snapped. "He hasn't been convicted of anything."

The officer said nothing.

"All right, what's his bail?" Mary Helen asked. "I'll post bond for him." It was a bravura gesture; the Dunns didn't have more than a few hundred dollars in the bank. But Mary Helen figured she could write a check and the police wouldn't try to cash it before Monday morning. The important point was to get Wayne out of jail so they could talk to him, find out the truth, and help him.

But the officer explained that in Maryland (in 1961) no bail was possible in murder cases.

"Is that what he's charged with? Murder? How can that be? He's a juvenile."

"I didn't say he was charged with anything. I'm just telling you there are two people dead and we're holding him till we get the story straight. Soon as we finish our investigation, it's up to the judge to decide whether he's juvenile or not."

"I hope you're going to look into his family life," Mary Helen said. "I'm sure there's a reason for what he did. Look, I know some things that might help you."

Wearily, the officer assured her they would look into everything. At their insistence, he took their names, address, and telephone number and said somebody would be in touch with them.

On the ride home, the Dunn family remained silent, as if transfixed by the dull groan of their old Buick's Dynaflow engine. Mike thought there should have been something to say, some dramatic gesture he should have made. Instead, he stared out the window at the leafless, wintry landscape. His eyes stung, but he didn't cry. He couldn't.

He knew this feeling from two summers ago, when a hysterical woman had appeared on their doorstep in East Riverdale and shrieked that her little boy had fallen into a nearby creek. Mike and his mother had thought the woman mad. The creek was no more than six inches deep. Why hadn't she reached in and grabbed him? Why had she wasted time coming to call them?

But they went with her and only as they stood on the bank of the stream did they discover that the water had turned a thick chocolate color from mud stirred up by a recent storm. Sticks and leaves floated sluggishly on the surface. The woman pointed, said, "There. He's down there," and Mike had waded in.

The first step took him up to his ankles, just as he had expected. But at the next step it was as if a trapdoor had opened under him. Down and down he sank, floundering, choking on silt. He never did touch bottom. Flailing his arms, he fought his way to the surface, crawled ashore, and crouched there in fear and shame.

He refused to go back into the water. He knew it was just a deep pool left by the storm. He was a good swimmer and knew he wouldn't drown. But suddenly he was panic-stricken at the thought of finding—of touching and grappling with—the clay-cold body of the little boy who he was now certain lay on the muddy bottom.

Minutes later, the rescue squad arrived and pumped the pond dry. The body, stiff and blue, came up spinning slowly, looking like a gigged frog. One man tried mouth-to-mouth resuscitation, but it was no use.

Mike had wanted to cry then, but couldn't. It had all happened too fast for him to comprehend.

He felt the same way now. He hadn't seen the Dresbachs' bodies. He had spoken just briefly to Lee, and not at all to Wayne. Yet there was no mistaking his feeling that something desperately important had happened, something he was inadequate to understand, and he could only sit here, realizing he had fallen again over the edge of the familiar into murky waters which stung his eyes with grit.

Finally Mary Helen broke the silence, echoing what Dallas Talbert had said an hour earlier. "If only Wayne had let us drive him home, none of this would have happened. The boys would have gotten back at the same time, and his parents wouldn't have been angry. Or if we hadn't given Lee a ride, he wouldn't have been home so much earlier than Wayne. Or if . . ."

"Don't, Mom," Karen said. "You make it sound like your fault."

"I feel it is." For years afterward, she would continue to believe this and play the same self-punishing game. If that evening in September she had only understood what Wayne was saying, and had warned the Dresbachs. Or if she had been able to break through to the boy, perhaps he would have confided more fully in her. Or if . . .

"What would you have done," Mike asked, "if they had let you see Wayne? What would you have said to him?"

"I don't know." Mary Helen shook her head, fighting the tears that had pooled in her eyes. "I guess I wouldn't have known what to say. I guess I would just have put my arms around him and held him. To let him know I still care about him."

She couldn't stem the tears any longer. They spilled over, streaming down her face, and she started to cry again. She couldn't help it, for she realized how far beyond her reach Wayne was now, and she feared they would put him in a place where no one could ever touch him.

6

Late that afternoon, Father Paul Dawson had finished one pastoral home visit and was on his way to another when he switched on the car radio to listen to the news. Short, slender, and intense, Father Dawson wasn't quite thirty, and he looked ten years younger. A graduate of General Theological Seminary in New York City, he had only recently been ordained; St. John's Episcopal Church in Shady Side was his first assignment as a priest. Yet in spite of his boyish appearance and his implacable earnestness, he was not naïve. He was a married man, a father, and he characterized himself as "a cynic," expecting the worst, but willing to believe the best about people.

A native of Baltimore, he knew, for instance, that these beach communities on the Chesapeake Bay were not at all as idyllic as some outsiders seemed to believe. For the true natives—the crusty, laconic oystermen, fishermen, and crabbers—times had always been hard. Liquor, sex, and fighting were among their few escapes from day to day drudgery. As for the newcomers, many of them had serious personal problems and, anxious to find a hiding place, they had left the city and driven to the end of the road, dragging trouble with them.

In Paul Dawson's opinion, however, there was no hiding place anywhere. His own father had been a Methodist minister, and although he was raised in a parsonage, Father Dawson soon learned that the cloth and collar, far from shielding a man, left him vulnerable, invited complications and responsibilities which he could not shirk. In his sermons he spoke often of the necessity of confronting the unexpected, life's dark side, the irrational element which made civilization so fragile and salvation so difficult.

Yet that day in January, when he heard the Dresbachs were dead and Wayne, their fifteen-year-old son, was being held for murder, Father Dawson reacted in disbelief. He couldn't say he knew the family well; they had been attending services at St. John's for only the past six or seven weeks. But he had been impressed by the politeness and exemplary manners of both boys.

There was one thing, though, that had impressed him even more. One day he had made an impromptu call at the Dresbach house and, finding Shirley there alone, he had had a most peculiar encounter. He knew now he should have recognized something was wrong.

Badly shaken, he drove to Edgewater, introduced himself as Wayne's priest, and asked to see him. Perhaps the police had reconsidered their hard-line position after their argument with the Dunns. Or maybe they had gotten what they wanted from Wayne and now didn't care whether he had a visitor. They showed Father Dawson to a dingy retaining room and left him there a moment to ponder what he should say. Nothing in his brief ministry, nothing in his entire experience, had prepared him for this.

And nothing could have prepared him for what he saw when the police led in Wayne. If Father Dawson was shaken, the boy looked shattered. Disoriented, unsteady on his feet, he was trembling and stared out through glazed, rheumy eyes. Father Dawson would never understand how the police could characterize him as "outwardly calm."

Wayne sat down, and the police left them alone. The boy had never been effusive, Father Dawson recalled, and when forced to talk, he was invariably monosyllabic and inarticulate. Now he was worse than that—almost mute. Every time he spoke, he cringed as if his garbled words were a reminder of some physical affliction. In answer to the priest's questions, he said he didn't know how or why it had happened; he was sorry it had; he had sure goofed up bad this time.

Father Dawson didn't believe he was doing much better than the boy at making sense of things and as he groped for a way to get through to him, he found himself paraphrasing scriptures, telling the story of the prodigal son. When there was no response from Wayne, the priest said surely he remembered the parable of the man who had left home, lived a decadent life, committed every conceivable sin, and touched absolute bottom. But when he repented, even he had been forgiven. No crime exceeded Christ's capacity for mercy.

Wayne shook his head; he'd never heard the story before and didn't appear to understand it now. Father Dawson decided the boy was in shock. Every Christian had heard of the prodigal son. Hadn't Mrs. Dresbach said the family was Episcopalian?

Despairing of any other contact, Father Dawson put a hand on Wayne's shoulder. It was a tenuous link, he knew, but better than none; so the sandy-haired young priest and the fifteen-year-old accused murderer sat there saying little, yet somehow resonating at the level of their mutual need.

Later, on his way home, it occurred to Paul Dawson that he hadn't asked the police anything about Wayne's legal situation. What was he charged with? Did he have a lawyer? Where would he be sent? But, like so many people, he assumed that the Dresbach family would look after these matters and, since the boy was fifteen, he thought Wayne would be held in a juvenile detention center.

What Father Dawson didn't realize was that although Anne Arundel County had a juvenile bureau, there were no holding facilities for underage offenders. And in many ways it was already too late to hire a lawyer.

7

It had been nearly noon when State Trooper Joseph Grzesiak reached the Edgewater Station. He took his prisoner upstairs to the detective room and turned Wayne and the .22 rifle over to Ashley Vick, who had just returned from the scene of the murders. Vick removed five rounds of live ammunition from the rifle, then started the interrogation.

At first there was only one other person present: a secretary, Mrs. Lamm. According to subsequent testimony, Lieutenant Vick offered no inducements and made no threats. When he advised Wayne that he could have an attorney anytime he wanted, the boy simply shrugged his shoulders.

After a few preliminary inquiries concerning name, age, and address, Lieutenant Vick got to the point.

Q. Now Wayne did anything unusual happen in your home this morning?
A. Yes, I shot my mother and father.
Q. Start at the beginning and tell me just what happened.
A. I went to the basketball game between Frederick Sasscer and Southern High School last night which was Friday night and I got home about 11:45 P.M. and my Mother and father was argueing [sic] with me about being late. I told them goodnight and I went to bed. I got up this morning about 9:00 A.M. went to the bathroom to get a drink of water and then I went to the office and got a 22 caliber automatic rifle and went back through the catwalk to my room then I went downstairs when I heard them moving around downstairs. I went to the living room and stood behind the television so that I would not be seen easily and waited for my father to come out of the bedroom. I waited for about two or three minutes and my father came out of the bedroom and started towards the kitchen, as he got about five feet from the kitchen door I shot him in the back. I'm not sure how many times but I think I shot him about four times. He hollered, "Shirley" and my mother came out of the bedroom. I moved out to the middle of the living [room] and while she was

standing about at the foot of the steps I shot her about three times. I think the bullets hit her in the front chest and shoulder. She, Mother, ran back in the bedroom downstairs. I then went to the bathroom downstairs and got a Blue towel and wiped up the floor in the hallway, then threw the towel in the bathtub downstairs. Then I went upstairs and got dressed and came back downstairs and looked to see if the car keys were on the table and they weren't so I took the gun and put it in the car and the keys weren't in the car so I looked at fathers [sic] car and his keys were in the car and I knew that he had a key on his ring to fit mothers [sic] car so I took them and got mothers [sic] car and left and went to Southern High School by Deale way. When I got to Southern High School I went inside and they were playing basketball. Denny Zang, Covington Scotten and myself went up to Moreland's gas station to get something to eat and that is where I was picked up.

Q. Where was your brother Lee when the shooting occurred?
A. In the kitchen.
Q. What did he say?
A. He yelled stop it and he came out of the kitchen just as I finished shooting mom and hit me on the arm and he ran upstairs and in his room.
Q. Did he know what you were going to do?
A. No.
Q. When did you first plan to shoot your mother and father?
A. I had planned it before but I never did it, then last night I made up my mind that I was going to do it.
Q. When did you load the gun?
A. I already had some in it and I put four more in it this morning.
Q. How many does it hold?
A. About 15 long, which was in the gun.
Q. I show you a 22 cal. rifle and ask you if this is the rifle you used to shoot your mother and father with. Model No. 550-1 Remington Automatic.
A. Yes.
Q. When the rifle was recovered from you it had only five

rounds of live ammunition in [it]. What happened to the rest of the ammunition?

A. I shot the rest of them at my mother and father. I don't know exactly how many I shot at each.

Q. Can you give me any reason for shooting your mother and father?

A. Only that they were yelling at me.

Q. Have you ever been in trouble before?

A. Yes sir.

Q. For what?

A. Running away and stealing guns.

Q. What happened that time?

A. I talked to Lt. Smith first and then a couple weeks later my mother and father took me in to talk to Mr. Ogle of the Juvenile Probation department and they decided to drop the whole thing.

Q. Is there anything else that you wish to tell us about this case?

A. I can't think of anything.

Q. You have read the above statement are they your answers and are they true and correct to the best of your knowledge?

A. Yes.

It is worth noting that these questions and answers were not tape-recorded and although the secretary, Mrs. Lamm, was present, Lieutenant Vick typed the entire statement himself. Describing the process later under oath, he said, "I type the question and ask it to him and then type the answer after he answers." As for the long response which followed "Start from the beginning and tell me just what happened," Vick said, "As he began to talk, I would type and tell him to stop. After I caught up, then he would make other statements which I would write in there."

No doubt the method in which the statement was transcribed provides a partial explanation for its sometimes stilted, sometimes staccato, sometimes rambling and run-on quality. Still there is something troubling about its tone. In places it does not sound like a fifteen-year-old boy. Or rather it sounds like a boy mechanically repeating phrases that may have been suggested to him. And it is hard to believe he so casually accepted the blame without saying anything to mitigate his guilt or explain his motives.

When asked in court to characterize Wayne's demeanor during the confession, Vick testified, "He was calm and unemotional completely through . . . as we got down to the immediate investigation he talked very straight forward and was very unemotional."

If Wayne's calmness or anything else roused Vick's suspicions, he never said so. But during the interrogation, Lieutenant Lloyd Smith, director of the Juvenile Bureau, came into the office and was struck by the strangeness of the proceedings. He had dealt with this boy before, a few months back when he ran away from home and had supposedly stolen his father's guns. As it turned out, he had taken and sold his own gun, and Lieutenant Smith, though perplexed by that incident, had decided Wayne was not a delinquent. He certainly had shown no signs of being a potential killer.

As he listened to Wayne now, Lieutenant Smith was astounded at how detached and careless he was. During his decades on the police force, Smith had heard a lot of criminals confess their guilt—but always with qualifications, excuses, lame attempts to explain. This boy, however, sounded eager to accept all the blame and to put himself in the worst possible light. Whatever the degree of his culpability, it seemed to Smith that Wayne was trying to protect someone.

After signing the confession as a witness, Lieutenant Smith left the station for Franklin Manor to start his own investigation. Ultimately it would focus as much on Harold and Shirley Dresbach as it would on Wayne and it would prove to be the most confusing, frustrating, and infuriating experience of his career.

8

That same afternoon, Lee arrived at the Edgewater Station. Wayne was never told of this, for his younger brother had not come to visit him, but to give a statement.

Lieutenant Vick, working this time with Captain Elmer Hagner, conducted the interrogation. Although the information never emerged at the trial, it seems that Wayne was not the only one who impressed people as being calm and unemotional. Many years afterward, Hagner recalled that Lee, like his brother, had appeared to be in complete control of himself.

After the preliminaries, Lee was asked:

Q. Were you present when your mother and father was [sic] shot this morning?
A. Yes sir.
Q. Tell us just what happened?
A. I was downstairs and my brother came downstairs and said that he was going to shoot my mother and father but I didn't believe him. I was sitting at the table when I heard the shots[.] I looked up and saw my father crawling in the kitchen[.] He had screamed Mother . . . I got to the door leading into the living room and told my brother to stop and went back to help my father[.] While I was in the living room I hit my brother. I never did see my mother. Then my brother went upstairs and I went up behind him and then he got dressed and left in the car and I called the police. Then I went over to the Talberts.
Q. How many shots did you hear?
A. I couldn't be sure but I think it was about eight.
Q. Is there anything else that you wish to tell us about this case?
A. No.
Q. You have read the above statement[.] Are they your answers and are they true and correct to the best of your knowledge?
A. Yes.

Interestingly, Lee wasn't any more expansive or forthcoming with details than Wayne had been. Perhaps the police simply didn't ask the right questions or enough questions. They certainly made no recorded effort to correlate Wayne's confession with Lee's deposition, and it is puzzling that Vick, who interrogated both boys, did not spot discrepancies in their versions of the killings.

For example, Wayne had claimed that Lee hit him, then fled upstairs. But Lee stated that Wayne went upstairs first, and for some reason, he ran up after him. Neither mentioned what—if anything—happened while they were upstairs or how much time they spent there.

More importantly, Wayne swore that Lee did not know that he intended to kill his parents. Yet Lee admitted that Wayne had told him of his intentions beforehand. Although Lee said he hadn't believed his brother, he didn't explain why, and apparently the officers didn't ask him to.

Furthermore, Wayne, in response to Vick's questioning, had described *when* he had loaded the rifle. Presumably Vick wanted to establish that the boy had had a plan and knew precisely what he was doing. Since Wayne took the time to load the .22, one can assume—at least, Vick and a jury might assume—that there had been premeditation, and thus this was murder in the first degree.

But it appears not to have occurred to Vick to ask *where* Wayne had loaded the rifle. Perhaps, having made his search of the Dresbach house, the lieutenant already knew that the ammunition was kept in the kitchen cabinet. This would suggest that, in addition to telling his brother what he intended to do, Wayne had loaded the rifle in front of Lee.

It is possible that in unrecorded conversation Captain Hagner and Lieutenant Vick pressed Lee and satisfied themselves that they had the full story. But, if so, this was never brought out at the trial and, when interviewed years later, neither man recalled that there had been any inconsistencies or conflicts in the original statements. Hagner did concede, however, that had Lee been older, he would probably have come under closer and harder questioning. But Lee was fourteen, and everybody wanted to protect him from further trauma. After he gave his deposition, he was driven back to the Talberts' house.

Wayne, who was eleven months older than Lee, was clapped into handcuffs and leg irons and driven from the Edgewater Station to Spring Grove State Hospital in Catonsville, outside of Baltimore.

On the way there, the police had to stop in Severna Park at the home of Judge Benjamin Michaelson. Because it was a Saturday, there had been no one at the courthouse to authorize this transfer. According to Wayne, the police led him into the house, still manacled hand and foot, and the judge seemed irritated by the intrusion upon his privacy. After signing the transfer papers, he spoke to the boy, who concluded from his questions that Michaelson knew his parents. The judge said the Dresbachs were good people, and asked Wayne why he had killed them. Wayne said he didn't know.

9

Sunday morning, January 8, 1961, newspapers as far west as Kansas carried accounts of the Dresbach murders, and in each one Harold and Shirley Dresbach were described as "socially and politically prominent." A native of Nickerson, Kansas, Mr. Dresbach, age forty-seven, had finished Hutchinson Junior College, then moved east to Washington, D.C., where he worked his way through law school. After graduation he went into private practice, specializing in divorce cases, but he also took an active role in civic affairs. A member of the Elks, the Lions, the Prince Georges County Chamber of Commerce, and the County Council of Democratic Clubs, he twice made unsuccessful runs for a seat in the Maryland General Assembly.

Mrs. Dresbach, age forty-six, hailed from Elk City and was the niece of Harry Woodring, who had been Governor of Kansas from 1931 to 1933, then Secretary of War during the early years of the Roosevelt administration. Mrs. Dresbach had served as a Cub Scout den mother, president of the Study Club of Lanham, and treasurer of the Prince Georges County Federation of Women's Clubs. She had, however, reduced her outside activities after the family moved to Franklin Manor in 1958.

Nathaniel Blaustein, a lawyer who shared offices with Dresbach in Washington, characterized him as an "active, healthy man," not given to excess worrying. Mrs. Dresbach, Blaustein said, was "quiet, but very pleasant."

Hearing of the Dresbachs' deaths, neighbors, family friends, and business associates professed "amazement," "shock," "disbelief." They had noticed "nothing about the boy [Wayne] which could have foretold yesterday morning's shocking eruption." Colonel Philip Boone, a retired Army officer who lived near the Dresbachs, said Wayne "seemed such a cheerful, happy kid, a real outgoing boy who seemed never at a loss for something to talk about."

Others told newspaper reporters that the Dresbachs were "a happy, normal family" that enjoyed picnicking and swimming. Harold and Shirley were described as doting parents who "took a great interest in their children and 'gave them everything they wanted' . . . the two Dresbach boys seemed quite close. Of the two, Wayne appeared the more introspective, but both joined wholeheartedly in a variety of neighborhood projects, both civic and recreational. They trimmed lawns, made themselves available for errands, and enjoyed reputations for politeness and good conduct."

"Wayne," neighbors told the Washington *Post*, "appeared especially close to his father, who was an avid boating enthusiast. Together, father and son motored out in the pre-dawn during duck season to lay in wait for the birds with shotguns in the blinds that dot the bay.

"The Chesapeake was their front yard. On the porch of the Dresbach home . . . the lawyer had installed a powerful floodlight and in its beams he and his boys often swam, fished, or . . . water-skied in the evening. Mrs. Dresbach flicked it to call them from the water for meals."

Just recently, at Christmas, Mrs. Dresbach and the two boys had worked at St. John's Episcopal Church in Shady Side, making candles and wrapping presents for the underprivileged.

In these early reports there were only a few faint shadows to mar the otherwise idyllic portrait of familial love and tranquillity.

To the surprise of some people in the community, it was revealed that the boys were not the Dresbachs' children. But even this appeared to put Harold and Shirley in a glowing light. Unable to have children of their own, they had adopted Lee and Wayne and, according to long-time family friend Jean Taylor, Shirley frequently "told the boys she and her husband felt very lucky because they had been able to choose just the children they wanted."

"Mrs. Taylor said Dresbach represented one of their parents in a divorce proceeding and had been asked to handle details of putting the boys, who were then infants, in the custody of an adoption agency."

"'But the Dresbachs fell in love with the boys and adopted them themselves,' she said."

Still, there were nagging suggestions that things weren't altogether right at home. As Nathaniel Blaustein expressed it, Wayne "had a wanderlust." In the last two years he had run away half a dozen times and although he had "high average ability" he had failed every subject in the ninth grade and was repeating the grade this year. When his teachers complained that he "daydreamed a lot," Wayne told the school counselor that "he was discontented at home." His parents had had him examined by a psychiatrist the previous summer.

On Monday, January 9, darker shadows appeared. Wayne, the Washington newspapers reported, had been arrested in October for stealing guns from his father. The Dresbachs had declared him incorrigible, charged him with larceny, and left him in jail several days. The charge was later dropped, but at the encouragement of the Juvenile Probation officer, the Dresbachs had taken Wayne to the County Mental Health Clinic, where both the parents and the boy were interviewed by a psychiatrist, Dr. Elizabeth Winiarz.

She had seen Wayne as recently as December 29, 1960 and noticed some emotional instability, but did not believe he displayed any violent tendencies. Of that last visit, Dr. Winiarz told reporters, "He and his mother were in a good humor. . . . They talked about how wonderful Christmas had been . . ."

As for her evaluation of Wayne, " 'He could get excited and act on impulse,' she said. However, when angered, he appeared more likely to sulk quietly than talk back. . . ."

In the following days the articles about the Dresbach case grew shorter and shorter, then drifted off the front pages. The bodies of Harold and Shirley, still described as having been shot in the back, were in Baltimore. Final arrangements and burial services had been delayed pending the arrival of relatives from Kansas.

10

The office of the Chief Medical Examiner, a dingy two-story building where autopsies were performed, stood behind a sewage-treatment station on a pier overlooking the oily iridescent waters of Baltimore harbor. In that neighborhood one never knew whether the stench was of chemicals, low tide, or corpses. Still it was a convenient location. A police boat, *The Gaither*, chugged up to the pier several times each week to deliver bodies it had fished from the harbor.

The Dresbachs arrived at 3:10 P.M., the day they died. One of the dieners, or morgue assistants, logged them in, scribbling the case numbers on cards which he placed on the chest of each corpse. Whatever she might have been before, Shirley was now 43938; Harold was 43939.

Oblivious to police reports or news accounts, the diener recorded the stark facts. Each body was photographed, fingerprinted, measured, and weighed. Shirley was 5′2″ and 133 pounds. On the morgue record, the check list for clothing covered everything from hat to hose, shoes to bra. In this case the diener put an X next to None.

Harold Malone Dresbach was 5′4″ and 120 pounds. He arrived wearing a coat which someone had pulled over his bullet-riddled body.

Printing their identification numbers on manila tags, the diener tied one to the woman's right big toe, the other to the man's. Then he washed them with moist, sterile swabs. The authorities in Anne Arundel County had requested autopsies, standard procedure in cases of suspected homicide. But that would have to wait until tomorrow. The diener wheeled the Dresbachs into the cooler.

Although one generally assumes that coroners grow inured to their work, Dr. Charles Petty, the Assistant Medical Examiner, was not eager to go into the office on January 8, 1961. For one thing it was Sunday. For another, he knew that in winter the autopsy room was cold, damp, and downright unbearable. Still, he thought that was better than in summer when the old building was stifling with heat and humidity, and flies buzzed in through the rusty screens and laid eggs on bodies left outside the cooler.

But Dr. Petty, a graduate of Harvard Medical School, had no choice. He realized the police, the State's attorney, and perhaps even the attorney for the defense would need his report. Since their murders were front-page news, he might well have read about the Dresbachs, but, if so, that would have had no influence on him. His job wasn't to say *who* killed them; his job was to let the bodies tell him *what* killed them.

By the time Dr. Petty arrived after lunch, the dieners had assembled the necessary equipment—specimen containers, syringes, sharpened knives, scalpels, and a Stryker Saw. New Bard-Parker blades had been snapped into handles. Made of gray plastic and shaped to fit a man's palm, these scalpel handles were specially designed for long, tough cutting rather than for the meticulous incisions required in surgery.

The Dresbachs were brought in on stretchers—actually stainless steel trays whose sides were bent up to form a trough that could contain a body and the fluids which drained from it. Turning first to Shirley, Dr. Petty started at 1 P.M., working with great precision as he described the woman's external appearance. Unlike many medical examiners who tape-record their remarks as they proceed, Dr. Petty preferred to make handwritten notes and draw his own diagrams, then go upstairs to his office and dictate his findings to his secretary, Desma Usher—"as in House of Usher" he always quipped—who took excellent shorthand.

In the bloodless prose of his report:

> The body is that of a well developed and well nourished white woman approximately 50 years old. . . . The head hair is brown, well combed and 12″ to 14″ long. The eyes are grey and each pupil is 3 mm. in diameter. . . . All of the teeth are missing except numbers 27, 28, and 29. Tooth 28 has a metal cap. Otherwise, the mouth is negative. The fingernails are neatly cut and covered by red polish. A thin blood smear is found in the right palm. . . . A few drops of dried blood are found on the soles of the feet. . . . The external genitalia and anus are negative. The introitus is of the marital type. Two old, lower abdominal, surgical scars are found; one between the umbilicus and the symphysis pubis is 5″ long and the other 2″ to the right of the umbilicus is . . . 7″ long and its inferior end is depressed. Over the posterior surfaces of the body moderate livor mortis is noted. In the extremities there is moderate rigor mortis. The body is at icebox temperature.

He then focused his attention on the gunshot wounds, of which he found five. After carefully numbering them, he described the first as "a neat round hole ⅜" in diameter with a dark compressed edge." It was located in Shirley's chest, just above her right breast. Wound number two, another "neat round hole ⅜" in diameter," was on the left side of the chest, quite near the armpit. Wounds three and four were in the back, almost in the middle, just to the left of the back bone. "Gunshot wound number five is on the right forearm 6" below the elbow." Dr. Petty concluded that the same bullet may have been involved in both wounds one and five. "This possibility can be seen when the right upper extremity is raised." In other words, Shirley had lifted the arm in a vain effort to shield herself, and a bullet pierced it and struck her chest.

With the external examination over, one of the dieners opened the body, making twin incisions at each shoulder and cutting down to the sternum, then extending the line to the bottom of the belly. It was, as Dr. Petty wrote, the standard "crutch-shaped" or Y incision. But because this was a woman, the diener took care to cut beneath the breasts, rather than over them. You never knew when the family might want to bury the deceased in a décolleté, or otherwise revealing, dress.

Once the internal organs had been removed, Dr. Petty examined them closely, scrutinizing even those which were remote from the bullet tracks. In his profession, nothing was ever obvious, nothing taken for granted. "No lesion is found in esophagus, stomach, duodenum, intestines, anus or rectum. The vermiform appendix is surgically absent." The fallopian tubes and ovaries were also "surgically absent."

The trouble was located in the respiratory and cardiovascular systems. "Each lung has been penetrated by a bullet . . . and each lung is partly collapsed. A small amount of bloody mucus is found in the trachea and bronchi." As for the heart, a "bullet track passing through the pericardial sac, the superior vena cava, the pulmonary veins and the descending thoracic aorta is noted." As Dr. Petty later remarked, Shirley Dresbach probably could not have survived "even if she was shot right on the operating table and doctors had gone to work on her at once."

Yet although he was reasonably certain now of the cause of

death, he continued his examination, leaving nothing to chance, reducing Shirley Dresbach to facts and figures, not opinions. "The heart weighs 250 grams . . . together the kidneys weigh 380 grams. No lesion is found in pituitary, thyroid, pancreas or adrenals."

Then a diener slit the scalp across the crown of the head from ear to ear and drew back the skin. Plugging in the Stryker Saw, an oscillating, drill-like instrument, he went to work on the skullcap, spraying a fine shower of bone meal as he opened the cranial cavity like a pod. Originally invented to remove casts, the Stryker Saw is pressure sensitive and can cut through bone without destroying underlying tissue.

"The brain and meninges are removed and the brain weighs 1,380 grams." No signs of damage or pathology were discovered.

Dr. Petty's final opinion was that "In the case of Shirley Dresbach death is due to two gunshot wounds of the chest with massive internal hemorrhage." He found no bullets because the wounds were "through and through," meaning the slugs entered one side of her body and passed out the other. Considering the newspaper reports, Dr. Petty's most interesting discovery was that Shirley had not been shot in the back. She had stood face to face with her murderer.

At 1:30 P.M. Dr. Petty started on Harold Dresbach and, although during his years as Assistant Medical Examiner in Baltimore, he had seen the ravages of hundreds of homicides, he was struck by the number of gunshot wounds in case ⌗43939. There were six bullet holes in the back and five in the front. But the doctor knew better than to leap to the conclusion that eleven shots had been fired.

As he proceeded with his external examination, two dieners closed up Shirley's body. They stitched the Y-shaped incision back together, then sutured the scalp. Once an embalmer and a mortician were finished with her, there would be nothing to prevent the family from leaving the casket open at the wake.

Noting that "this is the body of well developed, well nourished, white male appearing of middle age," Charles Petty spotted something on Dresbach's wrists. "There are old scars present on the flexure surfaces of both wrists, the scar on the right wrist being of a hockey stick shape and those on the left wrist approximating two hockey sticks joined with an extension toward the medial aspect of the wrist. No other significant old scars are seen. There are no tattoos present."

Turning to the bullet holes, Dr. Petty remarked: "Because of the multiplicity of wounds present, these are considered in order with descriptions first of the external wounds and secondly of the internal manifestations of these wounds."

"Wound #1—This is a gunshot wound of entry, ovoid in shape . . . located over the mandible just lateral to the right . . . corner of the mouth." After fracturing the jaw, the bullet coursed downward, passing through the neck and chest, lodging "in the anterior chest wall on the left." Dr. Petty found "in the pectoralis major muscle, a lead pellet of approximately .22 caliber, partially deformed." He initialed the slug with the letters "CP" and saved it as evidence.

"Wound #2—This is a gunshot wound of entrance located . . . 3" to the left of the midline of the left upper anterior chest wall." After puncturing the front of the chest the pellet sliced "through the upper lobe of the left lung," cracked a rib and exited from a spot between Dresbach's shoulder blades, very near the vertebral column. The exit wound was labeled #5.

"Wounds #3 and #4—These are described together because of their location. Wound #3 is located on the interior axillary fold and Wound #4 is located on . . . the left upper arm, and the two wounds are so situated that they 'kiss' each other when the arm is close to the side of the body."

"Wound #6—This is located on the [back] of the upper left arm." And it is connected with Wounds #3 and #4. In brief, a bullet entered the back of the left arm, coursed upward, exited from the front of the arm, then grazed the skin near the left armpit.

"Wound #7—This is a gunshot wound of entrance located . . . on the right buttock." The bullet track passed through the right buttock, the pelvis, and the left buttock, exiting at Wound #10.

"Wound #8—This was an entrance wound, near the spine, just above the right buttock. The bullet coursed upward, puncturing the abdominal wall and peritoneum, lodging near the center of the torso. Dr. Petty located "a lead pellet of approximately .22 caliber," marked it with his initials and saved it.

Wound #9—This was another entrance wound, also "in the small of the back," just above the left buttock. It too coursed upward through the body, passing through the right kidney, the right lobe of the liver, and the upper and lower lobe of the right lung. Once again Dr. Petty found a "lead pellet of approximately .22 caliber," initialed and saved it.

To avoid any possibility of confusion, Dr. Petty made lists that recapitulated his findings:

> *Gunshot Wounds of Entrance*—Wounds #1, 2, 6, 7, 8, 9.
> *Gunshot Wounds of Exit*—Wounds #4, 5, 10.
> *Grazing of Skin*—Wounds #3, 11.

Although he went on in the usual manner to examine the internal organs, fluids, and brain, he observed that "The remainder of the autopsy is without particular note. . . . In my opinion death is due to multiple gunshot wounds with bleeding into both pleural cavities."

He concluded by returning to an old trauma, a hint that Dresbach's life, long before his death, was shadowed by violent forces which few people outside the family were aware of. "The presence of the bizarre old scars on both wrists may indicate a previous suicide attempt."

Investigators and lawyers were, of course, free to make of these scars what they might. Or to ignore them altogether. What they could not ignore—or at least should not have—was the nature of Harold Dresbach's gunshot wounds. The police and Wayne, for that matter, claimed Dresbach had been shot in the back as he crossed the living room. Yet the autopsy disclosed that he had been shot in the face and in the front of the chest. While still standing, he had also been hit on the side of the right buttock.

He had indeed been shot from behind three times. But the evidence indicated that Wound #6 in his upper left arm, and Wounds #8 and #9 in the small of his back, were made after Dresbach had fallen to the floor. The bullet tracks of Wounds #6, #8, and #9 coursed upward—which is what happens when shots are fired into a prone body from behind. Given the angle of the bullet tracks, it was unlikely these shots had been fired from any great distance.

In other words, it looked as if someone had come close and pumped three more slugs into Harold Dresbach as he lay wounded on the kitchen floor.

11

While everyone waited for the Dresbachs' relatives to arrive from Kansas, funeral arrangements continued to be postponed and Lee remained with the Talbert family. The Talberts had also been asked by the police to hold for safekeeping a number of valuable items: two diamond rings that had been removed from Shirley's fingers, another diamond ring belonging to Mr. Dresbach, a diamond bracelet, and an expensive camera, a Nikon or Leica, Lena recalls. They had taken Dede, the dachshund, into their house, and every evening Dallas walked over to the Dresbachs' garage to feed Wayne's dog, a Weimaraner named Mac, who was growing ill-tempered and unruly now that Wayne wasn't around. Lee was supposed to look after his brother's dog, but he seldom remembered to do so. Dallas could understand that. Most boys are absentminded and Lee was probably still upset, although, Dallas thought, he seemed to be recovering quickly.

Much as all this must have disrupted their own lives, the Talberts didn't complain. They felt, under the circumstances, it was the least they could do to help. But they did wonder why Dresbach's friends and business associates hadn't made a greater effort to lend a hand. And they worried that nobody was looking after Wayne's well-being. Like the Dunns, the Talberts had been denied permission to visit or even to write him, and they wished that his relatives would show up soon so the boy wouldn't feel he had been abandoned.

Their sense of urgency increased as they realized how many practical decisions had to be made. Above all, Wayne needed a lawyer. Since he still had not been charged and no one knew whether he would be tried as a juvenile or an adult, the Talberts retained the hope that he would be sent someplace for treatment, rather that left in jail. A good lawyer, they believed, could make

a crucial difference in the deliberations of Judge Benjamin
Michaelson who was said to be waiting for the results of Wayne's
psychiatric evaluation.

After the autopsies, the Dresbachs were laid out at Hardesty's
Funeral Parlor in Galesville. Since no family member had shown
up, the Talberts took Lee to see his parents, and it was an awful,
heart-wrenching scene, as they and others remember it. When he
came to Shirley's open casket, the boy broke down and cried un-
controllably. For several minutes he clung to Lena, leaning his
head against her shoulder and sobbing.

When he finally regained his composure, they moved on to Mr.
Dresbach's casket. Dry-eyed now, Lee passed by his father without pausing to look down and without showing any emotion.

Five days after the murders, one relative—and one alone—arrived in Maryland. It was Harry Woodring, the former Governor
of Kansas and Secretary of War under Roosevelt. He contacted
Father Dawson by telephone to discuss plans for the service.
He and Lee had had a talk, he said, and had decided on a
requiem mass. This pleased Father Dawson who believed that a
eucharistic service, with its emphasis on salvation, on Christ's ris-
ing again after Calvary, would partly redeem the dreadful situation.

Then, very tentatively, the young priest mentioned Wayne.
Had Mr. Woodring visited him? No. Well, then did he intend to
get in touch? And had a lawyer been hired?

With chilly urbanity, the result, no doubt, of his decades of political dealings, Harry Woodring cut the questions short. "There's
nothing we can do for the boy now except hope he gets help."

But he didn't specify what kind of help he had in mind or
what steps, if any, he had taken to ensure that Wayne would get
it. He gave Father Dawson to understand that this was none of
his business.

Next day at the requiem mass, Father Dawson was pleased to
see that Lee received communion. But afterward there was no
cortege to the cemetery, no graveside service. The Dresbachs were
shipped west to Shirley's home town of Elk City, where they were
buried on the sere winter plains of Kansas.

Neither the Talberts, the Dunns, nor Father Dawson ever heard from Harry Woodring again. And still nobody knew if a lawyer had been hired or whether anyone had been appointed to protect Wayne's interests. It was, Father Dawson thought, as if the boy had been swallowed up by the earth, along with his adoptive parents.

Autumn 1978

1

Through no effort and certainly no virtue of my own, I have always known more about the Dresbach murder case than most people. In fact, I was the first to know. I am the son of Mary Helen Dunn, the stepson of Tommy Dunn. The morning of January 7, 1961, I answered that long-distance call from Lee Dresbach and have not been able to cut the line ever since. Although I left the place and lost track of some of the people, I continued to feel myself linked to that time and those events.

Gradually, by an inexplicable process of alchemy, the Dresbach case came to seem the story of my life. It was the story I heard all through late adolescence and early manhood. It was the story I told during midnight bull sessions when I was in college, then in graduate school. It was the story I intended to transform into a novel once I felt equal to the task.

In retelling it, in garnishing it with rumor, gossip, and incremental repetition, as if it were some ancient saga or myth, I recognize that I wound up shaping the story. But if I shaped it, it also shaped me. It marked the end of my youth. This is literal truth, not some literary turn of phrase. For after the Dresbachs died, my family was never the same, and neither was I.

The practical changes can easily be catalogued. Within a year we sold our cottage and never again spent time together on the Chesapeake Bay, the place where we had lived every summer since I was born. My parents, who were then already middle-aged, accepted the responsibility for two more children, two boys who had been abandoned as infants, then re-orphaned as teenagers. Eventually Lee came to live in our home, and my parents, along with a small number of other people, contributed money and sacrificed great chunks of their lives so that Wayne wouldn't despair of his own.

There were also less tangible, though no less dramatic, changes. While the murders shocked and bewildered us, the events which followed were more profoundly confusing and, in the end, they left us feeling powerless and angry. If, as some have remarked, everybody in my family burns on a short fuse, is slightly suspicious and slightly cynical, cannot easily be flattered or cajoled, and bristles at the mere mention of most figures of authority, it is because of what happened to Wayne. Or what we believed happened to him.

The point is, no one could say with certainty what had happened. Close as my mother and stepfather got to Wayne and Lee, some sense of decorum—mixed, I suspect, with a large dose of uneasiness—prevented them from asking questions. Probing would have seemed to them a violation of their role as surrogate parents.

So, like me, they told the story, but could never fully account for it. Although they had heard rumors and formed their own opinions, they could not be sure why the Dresbachs had been killed. At times they even confessed doubts about who had done the killing.

I have said that in retelling the story, I shaped it. To be honest, I simplified it. I stayed on the surface, both to make it easier for others to understand and to make it easier on myself. Just as that day when I crouched beside the creek and refused to go back into the water, I was reluctant to confront the unknown, to grapple with the strange forms that drift through our deepest nightmares. But, in my defense, it was not death that frightened me now. It was the thought of what I might find out about the living and what damage my discoveries might do to the innocent and guilty alike.

So whenever I considered writing about the Dresbach murders, fiction seemed safer. I could select, I could reject. I imagined I could construct *a* truth, and thereby avoid the necessity of discovering *the* truth.

Eventually, however, this struck me as not just a cowardly evasion. It was an insult to the people I cared about most. Although a novel might well have done justice to whatever talent I possess and whatever personal significance I had invested in the Dresbach case, it would have been unfair to my parents, the Talberts, Father Dawson, and others who regard the events, with much better reason than I, as the story of their lives.

Long ago I had done these same people a serious, if secret, wrong and I knew I owed them an apology. As an eighteen-year-old seeing only absolutes, imperious about my own sophomoric perceptions, I had listened to them struggle to make sense of the Dresbach murders; I had watched them attempt to help Wayne; and I had judged them harshly. They seemed to me—all of them, even, I confess, my parents—a sad, dreary, uninspired lot. Impatient with their reticence, contemptuous of what I viewed as their overeagerness to compromise, oblivious of their generosity, I thought more should have been done for Wayne—although I could not say what. And I was smugly confident I could have done a better job—although, to be honest, I never did much for Wayne at all.

It is only now that I am married and have a family of my own that I recognize the extraordinary effort they expended. And it is only now, after I have confronted the resistance and hostility which they encountered, that I can appreciate the full extent of their dedication and courage.

Yet their example of selflessness still might not have been enough to convince me to forsake my novel. It took Wayne Dresbach to do that. Eager to lend the illusion of reality to my fiction, I went to ask him a few background questions, and he began to speak of subjects he had never mentioned in the twenty years I have known him. Finally I could not escape the obvious conclusion. If this is anyone's story, it is his. And it has to be told through facts, rather than artifice.

So, for several weeks, Wayne talked as I listened and let a tape recorder run. Then, with a transcript of his trial, an envelope of newspaper clippings, a box of old letters, and a trunk full of books on law, forensic medicine, and psychology, I moved to Europe and immersed myself in the case.

Six months later, I had hundreds of pages of notes, the names of several dozen people I wanted to interview, and over a thousand questions for which I intended to find answers. When, in the autumn of 1978, I flew back to the States to complete my research, I was convinced that Wayne Dresbach had been the victim of a monstrous miscarriage of justice and, I suspected, a cover-up.

2

Since I couldn't be sure who might be involved in such a conspiracy, it was difficult to decide where to start. I feared that the instant I began asking questions, all the guilty parties would be alerted and nobody would talk. The police, I thought, should have the most complete records of the case, but I wanted to postpone speaking to them and avoid all the principal characters until I had a better sense of where they stood.

Nibbling at the edges, searching for documentary evidence, I called the Remedial Education Center in Washington, D.C., where Wayne had undergone a series of academic and psychological tests in the summer of 1960. The director, Susan Zunzer, wasn't in, but a secretary confirmed that the center still had records from 1960 and quickly pulled the Dresbach file.

"Oh . . . I think there may be a problem with this one," she said, "There's been . . . ah, a family tragedy."

I told her I knew that, then explained that, with Wayne's notarized approval, I planned to do a book on the case and needed information from his file.

"Well, there's sure a lot here." She mentioned newspaper clippings, test scores, profiles, and handwritten notes made by a staff diagnostician and a psychologist.

"Are the notes about Wayne?" I asked.

"Not all of them. Some of them are about his parents and his family life."

"You mean Mr. and Mrs. Dresbach were interviewed, too?"

"I don't know. But there are notes about them."

"I'd like copies of everything. Can I pick them up this afternoon?"

Suddenly the woman seemed unsure of herself and said that, under the circumstances, she felt Mrs. Zunzer would have to give approval before she made copies available. And they'd want a written request from me. "Then you'll need permission from the boy's guardian."

"The boy is thirty-three years old."

"Well, I'll tell Mrs. Zunzer. She'll be back Monday. Call then."

Continuing to work over the telephone, I tried to find out who had handled Wayne's and Lee's adoption. The Dresbachs had been living in Maryland when they brought the boys home, but no agency in that state or in Washington, D.C. or Virginia had any record of the case. It looked, I was told, like a "black market" adoption: one privately arranged and involving the exchange of a considerable sum of money. Since Harold Dresbach was a lawyer, he could easily have handled things himself and never undergone any testing to determine Shirley's and his suitability as parents.

The next day I discovered that Osborne Duvall, the State's attorney who had prosecuted Wayne, was dead, and Dr. Elizabeth Winiarz, the psychiatrist who had interviewed him in December 1960, had been incapacitated by a stroke.

The Anne Arundel County Mental Health Clinic refused to release any of its records unless I got a court order—which prompted me to make another call, this one to the current State's attorney, Warren Duckett, who promised he would do what he could to help.

On Monday I contacted the Remedial Education Center again and spoke to the director, Mrs. Zunzer, who said she hadn't decided how to proceed with my request. She thought she might be able to provide Wayne's test scores and profiles. But she doubted she could disclose the contents of the handwritten notes without the permission of the staff members who had made them, neither of whom was currently working at the center. Myra Orleans, a psychologist, lived in California. I could call and try to get her approval. But Louise Lee, a diagnostician, was dead, and I would have to get permission from the executor of her will—if I could locate him.

Citing the Freedom of Information Act, I said I believed I needed only Wayne's approval. But Mrs. Zunzer said she'd consult her lawyer about that. Meanwhile, why didn't I send her a copy of Wayne's notarized statement, then call Myra Orleans?

During our first long-distance conversation, Ms. Orleans sounded interested in my book and eager to be helpful. She didn't know of any reason why I couldn't see her notes, but she said she'd like to review them before releasing them to me. Why didn't I have the Remedial Education Center send her copies?

While waiting for Mrs. Zunzer to mail this material to Ms.

Orleans, I called the Anne Arundel County Police and spoke to
Ashley Vick, who was now Chief of the Department. Though he
remembered the Dresbach murders, his recollections were vague
and he said he'd have to review his files. He would ask the Information Office to reassemble all the data on the case.

Convinced this would produce quick results, I decided it was
time to contact some of the principal characters.

3

Lieutenant Lloyd Smith, former Director of the Juvenile
Bureau and previously the departmental public relations officer,
was retired and living outside Annapolis. He had no trouble
recalling the Dresbach murders, and he didn't sound particularly
surprised to have somebody ask about them after seventeen years.
Of the tens of thousands of cases he had handled, this was, he
said, the one which stuck out in his mind—the one he still wasn't
sure about.

"Why's that?" I asked, the telephone receiver suddenly moist
in my hand.

"I don't think the whole story ever came out. Seemed to me
somebody didn't want it all to come out. You know, I did an investigation. I went around and talked to a lot of people and
gathered evidence and made phone calls all over the east coast.
But at the trial, they swore me in, then wouldn't let me testify.
They threw me right off the stand. I never did understand it."

Much of this I knew from reading the transcript and, as intrigued as I was by Lieutenant Smith's belief that the whole story
hadn't come out, something else interested me more immediately.
"The evidence you collected—what did it include?"

"I had a whole briefcase full. I had it right there in court with
me. But I never got a chance to show it."

"What was in the briefcase?"

"Well, there was my report, the summary of the interviews and
telephone calls I made. And then there was all the pornography
and dirty pictures we found at the house, and the statements I
took from people who saw the Dresbachs at various nudist
camps and—"

"Excuse me, but do you know where that material is now?"

"Why, sure!"

"Where?"

"Down in my basement. You see, I kept copies of everything at home. After I retired, I just held on to them."

"Look," I said, struggling to conceal my excitement, "I'd like to talk to you in person and maybe glance at your files."

"Why, sure, come on over."

I left for Annapolis at once, but it was late evening, just getting dark, and I was startled after all these years to find I was unfamiliar with the area. Although it is, I suppose, a common—even a cliché—experience in America to discover that the countryside of one's youth has disappeared beneath acres of asphalt and gas stations and shopping centers, I had the sensation of being unhelmed, of drifting aimlessly on a stream of cars that cruised through countryside which had once been cow pasture and woods.

Off the main highway, the roads seemed to wander through time warps. Suburban subdivisions ended abruptly at tobacco patches; a community college merged into a cornfield; sharecropper shacks surrounded a television transmitting tower. City and country, North and South, stood in bewildering juxtaposition, as if Maryland was still trying to make up its mind what side it was on and what direction it was going.

Lieutenant Lloyd Smith's house looked like a farmer's cottage that had been rejuvenated and expanded by someone handy with tools and reluctant to waste spare time. Once it had probably stood alone on a rural free delivery route; now there were houses lining the road for miles.

Pulling into the driveway behind a Shasta camper, I picked up my notebook and tape recorder and started for the door. Then, for some reason, I had misgivings about the tape recorder. Thinking it might seem pushy, I put it back in the car.

The instant Lloyd Smith opened the door, I was glad I wasn't carrying the Panasonic. I sensed trouble. I could see it on Smith's face and in the rigidity of his wife's spine. She sat at the dining-room table and barely nodded when I said hello.

Smith led the way to what used to be called a "recreation room" and is now known in real estate argot as a "family room." It had all the earmarks of a major do-it-yourself project. Wood paneled, decorated with knickknacks and souvenirs, the room had a bar and a gaudy display of liquor bottles, but was most unfestive and appeared not to have been used recently for "recreation" or a "family." A faint sulfuric smell clung to the furniture as it sometimes does in country houses that have their own wells.

Smith said I was lucky to catch him at home. He was leaving in a few days for a Shasta camper convention in Ohio. He'd been to these conventions all over the country. He drove everywhere, didn't feel comfortable flying. I admitted I didn't either.

"Afraid I have some bad news," said Smith, as we sat down. He was a big, heavy-set man dressed in khaki work clothes which looked not unlike a police or military uniform. But he also wore a pair of horn-rimmed glasses, which lent him the incongruous air of a professor emeritus. "My wife reminded me we had a big rainstorm a couple summers back. The basement flooded, and it ruined a bunch of my files."

"What about the Dresbach material?"

"Yeah, that rain—it ruined just about everything. Sorry I didn't mention it on the phone. But I didn't remember."

Much as I wanted to press him, I gave the pretense of being calm and unperturbed. I suspected Lloyd Smith had those documents, but after discussing the situation with his wife, had decided not to show them to me. Maybe he thought they weren't really his property and he shouldn't have kept them. Maybe he feared legal action—it is a litigious age.

Whatever his reason, he was waiting for my next move, and I had the impression of playing poker with somebody who not only held all the cards, but was much better suited to the game than I. Although once a PR man, he bore no resemblance to the usual smiling, facile mouthpiece who puts the best face on the worst news. Throughout that evening, he paused an uncomfortable length of time before speaking and took special care in phrasing his sentences.

I said, "You mentioned the papers you had were copies. Where are the originals?"

"They should be in the boy's police files. They keep all the official records. Call the station and they'll dig them out for you."

"I have called. They said they'd see what they had."

"Good. You get that file, then we'll set down and go over it."

He wanted to cut the conversation short, but I said, "I'd like to talk to you about the evidence you gathered."

"It's been so long, I don't think I better trust my memory."

"You mentioned pornography."

"Like I say, it's been a long time."

Though exasperated by his waffling, I politely reminded him that the trial transcript referred to pornography "and other devices" confiscated from the Dresbach home. What exactly had been there? Films? Pictures? And about those devices—

"Before I go speculating what might have been there," Smith said, "I think you better get the file."

"Sure, I'll do that. But I'd like to know who you interviewed for your report."

"No way. I slip up and tell you I talked to somebody and it turns out I didn't, I'm liable to get sued."

"We'll keep this off the record."

"That's not good enough. I'm retired now, you know, and this house is paid for and I don't feel like losing everything I worked for."

I was tempted to ask whether this was why he wouldn't let me see his files, but I doubted I'd get a straight answer that way. So I started over, trying to allay his fears, explaining my plans for the book, and emphasizing that I had Wayne's approval and full cooperation.

"I'd sure like to help the boy," he said quietly. "I always liked him. I just couldn't believe he did it." As he went on in his elliptical, cautious fashion, he invariably spoke of Wayne's "alleged crime."

"Why do you call it that?" I asked. "He confessed."

"I never believed it. I'm still not convinced he did it. Look, I worked on over 25,000 cases, and you get to know who's a killer and who's not."

"You really think he didn't do it?"

"What I think is I'm not sure. I'm not sure how it happened or why it happened. Too much was covered up. A lot of fellows at the station felt the same way I did."

"What do you think happened?"

"I'd just be guessing. I'm not going to go accusing anybody without evidence."

I tried a new tack. "What did other people think?"

He hesitated, once more displaying the caution of an experienced cop—a cop as reluctant to make hasty accusations as to accept easy excuses. "Well, a lot of people said Mr. Dresbach must have been mighty important. He had an office in Washington. Maybe he was doing government work. You know, secret work, and somebody didn't want us to dig too deep into his life or talk at the trial about what we found out. Otherwise, why didn't they let me give my report? Why didn't they question certain people harder? Why didn't they follow up all the leads? And the trial— why did it go so fast?

"Of course, I'm no lawyer. There may have been reasons I don't understand. But whether the boy did it or didn't, everything should have been out in the open so people could see what kind of home he came from and the way he was treated. I know there are rules of evidence and all. But what I always wondered, the whole time I was on the force I wondered, why does Justice wear a blindfold?"

Lloyd Smith stood up. It was a Monday night. The Baltimore Colts were playing the Dallas Cowboys, and he wanted to watch the game on TV. As he walked me back through the living room, I asked, "Were the Dresbachs nudists?"

"You get that report from the police and see what it says."

We lingered at the door; moths and beetles blundered against the screen.

"If you have a chance," I said, "I'd appreciate it if you'd check your basement again. Maybe the Dresbach file was one that wasn't ruined."

Smith nodded. "You've talked to the boy, haven't you?"

"Yes." Then, as I was to do so often in the next few months, I reminded him that Wayne was now thirty-three. It was as if people believed he had been frozen in childhood; actually, he had aged prematurely.

But Smith was pursuing his own thoughts: "If I'm wrong and he did kill them, I'd understand why he shot his father. But why his mother? That's another thing I could never figure out."

Then he unlocked the screen door and let me out, and on the drive back to Washington I considered his question, as well as many others. Though disappointed not to have seen Lloyd Smith's files, I thought I was on to something. Now I knew the chief investigating officer shared many of my suspicions. But I had no evidence and Smith wasn't going to risk giving me any. Not yet, at any rate. I hoped, however, that he would change his mind once I had Wayne's records.

4

Next morning I called the Information Office of the Anne Arundel County Police and spoke to Captain William Lindsey, an affable man who had been one of the first officers at the scene of the crime and who readily described his brief involvement in the case.

But searching for the Dresbach file, his department had encountered some difficulty. Thus far, they hadn't found it at the main station in Millersville. It might be at the Edgewater Station, he said, or in a warehouse in southern Maryland where many of the old records were stored. Would I call back later that week?

Meanwhile, I visited the community in Lanham where the Dresbachs had lived before moving to Franklin Manor. Several of their old neighbors were still there, among them Evelyn McCracken who, along with her husband Bob, had taken an early interest in Wayne and Lee. After the murders, the McCrackens had contributed to Wayne's appeal and, for a time, let Lee live with them.

Now Mr. McCracken was dead and his widow didn't care to talk about the Dresbachs. She conceded she had heard about nude swimming parties in their pool and beatings Mr. Dresbach inflicted on the boys and his wife. But she claimed this was hearsay; she had no firsthand knowledge. All she offered for quotation was: "Wayne was always a good boy. A good, sweet, gentle boy. I know what he did was wrong, but I think he must have been pushed into it. The situation pushed him into it."

What situation? Just the situation at home. And whatever that was, Evelyn McCracken didn't intend to discuss it.

At first, on the phone, another old neighbor sounded brutally candid and outspoken. "Lemme say this. If Wayne hadn't killed his father, somebody else would have."
"Who?" I asked.
"An irate client, a jealous husband, a jilted lover. Take your pick. There were dozens of people who'd have liked to see him dead."
But when I said I wanted to discuss the subject with him in person, the man wavered. He'd have to think that over and call me back.
Instead his wife called back to say how "sick" and "disgusting" she thought it was to use other people's misery for a book. It was like all that Watergate business, everybody prying into everybody else's private affairs. What was the point?
"The point," I said, "is to find out the truth."
"What good will it do? It'll just stir up bad blood and hurt Wayne."
"Wayne doesn't see it that way. He wants to tell his side of the story; he wants people to understand what went on. He thought you'd help."
At this the woman relented. She said if Wayne gave his go-ahead, she and her husband would agree to see me.
Yet, even after Wayne urged her to tell whatever she knew, the woman was hesitant and it took me another half hour on the phone to convince her that if she cared so much about him, she should do what he asked of her.
It was hot and humid the day I went to their house, and these people were of the school that believes it is better during such weather to keep the windows closed, the blinds drawn, and the lights off. I was handed a glass of cloyingly sweet iced tea, then shown to a rocking chair next to a table covered with religious magazines.
Before we started, the man set some ground rules. They would talk only if I guaranteed them absolute anonymity. Moist with anticipation—or perhaps just from fighting for air in that sealed room—I gave my word.

"Okay, then," the man said. "We really don't know anything."

"Wait a minute! On the phone you told me if Wayne hadn't killed them, someone else would have. You mentioned irate clients, jealous husbands—"

"Those are rumors," the woman said. "Things people told us."

"People you trust?"

They glanced at one another. "I suppose so. You see, we had a friend who was a business acquaintance of Mr. Dresbach's. He told us . . . well, he said Mr. Dresbach ran around on his wife."

"Isn't it true," I asked, "that he brought these women home while his wife was there?"

"Yes, that's what we heard."

"Did you ever see anything?"

"Just a lot of people going in and out. In summer they always had parties around the pool."

"Skinny-dipping," the woman said with distaste. "I don't know how they could stand it. Their stables were right near the pool, and the paddock used to stink to high heaven. We complained about it. This neighborhood is zoned residential. They had no right to keep horses. But of course they had no right to do most things they did."

"What things?"

"They drank a lot," the man said. "And Dresbach, he beat the boys. Shirley told me she was afraid he'd hurt them someday. Really hurt them."

"He beat her almost as often as he did the boys," said the woman. "I saw the bruises. I think Shirley was a good mother. Anyway, she wanted to be. But what could she do against him?"

"How often was Wayne beaten?" I asked.

"All the time. He got the worst of it. Who knows why? I guess there's just no saying why parents like one kid more than the other. They probably couldn't tell you themselves. Me, though, I liked Wayne."

"Would you have been willing to testify at his trial?" I asked.

The man shrugged. "Sure. But nobody asked me. Not that it would have done any good."

"Why not?"

"The Dresbachs had friends. He was always bragging about the powerful people who looked out for him. The boy never had a chance."

"Who were these powerful people?"

"I don't know."

"What about your friend who did business with Dresbach? Was he one of them?"

"We said we'd tell you what we know," the woman interrupted. "We didn't say we'd drag in the names of our friends. I'm sorry. We'd like to help Wayne. But we don't care for writers. We don't trust them."

I wanted to ask, "What about the ones who publish in *Christian Living?*" But I finished my tea and left.

5

Almost two weeks had passed since I had spoken to Myra Orleans, and I still hadn't received the notes she had promised to send once she had reviewed them. So I called California and discovered she had changed her mind. Her handwritten notes, she explained, had never been meant for anybody but herself; they contained sensitive material about Wayne and his parents which might cause Wayne torment if it were made public.

I said I found it strange that so many people were suddenly worried about his well-being now, seventeen years too late. "Whatever is in those notes, do you think it'll be harder on him than what he's been through?"

Myra Orleans didn't answer. She had already sent her notes back to the Remedial Education Center, explaining that since she no longer worked there, it wasn't her place to decide who should see them. She just wouldn't release them to me herself.

Immediately I phoned Susan Zunzer, who claimed that the center was still considering my request for the material. She hoped I would understand the delicacy of their position and allow her to discuss it further with their lawyers.

Though my patience was wearing thin, I wanted to be cooperative and I believed she would soon see that the center had no legal, ethical, or medical reason to deny me full access to Wayne's files. I agreed to call back.

Life for Death

After several weeks' research, however, I noticed a pattern. People admitted they had information, declared themselves willing to share it, then abruptly changed their minds. Although I'm as paranoid as the next person, I couldn't believe they were all part of some conspiracy. They just seemed cautious and self-protective, in the manner of bureaucrats everywhere.

I began to wonder whether similar problems had plagued the police and Wayne's lawyers when they were preparing their case. Was it possible that the boy had been the victim, not of a cover-up, but of a clutch of feckless, timid, or inefficient people?

I continued to call Captain Lindsey at the police Information Office once or twice a week. But the Dresbach file still hadn't turned up. With Warren Duckett's assistance, I had the records at the State's attorney's office searched, but the file wasn't there either. Then I combed the records in the County Courthouse, but discovered nothing I didn't already know. Now, in addition to half a dozen people who refused to talk or to supply documents, I was faced with the prospect that all the case reports had disappeared.

One thing, however, had remained in place: the Dresbach house in Franklin Manor. Since it now belonged to a family whose daughter I had dated in college, I thought it would be easy to arrange to get inside and study the floor plan.

I was wrong. Mr. and Mrs. Rollins didn't remember me. What was worse, they seemed not to understand what I was doing.

"Is this some sort of school project?" asked Mr. Rollins.

"No, I'm writing a book."

"That's what I mean. Are you doing it for a course or what?"

"I'm doing it for a living."

That produced a moment's pause. "You ever published anything?"

"Five novels."

A longer pause. "Well, I don't guess there's any harm in having you look around the house."

The next day when I arrived, however, he had had a change of mind. Bare-chested, deeply tanned, his sparse hair cut short as the bristles of a brush, he met me on the front lawn.

"Wait just a minute," he said. "Before we do anything, let's see some identification."

I showed him my driver's license.

"Don't you have any professional identification. You know, a press card?"

"I'm a novelist."

"I thought you said you were writing a book?" His eyes narrowed with suspicion, and I realized that he wouldn't look kindly on a lecture about literary genres.

"Sure, I have a press card." The previous spring in Rome, a friend had gotten me a journalist's pass for the Italian Open Tennis Tournament. Taking it from my wallet, I handed it to Mr. Rollins who, judging by his expression, didn't think it strange that my card was inscribed *Campionati Internazionale d'Italia.*

Hanging on to it, he led me into the house, to the kitchen where his wife sat at the table. "Here's his press card, honey."

She studied it a moment and copied the information onto a legal pad. *Gran Premio Lebole, 17–28 Maggio, Foro Italico.*

Then Mr. Rollins gave a tour of the place, assuring me that, with the exception of some new carpeting, paint, and paneling, things were pretty much the same as they had been seventeen years before. Leaving the kitchen, we mounted the half-flight of steps to the room Mr. Dresbach had used as an office. A brace of rifles and shotguns had hung on the wall behind his desk. Then we went up another half-flight of stairs to a smaller room where Mrs. Dresbach had done her sewing and some sketching and painting.

From here a door led into a large storage space. Under the eaves of the roof, it ran almost the entire length of the house, and at the opposite end a door opened into what had been Wayne's bedroom. The Dresbachs had referred to this storage space, which connected the north end of the house with the south, as the catwalk.

Across a narrow hallway, Lee had had his own bedroom and a bathroom which the two boys shared. Then yet another staircase allowed access to the ground floor, where Mr. and Mrs. Dresbach had had the master bedroom and bath just off the living room.

The living room and dining room were one long, open space

with armchairs, a sofa, and the TV clustered near the fireplace at the south end, and the dinner table and an electric organ at the north end. The distance from the TV to the kitchen was at least twenty-five feet.

On a sheet of yellow legal paper Mr. Rollins sketched a diagram of the house, top floor and bottom, so that I would not forget this curious arrangement of rooms. I thanked him and was about to take my leave. But he wasn't finished. Saying he wanted my photograph, he went to fetch his camera.

Puzzled, I asked, "What for?"

"Just to make sure you are who you say you are. I'll send it to my daughter to check it out."

"Who do you think I am?"

"You could be Wayne Dresbach, for all I know."

There was no sense objecting. That would only have confirmed his already rampant suspicions.

Outside, Mr. Rollins had me stand in the driveway, with the big red-brick house as a backdrop. It occurred to me that his daughter wouldn't recognize me—not after more than fifteen years. I wore glasses now and a moustache, and my hair had gone completely gray. Uncomfortable under Mr. Rollins' remorseless gaze, I didn't know what to do with my face. Should I smile? Or strike a somber pose?

Before I made up my mind, Mr. Rollins clicked the shutter. I'm sure the photo came out looking like a mug shot.

After that reception by Mr. Rollins, I felt the need for something familiar and reassuring. Pausing at an asphalt basketball court up the road from the Dresbach house, I jumped and proved to myself I could still touch the rim—barely. Then I walked onto the communal pier and found my initials carved in a railing. But after so many years of exposure to the sun and the damp salt air, the wood had been bleached almost silver and the letters MM were smooth and shallow, like an inscription on a coin that is slowly being effaced.

On the way out of Franklin Manor, I drove by our old cottage and considered stopping to look around. But the present owners had painted it a high-gloss flamingo pink, and I didn't bother slowing down.

6

After more than a month, Captain Lindsey said it was hopeless. They had searched everywhere and could not find Wayne
Dresbach's file. "Usually in a case of this kind, where there's been
a capital offense," he said, "we hold on to everything. But it's
been a long time, and there've been a lot of changes since 1961.
His file could have gotten lost when they moved the old records
to the warehouse."

When I told Lloyd Smith the news over the telephone, he
couldn't believe it. His voice seemed to betray anger as well as in-
credulity. But then the emotion leaked from his words. That was
just the way it had been with this case. Information was gathered,
then never used, evidence was collected, then lost.

Under the circumstances, I said, since it looked unlikely I
would ever track down his report, wouldn't he reconsider and tell
me what had been in it and whom he had talked to? Maybe then
I could reconstruct the file.

"Nope," he said, "I think I've told you about all I have to say."

Still hoping to shake something loose, I drove to the Millersville station to interview Chief Ashley Vick. He was big and
fleshy and wore a shiny gray suit and silver-rimmed glasses. But
his voice was out of keeping with the surface flash. A soft-spoken
native of North Carolina, Chief Vick was polite, if slightly distracted. In the next few weeks he would leave the police force
and go into private business, and maybe his mind was on that. He
apologized, but could not even recall whether he had testified at
the trial. Oh, he remembered the murders, all right, but he had
no recollection of details.

When I mentioned Lloyd Smith's misgivings, Vick smiled
ruefully. "Old Lloyd, he never thought any boy was guilty."

Then when I mentioned that there appeared to have been serious problems in the Dresbach family which might have explained
Wayne's behavior, he said, "But you can't have people going
around killing their parents just because they don't like their
home life. Did you see the Dresbach house? I did and it was a
beautiful place. Believe me, those boys were very well provided

for. Me, I came from a poor family and I know what it's like not to have everything handed to you on a silver platter. But I didn't kill my parents. The thought never crossed my mind. To my thinking nothing justifies that kind of crime."

As the interview limped to a close, I knew there was no sense calling the Anne Arundel County Police again.

7

While reviewing the trial transcript for the eighth or ninth time, I paused to consider something I had passed over before. Lloyd Smith had been a witness for the defense, summoned to the stand by Wayne's lawyers. This suggested that the lawyers must have been aware of the information Smith had gathered. In fact, if they intended to introduce his report into evidence—and the transcript indicated that they did—then they had probably made copies of it for their files.

The same should hold true, I reasoned, for all the other documents and reports. By law, the prosecution had to make everything available to the defense, and Wayne's lawyers could have subpoenaed information from every agency that had dealt with him.

But while in theory things worked this way, I had learned to curb my optimism. By that point I counted on nothing—especially not on people's willingness to cooperate—and I had come to expect constant frustration.

Phoning the law firm of Albert Goodman and Theodore Bloom, I asked whether they kept records from cases as far back as 1961.

They said yes.

Might they remember the Dresbach murder case?

Indeed, both men did, and when I inquired about Wayne's file, they assured me I could have it—if I got his written permission and a court order.

Late that afternoon, a heavy overcast day that threatened rain, I tried to guard against disappointment as I drove to Annapolis to pick up the court order at the State's attorney's office. And although nothing went amiss there, I was still waiting for something to go wrong as I walked across the street to the offices of Goodman and Bloom.

Even when they produced the file, I expected to find it empty or stripped of important papers. But standing in the lobby, too anxious to wait until I got to the car, I opened the manila folder and there, neatly bound, was almost everything I had sought for the last two months: confidential comments by the counselor at Southern High School, records from the Juvenile Protection Bureau, test scores and profiles (though not the handwritten notes) from the Remedial Education Center, memos from Dr. Elizabeth Winiarz at the Mental Hygiene Clinic, depositions and statements about the Dresbachs from neighbors and friends, and dozens of psychiatric evaluations done in the months after Wayne's arrest. Whether this constituted all the evidence Lloyd Smith had collected, I never learned. But it gave me more than enough to go on as I set out to file my own report on the case.

Before I began, however, I made a call which I had postponed until the last moment.

When I phoned C. J. Pettit, a close friend of the Dresbachs and the court-appointed guardian for Wayne and Lee, he refused to be interviewed and said he didn't want to get involved.

Since he had sworn to protect both boys' "interests," as well as their "person," I suggested he was already involved and had been for years.

"Well, I'll tell you this," Mr. Pettit said, "I made sure Lee got a good education."

What had he made sure Wayne got?

Mr. Pettit didn't care to discuss the matter any further.

September 1960

That evening in early September 1960, Wayne Dresbach went walking with his dog, Mac, along the shore of the Chesapeake Bay, clambering over big boulders that formed the jetty, thrashing his way through the tangle of cattails and marsh grass. For the dog, this was an unexpected treat. Wayne had been restricted to the house most of the summer, and the Weimaraner had remained in the garage, loyally waiting.

Then finally, over the long Labor Day weekend, Wayne's parents let him go out. But while Mac exploded after all those weeks of inactivity and flashed in and out of the water, his silver-gray coat glistening, his cropped tail twitching in delight, Wayne walked slowly with his head down, his hands deep in his pockets. He didn't bother throwing sticks for Mac to fetch, nor would he stop and play tug-of-war with the garland of seaweed the dog had dredged from the shallows.

In his young life Wayne had already endured some bad seasons. Now the worst so far—his fifteenth summer—had ended. But as a breeze blew in off the bay, combing the water into white-caps, it carried the first chilly hint of autumn, and he worried what winter might bring.

He was a small boy—though not nearly as small and weak as he imagined. At 5'6" and 130 pounds, he was bigger than his father.

He also imagined himself ugly. His eyes were tiny and lifeless, he thought, his mouth too large, his cheeks puffy and immobile. His light brown hair always seemed the wrong length. When he cut it short, it wouldn't stand up in a flat-top no matter how often he brushed it. When he let it grow long, it couldn't be combed back no matter how much hair oil he used.

But his hands, he believed, were his worst feature. The palms were perpetually wet, the nails bitten down to nubs, and just

recently the shaking that he had long felt deep inside him had
appeared at his fingertips. They had started to tremble the way
his parents' hands sometimes did in the morning. He could cope
with that by keeping them hidden in his pockets, but he had no
idea what to do about the shaking inside him.

His thoughts were jumbled, disjointed, and he despaired of expressing them. He imagined his mind was like one of those traps
he had seen bobbing beneath the surface of the bay. Crabs
swam into them, then couldn't escape. Fighting, clawing at each
other, they clung to the wire mesh in helpless clusters.

Although his expression might seem placid, Wayne's mind
swirled with ideas and impressions that gnawed to get out. But he
found himself thinking one thing and saying another. Or worse
yet, he opened his mouth, only to have the words die before they
reached his tongue. When his father saw this, he was liable to
say, "What are you doing, catching flies? Shut your trap."

It happened to him at school, too. Sometimes Wayne knew the
right answer, yet couldn't put it into words.

At other times, when he managed to order his thoughts and
marshall the words, he discovered he had lost track of the question and responded to one that had been asked minutes ago. His
classmates thought he was clowning around, making fun of the
teacher. But for Wayne, this was no laughing matter. He was
soon as afraid to speak at school as he was at home.

His eyes wouldn't work right either, especially when he tried to
do arithmetic. Numbers appeared to squirm around on the page,
turning topsy-turvy, their order reversed. Sometimes Wayne saw a
9 instead of a 6, a 3 where there should have been an 8.

Letters didn't cause the same trouble, and he liked to read po-
etry, particularly if it had a strong rhyme scheme and a metronomical rhythm. As he and Mac walked along the shore, he
gazed at the ship channel and saw freighters headed out to sea
and, recalling the verses of Robert Service, he dreamed of travel
and adventure in exotic places. But he knew that tomorrow he
would be back in school, and the thought filled him with dread.

Wayne should have been a sophomore, but he had failed the
ninth grade and had to repeat it. Last fall, despite his pleas and
despite the fact that he had previously failed the seventh grade,

his parents had made him take a college preparatory course. Even as it became obvious he couldn't keep up with the work, they refused to let him transfer to the general curriculum, and when he flunked every subject from gym to algebra, his father had beaten him with a garrison belt. The brass buckle cut through his shirt, drawing blood from his shoulders and back.

After that, the real punishment began. Laying on a heavy load of domestic chores and remedial schoolwork, Mr. Dresbach ordered him to stay indoors all summer. While Lee ran off each day to swim or fish, play baseball or zip about in one of the family's two speedboats, Wayne sat at the desk in his room, studying, reading, or staring out the dormer window, from which he could watch the pier where other kids his age congregated. He was allowed outside only to mow the lawn, wash the Chryslers, or carry pitchers of martinis to his parents as they sunbathed nude on the secluded patio in the back yard.

There was one small consolation, however. This fall, in spite of his father's objections, Wayne would enroll in the general-commercial course. But he would be in the ninth grade again—the same grade as Lee, who had registered for the academic program. As Mr. Dresbach delighted in reminding him, his younger brother was leaving him in the dust. Not only did Lee do better at school. He was a superior athlete and more popular with girls. It was useless for Wayne to point out that he couldn't improve at sports unless he was allowed to play, that he couldn't very well become popular with girls when he was forbidden to date or go to dances.

Even if he had miraculously discovered a solution to his other problems, Wayne would not have wanted to remain in Franklin Manor during the gloomy desolation of winter. After the summer people locked up their cottages and left, Harold and Shirley held a round of parties which were the subject of much gossip in the isolated community. But the Dresbach boys weren't included, and with the change in seasons, the routine of their lives diverged more dramatically from that of their parents. Wayne and Lee went to bed early, especially when there was company. Then each morning they woke before daybreak, walked in darkness to the school bus stop, and stood there with their backs to the wind, while marsh grass moaned all around them and loose shutters banged on the abandoned houses.

Late in the afternoon, just as the light was failing and the bay
was acquiring a rim of salty ice, the bus would bring them home,
where there were few kids to play with and little to do. Although
they sometimes sneaked off in the family cars, both boys were legally too young to drive, and while their father and mother refused
to chauffeur them around, they also had forbidden them to ride
with teen-agers who did have licenses. By the time he was fifteen,
Wayne had been to the movies only twice in his life, and he felt
that he lived in a ghost town. In winter he could walk the gravel
roads of Franklin Manor for hours and never see another human
being; he could sit on the pier and never hear anything except the
slosh of water against the mossy pilings.

The Talberts urged Wayne and Lee to join the same Boy
Scout troop as their sons, Danny and Chris, but Mr. Dresbach
wouldn't hear of it. He said the Talbert boys were "sissies,"
"goodie-goodies," and he detested them almost as much as he did
the kids whom he called "hoodlums." Anyone who wore blue
jeans and T-shirts fell into that category. There was yet another
neighborhood boy whom Mr. Dresbach disliked because he had a
speech impediment.

Aside from schoolwork—and sports for Lee—there was only
one activity which Dresbach encouraged. He liked the boys to go
duck hunting with him. Lee, always impatient and restless,
couldn't endure the hours of huddling in a duck blind while cold
wind sluiced through the gun slots. Fortunately for him, he could
beg off, claiming he had football or basketball practice.

But this winter Wayne would have no excuse. Since his father
had forbidden him to participate in any extracurricular activities
until his grades improved, he would be at home every weekend
and knew he would be dragged out to the blind to watch Dresbach drink Bourbon from a flask and fire at anything that flew
past.

Once when his father had aimed at a swan, Wayne begged him
not to kill it. Ignoring the boy, he pumped two shots into it.
Then to punish him for speaking out of turn, Dresbach had made
him pluck it, clean it, and eat it.

Wayne, whose ambition was to become a veterinarian or a forest ranger, didn't like killing animals, and although he had been
schooled in the use and maintenance of firearms, he felt consider-

able wariness of them. Perhaps this came from seeing his father carelessly sling shotguns around the duck blind. Then again, it could have come from the way Wayne was taught to shoot.

When he was eleven and the family was still living in Lanham, his father had taken up a twelve-gauge shotgun and marched the boy into the woods. Reaching a clearing, Mr. Dresbach said, "Watch what I do."

He pressed the gun stock to his shoulder, aimed over the tree-tops, and squeezed the trigger. Then, as the noise was subsiding, he handed the twelve-gauge to his son. "Now you try it."

Not much more than 5′ tall at that time and weighing 80 pounds, Wayne knew the shotgun had a vicious kick. He also knew better than to admit he was afraid. That was apt to send his father into a rage. So he tested the weight of the gun, then glancing around, he spotted a thick-trunked maple and moved back to brace himself against it. Raising the twelve-gauge to his shoulder, he hesitated an instant, hoping for instructions. But when Mr. Dresbach said, "Go ahead," Wayne tensed his small body and pulled the trigger.

The noise and power were enormous, deafening him, knocking his head against the maple, and wrenching the shotgun from his hands with such force that he feared it had ripped off his trigger finger. Spasms of pain forked up his arm, through his chest, down his spine. Cradling one throbbing hand in the other, he sank against the tree and cried.

Dresbach picked up the shotgun and reloaded it. "Now you know how *not* to do it. Never brace yourself like that."

"Why didn't you tell me?" Wayne sobbed.

"If you learn something the hard way, you never forget it. That's how I learned. And that's how you're going to. Here, try again."

As he approached Franklin Manor's north pier, Wayne saw several people sitting in the gazebo at the end of it. Recognizing Mary Helen Dunn and her thirteen-year-old daughter, Karen, he started toward them. He liked the Dunn family—especially Mrs. Dunn, who was friendly and talkative and always appeared interested in him.

But then he noticed that Lee was with them, and he paused. Tired of being ignored, Mac trotted home, while Wayne stood there wondering whether he shouldn't go home, too. He didn't dislike Lee; he didn't want to blame him for his troubles. It was just that he didn't care to see him with Karen. Wayne had met her first and liked her. Then Lee had come along, and Karen clearly preferred him. Though he had gotten used to having girls drop him for his younger brother, it wasn't easy to accept or to understand.

Part of what Wayne didn't understand was his parents' attitude. While they restricted his social life and wouldn't let him date, they seemed to encourage Lee with Karen. At least they never made fun of him, or warned him about girls the way they had Wayne.

Just last summer, when he was fourteen, his mother had caught him holding hands with a girl. It was afternoon—"in broad daylight," as Wayne had tried to explain—and he and the girl were sitting on the bulkhead in front of the Dresbach house when his mother had summoned him inside and sent him up to his father's office.

As was so often the case, Mr. Dresbach was furious. "What the hell do you want to do?" he demanded. "Get her pregnant?"

"I was holding her hand."

"It's not you I'm worried about. Something like that, it reflects on the whole family."

"But I tell you, I wasn't doing anything."

His father slapped him in the face. "Don't argue with me. You don't have any idea how easy it is for a woman to ruin you. Stay away from them until you're old enough to know what the hell you're doing."

If this wasn't enough to baffle Wayne, there was the glaring contradiction of Dresbach's own behavior. Frequently foul-mouthed, a habitual teller of off-color stories, he made no secret of his fondness for women of all ages. Over the past weekend, a friend of the family had stopped by the house with his teen-age daughter whose swimsuit could scarcely contain the new fullness of her breasts and buttocks. When she was out of the room, Mr. Dresbach glanced at her father and grinned, licked his lips and made a moist smacking sound. "Jesus, she's just about ripe. I can't wait to get my hands on her."

The man laughed, but Wayne didn't. He knew the things his father was capable of doing.

2

Someone called to Wayne. It was Mrs. Dunn, beckoning him to the end of the pier.

In her early forties then, Mary Helen Dunn had spent almost every summer of her life on the Chesapeake Bay. She didn't fish or crab, sail or water-ski; she seldom even swam anymore. Still, all her best memories, especially of childhood, were tied to "the beach," as she called it—although there was no broad expanse of sand either at Franklin Manor or at Back Bay, where her parents had had a place. Soon after she married and had children, she and her husband, Tommy, started saving for a beach cottage of their own.

Mary Helen couldn't account for this urge she felt to be near the water; nor could she explain the drowsy reassurance it gave her to hear the muffled waves at night, or the joy she got from seeing the sun rise out of the bay at dawn. But she was determined that her children would share these same emotions and someday cherish memories identical to her own.

Simple as they might sound, her ambitions for her children's happiness were not easily accomplished. The Dunns had had to work hard. "How do you think I wound up this way?" Mary Helen often asked, grabbing a handful of her coarse hair that had gone prematurely gray. But she laughed and gave one to understand she wasn't complaining.

The Dunns were Catholic, and their children attended parochial schools. In addition to the usual expenses, there were always tuition bills to pay, books, supplies, lunches, and uniforms to buy. For fifteen years Tommy managed the Naval Exchange laundry in Washington, D.C., and worked a second job at night, tending bar at the Bachelor Officers' Quarters. To help make ends meet, Mary Helen ran a day nursery in her home. According to her calculation, she had raised more than four dozen children from infancy to adolescence.

It was a lot of work, but she loved kids, and that nursery and Tommy's second job meant the family could afford a few extras. Finally they scraped together enough for a down payment and found a white cottage with green trim. A tiny cracker-box of a place, it had only two rooms; the first summer, the kids had had to sleep on the screened-in front porch. Later the Dunns added a large back porch which served as a dormitory for the kids and their friends.

In that community of larger, much more expensive houses, the cottage looked out of place, and among neighbors who were lawyers, doctors, private businessmen, and affluent retirees, the Dunns sometimes felt out of place. But they sacrificed to make the monthly payments and wouldn't have dreamed of giving up the cottage. Things had gone smoothly in the last few years, and Mary Helen thought they'd be all right if nothing drastic happened.

But with a family of six and a tight budget, it didn't take much to knock the most reasonable plans cockeyed. Medical bills were what worried her. You never knew when one of the kids might get sick or seriously hurt. She herself suffered from a thyroid condition and had had a number of operations. When it looked as though that danger was past, Mike had come down with polio and had spent months in the hospital. Then Kris had run into the street and been struck by a bicycle, had gone into a coma and nearly died. Just a few years ago, Mike had been hit in the shin by a baseball and had developed osteomyelitis.

Every time something went wrong, the damage was not simply to the Dunns' bank account. Mary Helen sometimes felt they were dangerously overdrawing their emotional reserves. Just as a budget could be stretched only so far, nerves, too, had a snapping point. But worried as she was, she kept things to herself. Recently she had been experiencing some trouble with her left eye. Her vision had begun to blur and sometimes she saw double. Maybe she needed new reading glasses. She'd go to a doctor as soon as they got far enough ahead on the monthly bills. Meanwhile she told nobody. She didn't want to worry Tommy and the kids.

As a corollary to her experience with child rearing, Mary Helen took pride in her knowledge of human nature. That evening, as

Wayne walked onto the pier, she sensed something was wrong. All along she had realized that Wayne, as well as Lee, had a crush on Karen, and that her daughter, consciously or not, was playing one brother against the other. But she didn't believe there was anything she could say that wouldn't make the situation worse.

Like Lee, Wayne was short and sturdy. Mary Helen thought he was a healthy, good-looking boy with a nice grin—when you could get him to smile.

But his younger brother was taller by an inch, heavier by about fifteen pounds. Small differences, yet telling ones at that age. An avid weightlifter, Lee already had the build of a mature man, every muscle as neatly defined as the examples in an anatomy textbook. Broad-shouldered, burly in the chest and arms, he walked with a cocky, rolling strut and after a summer of water skiing and swimming, his skin was bronze, his hair tawny gold. Tonight he wore a pair of plaid Bermuda shorts and a football jersey with the sleeves cut off to show his biceps. More than anything, though, it was his expressive features which set him apart from Wayne who often looked wooden and blank.

Mary Helen understood why her daughter liked Lee and recognized that, physically at least, they were well matched. Karen too was short, blond, and burnished by the sun. But Mary Helen couldn't help sympathizing with Wayne. Although she had called him onto the pier so that he wouldn't feel excluded, she feared she had made a mistake. Now he couldn't avoid seeing Karen and Lee sitting close together, talking in low voices, then laughing at some secret joke, touching one another with the kind of playful exuberance in which shoving, poking, and tickling are acts of affection, puppy-love caresses.

To divert his attention, Mary Helen asked Wayne whether he was ready to go back to school. What was his favorite subject? What were his goals this year?

In the next few months, school counselors, lawyers, and cops would lament that Wayne would not communicate with them. But that night, after his months of solitude, the words poured out of him on a riptide of raw emotion and his answers were only vaguely related to her questions. Subject led to subject, grievance to grievance, open sore to open sore.

He told her how much he missed his old neighborhood in Lanham, where the Dresbachs had had a swimming pool, several horses, stables, and a corral. He had had friends there and had never been lonely. Why had his father insisted on moving to Franklin Manor? And why wouldn't he ever let the boys do what they wanted? Why wouldn't he let Wayne take the courses he felt capable of passing?

He complained of his father's strictness, of frequent punishments, and said the man beat him with his fists, blackening his eyes and bloodying his mouth. When he started to talk about his parents' fights which sometimes turned into slugfests, Mary Helen thought she should put an end to this. It was wrong to let a child reveal intimacies about his family. She knew how kids could exaggerate. But his desperate inarticulate groping was too powerful for her to deflect.

As he rambled on, he gnawed his fingernails, then started tearing at the dead skin around them.

"Don't do that," she begged him.

He removed his fingers from his mouth and gripped his knees. Then, abruptly, he shoved his hands into his pockets. His damp palms had left smudges on his pants.

"Wayne," she said, "haven't you ever discussed any of this with your mother and father? Have you told them how you feel?"

"I can't talk to them."

"Do you want me to try?"

He gave her a startled glance. "No, don't do that! Please, Mrs. Dunn, don't mention anything to them. Promise me you won't."

Though she tried not to show it, Karen was worried. As evening lengthened toward night, Lee darted looks over his shoulder at the Dresbach house. The instant that darkness fell, Mr. Dresbach would flick on the spotlight and expect the two boys to dash home. If they didn't hurry—if they were even a few minutes late—they got a whipping.

But with characteristic bravado, Lee sometimes ignored the signal. Embarrassed that he had to be in earlier than Karen, he would stay and talk a little longer. He would tell her not to sweat it. But this was always nerve-wracking for Karen, who didn't want him to get in trouble and be forbidden to date her.

To avoid the problem tonight, she said she was tired; she had to get home. For once he didn't argue, and fortunately Karen's mother was also eager to leave.

Wayne alone seemed reluctant to go and lagged behind, hands in his pockets, head down again. At a fork in the road where the boys branched off to the left and Mary Helen and Karen continued straight ahead to their cottage, the three of them waited for him to catch up.

"Well, see you next weekend," Lee said. Then as Wayne drew near, Lee gave his brother a playful poke in the ribs, shouting, "Race you home." While he dashed off, churning up gravel with his sneakers, Wayne kept to his own slow pace, as if to emphasize the distance yawning between them.

3

As they often did on summer evenings, Dallas and Lena Talbert sat on their screened-in front porch and they saw the boys go by. Although they had been neighbors nearly two years, they didn't know Mr. and Mrs. Dresbach well, but through their own sons they had become friendly with Wayne and Lee, and they were particularly fond of Wayne, who was polite and always ready to lend a hand. He had a keen interest in cars and sometimes helped Mr. Talbert work on his.

In many ways the Talberts were old-fashioned and strict with their children. They expected to be obeyed, and they disciplined Danny and Chris when necessary. But although they would never intrude or "stick our noses into another family's business," they had difficulty comprehending the way Mr. Dresbach dealt with Wayne and Lee.

For one thing, he punished the boys by forcing them to do housework. This seemed to the Talberts senseless and self-defeating, for it virtually ensured that Wayne and Lee would avoid work and flee the house whenever possible.

Dresbach also had a penchant for concocting bizarre punishments. Once when Wayne broke a window with a baseball, his father had made him sit for several hours and contemplate the jagged hole in the glass. Another time, when Wayne was mowing the lawn and missed a two-inch strip of grass that bordered a flower bed, Dresbach ordered him to mow the entire yard again. For hours the boy had stumbled through sweltering August heat, shoving the mower back and forth over grass that had just been cut.

Like everyone else, the Talberts could see that Mr. Dresbach favored Lee and delighted in humiliating Wayne. Yet even when his father punished him for things the boys had done together, or which Lee had done alone, Wayne protected his younger brother and quietly took the blame.

Not long ago, the Talberts remembered, the boys had had a Sunday-morning paper route. While Harold and Shirley slept late, Wayne and Lee delivered the Washington *Post* to customers scattered widely throughout Franklin Manor and the adjacent community of Cape Anne. Eventually they began to sneak off in their father's Chrysler and, with Wayne doing the driving, they hurried back before anybody noticed the car was gone. But then one day Lee demanded to have a turn at the wheel—and promptly ran into a ditch.

When Mr. Dresbach discovered this, he was livid, and both boys feared they were in for a fierce whipping. To spare his brother, Wayne said he had been driving; it was all his fault.

Surprisingly, Dresbach didn't beat Wayne. Instead, he made the boys quit the job—their only steady source of pocket money —and confiscated twenty-six dollars they had saved. Keeping ten dollars to cover the cost of the gas he said they had wasted, he gave the rest of the money to Lee. Since Wayne was the guilty party, Mr. Dresbach explained, he got nothing. Still, Wayne didn't betray his brother.

There was one area, however, in which Dresbach treated his sons with something close to equality. He did his best to prevent them from forming friendships at school and in the neighborhood —or so it seemed to the Talberts. Lee and Wayne were seldom permitted to go on class trips, join clubs, or take part in local youth organizations.

Once she got to know Shirley Dresbach a bit better, Lena Talbert decided she wasn't as despotic as her husband. She wanted the boys to have friends and lead a normal life, but she didn't dare cross Mr. Dresbach. Although Shirley wasn't the sort who warmed quickly to new acquaintances or exchanged easy confidences, she admitted to Lena she was worried about Wayne. At that point he had run away from home several times and was failing all his subjects. Frankly, Shirley said, she didn't know what to do. She had tried to help him with his homework, but it upset her too much. She didn't have the patience to put up with Wayne's academic problems.

She confessed that her husband was too harsh. But that was how he had been raised, and that was how he intended to bring up the boys. At the least sign of defiance—and sometimes for no reason at all—he'd take his belt to them, with no qualms about which end did the damage. "I've talked to him. I've tried to reason with him. I've tried everything." Then in a distant, weary voice, Shirley added, "Sometimes I get so tired, I just don't want to go on. But what can I do? I've tried to commit suicide. Several times."

For a few moments Lena said nothing. Shocked, she was unsure whether it was better to speak or remain silent. But assuming Shirley wouldn't have mentioned this unless she wanted help, Lena asked if there was anything she could do.

Shirley shook her head irritably, as if angry at herself for that brief loss of control. The conversation was closed. It never opened again.

4

While all around them the night throbbed with insects, Mary Helen and Karen walked silently up the dark road. Both mother and daughter were absorbed in thought, unable to discuss what they had each learned about the Dresbachs.

Karen was troubled by two things Lee had told her. First he had said he loved her—which was disturbing enough for a thirteen-year-old girl. Then before that news sank in, he had admitted that Wayne and he were adopted. They had no idea who their real parents were or how they had come to be with the Dresbachs. Lee felt that if Karen cared for him as he cared for her, she had to know this; he couldn't keep that kind of secret from her. Was she surprised, he asked? Did she like him less now that she knew the Dresbachs weren't his parents?

It surprised her, all right. But it didn't change her feelings for him, she said. It was just . . . just strange and sad.

"Do you suppose your real parents are dead?" Karen asked.

"I don't know."

"Haven't you asked your . . . Mr. Dresbach?"

"We don't talk about it. Don't ever mention it around him. Okay?"

"But aren't you curious?"

"No," Lee said in a flat, dry voice. It sounded as if he might get angry and sulk, as he sometimes did.

Still, she couldn't help asking, "Are you happy with them? Are they nice to you?"

"I don't want to talk about it."

While Karen was baffled more by Lee's attitude than by what he had revealed, Mary Helen was as frightened by what Wayne had said as by the vehemence with which he kept repeating it.

He had finished by telling her he hated his father and wished Mr. Dresbach were dead.

"You don't mean that," Mary Helen said.

"Yes, I do. If you knew him, you'd understand. He's always yelling at me, always beating me and punishing me." Then after a pause, "There are other things, too. Things I can't tell you."

Over the years Mary Helen had heard a lot of kids complain about their parents, and she had made it a rule never to repeat what the nursery children told her, never to pursue any conversation about their family lives. But then none of them had ever spoken like Wayne, with a voice that cried out in accusation at the same time that it begged for help. Finally, she asked him about those "other things."

"No, I can't talk about them," he said.

"It might help to tell somebody."

"Not you. I don't want you to know."

"Then explain to your parents what's bothering you."

"That won't help. Nothing will help as long as he's alive."

Although not formally educated, Mary Helen was an avid reader of self-help books and articles on commonsense psychology, and she believed she knew something about the way the human mind works. When people started talking about murder and suicide and such, it might mean nothing; Wayne might just be blowing off steam. But you couldn't take the chance. Mary Helen felt that his parents should be alerted and the boy should see someone—a professional counselor of some sort—just to be on the safe side.

Were it any other family, she wouldn't have hesitated to telephone or drop by. But the Dresbachs were different. Nobody in the neighborhood was on a first-name basis with them, and they struck Mary Helen as standoffish, condescending.

Still, she would have swallowed her pride and called them, if she hadn't been afraid how the Dresbachs might react. Wayne and Lee were terrified of their adoptive parents, and they had transmitted some of this emotion to Mary Helen. Not that she feared what the Dresbachs might say to her. She feared what they would do to Wayne.

She couldn't forget how fervently Wayne begged her not to repeat what he had said, and she remembered an evening a few months ago when Lee had stopped by after dark to visit Karen. The Dunns had been surprised to see him out so late. But he had brushed aside their questions about his curfew, stayed an hour, then left around eleven o'clock.

Fifteen minutes later, he was back, sobbing as he banged at the door. He was trembling too hard to speak, and Tommy Dunn led him to a chair and told him to put his head between his legs before he fainted. With the blood drained from his face, his skin looked like parchment.

Seeing him that way, Karen too went pale.

"What's wrong?" Tommy asked. "Get a hold of yourself and tell us." He feared there had been an accident at the Dresbach house, and they were wasting time waiting for Lee to talk.

"I'm locked out," Lee sobbed.

"What do you mean?"

"I'm locked out of the house." Lee confessed that earlier, when the porch light clicked on, he had run home, as he normally did, and his parents believed he had gone upstairs to bed. But he had crossed from one end of the house to the other on the catwalk, then had crept down the staircase to the carport door and sneaked off to see Karen. When he returned, however, the carport door was locked.

"Did you knock?" Mary Helen asked.

Shaking his head, Lee broke into tears again.

"Well, you'll just have to go back and take your medicine."

"You don't understand. You don't know my father."

"I know he'll be mad. I don't blame him. I am, too. You shouldn't have sneaked off like that. You've put us in a bad spot too."

"But you don't know what he'll do to me!" Lee wailed.

Tommy and Mary Helen exchanged uneasy glances. They couldn't believe a cocky, self-possessed boy like Lee would act this way, especially in front of Karen, unless some unspeakable punishment awaited him.

"Look," Mary Helen said, "you go on home, and I'll call ahead and explain what happened."

"That won't help."

"Sure it will. Now you get started."

While Tommy walked Lee to the gate, Mary Helen dialed Mr. Dresbach.

"Lee just left our place," she told him. "I thought you might be worried."

"Yes, I wondered where he was." There was no warmth, no relief in his voice.

"We didn't know he was supposed to be home in bed. He didn't tell us that until he couldn't get back in the house."

"Yes. I see."

"I realize he shouldn't have done it. But he's very upset, and I'm sure he won't pull a trick like this again."

"Good night, Mrs. Dunn."

"Listen, I know it's none of my business, but—"

"You're right, Mrs. Dunn, it's none of your business."

As Mary Helen stood there with the dead receiver in her hand, she experienced a mixture of anger and something close to dread. She had an irrational impulse to run after Lee and protect him. But Tommy convinced her that much as she might dislike the man's tone of voice, Mr. Dresbach was right. It wasn't their business. Just think how furious she'd be if somebody interfered in their family affairs.

The next day, however, Mary Helen was still worried. When she saw Mrs. Dresbach on the pier, she again tried to explain. But

Shirley Dresbach had a detached manner and a dry, thin voice. The few people who knew her well claimed that she was shy. Others said it was just her formality that made her seem brittle. Whatever the truth was, Mary Helen felt she couldn't crack the woman's veneer; she had the sort of remoteness you saw on the faces of mannequins. The conversation ended with Shirley protesting, "If people would leave us alone, everything would be all right."

After that—after confronting Mr. Dresbach's coldness and Mrs. Dresbach's eerie detachment—Mary Helen couldn't bring herself to go to them now and say that their son wished Mr. Dresbach were dead.

5

Bare-chested, dressed only in Bermuda shorts, Harold Dresbach stood at one of the large picture windows in his living room, staring out at the bay. Over the long weekend, his skin had crisped in the sun and the hair on his chest had turned a copper color. Although not a big man—he was 5'4" and seldom weighed more than 120 pounds—he had a habit of striking poses and "strutting like a banty rooster, the cock of the walk," particularly when there were women around or he was in court pleading a case. As he often did when he was at home, he wore a captain's hat, as much to conceal his baldness as to assert the image he liked to project—that of a leader of men and a lover of many women.

He knew his wife Shirley and a young couple named Darlene and Nick sat in the room behind him, and he was sure they were watching him. But since he was also sure they were waiting for him to start the evening's activities and would be ready whenever he was, he luxuriated a moment longer in standing apart, biding his time, combing his fingers through the hair on his chest.

Illuminated by the spotlight which Dresbach had just switched on to call home Wayne and Lee, his lawn stretched toward the water. His two Chryslers glistened in the driveway. He knew how the house appeared to anyone passing in a boat; it looked like a mansion. The place was only a story and a half high, but it presented its broadest, most impressive side to the bay.

Dresbach believed he had come a long way and done all right for a small-town boy from rural Kansas. Born in Nickerson, the son of a stockman, he had been raised on a hardscrabble farm outside of Hutchinson. Of his early life there, he told his adopted sons very little except that it had been difficult and that he had had none of the advantages which he provided them and which they took for granted. Family friends and acquaintances amplified this, recalling that Dresbach claimed to have been abandoned by his parents as a child and brought up by an aunt.

By the age of seventeen he had developed an abiding interest in politics and served as a Democratic precinct clerk in the staunchly Republican state. Perhaps recognizing the futility of this, he finished Hutchinson Junior College and left the area during the depths of the Depression, moving to Washington, D.C., where he worked his way through the National University Law School at George Washington University.

Graduating in 1936, he married Shirley Shaffer, who hailed from Elk City, but came from a much different—and to his thinking, much better—family than his. While he never had much to say about his own background and his efforts to rise above it, Shirley often spoke of her childhood and of spending months in the Governor's mansion in Topeka. Then when her famous uncle, Harry Woodring, moved to Washington and married Helen Coolidge, the daughter of Marcus Coolidge, a senator from Massachusetts, Shirley lived with them for a while at Woodlawn, the house George Washington had built near Mount Vernon. Although all this had ended abruptly in 1940, when Roosevelt forced Woodring to resign as Secretary of War because of his isolationist views on World War II, Shirley cherished the memories and until the end of her life was eager to share them with anyone who would listen.

Harold Dresbach—Pat, as his close friends called him—had never attained anything comparable to the Governor's mansion or Woodlawn, but he thought he had made the most of his opportunities. With income from several sources besides his legal practice, he had invested in stocks, oil leases in Kansas, and real estate in the Washington suburbs. Leaving the boys with a series of maids and baby-sitters, he and Shirley drove down to

Florida almost every winter and had traveled in Europe and
Africa. They entertained often and numbered among their friends
dozens of politicians, labor leaders, lawyers, businessmen, military
officers, and the vice president of a major national airline—none
of whom would come forward to assist in the investigation of the
Dresbachs' deaths or to give testimony about their lives.

Even a man of Pat Dresbach's sizable ego, however, could not
have deluded himself that his life had been without failures. Perhaps in emulation of Shirley's Uncle Harry, he had twice run for
political office—for the Maryland House of Delegates in 1954 and
the State Senate in 1958—and had lost badly both times.

What was worse, his wife was unable to have children.
When drunk, Pat complained of her infertility and criticized her
so mercilessly she sometimes fled the house. After they adopted
Wayne and Lee, he still said he wanted kids of his own.

But perhaps the darkest episode in his life—the suicide attempt
which had left scars on both his wrists—remained a mystery
which he never mentioned to anyone. He would, however, publicly mock his wife for her failed efforts at suicide.

6

Reaching the house, Wayne paused at the edge of the lawn,
just beyond Pat Dresbach's range of vision, and peered at his father framed in the picture window. He could see Dresbach's bare
upper torso, but not his shorts, and he feared he was naked. That
meant his mother probably was, too.

The Dresbachs were nudists—had been for years—and it was
not at all uncommon for the boys to see their parents walk
around the house without clothes. Neither of them liked that; it
made them acutely uncomfortable. But it was far better than seeing Pat and Shirley naked in front of strangers. There was an automobile with out-of-state license plates in the driveway, so
Wayne and Lee decided to use the carport door and slip upstairs
without going past the company in the living room.

Although their parents had taken them to nudist camps from
the time they were just beyond the toddling stage, Lee and
Wayne had recently started to protest. No matter how much

their father assured them nudism was normal and healthy, they thought it was wrong, shameful. As he blundered through puberty, Wayne, in particular, felt self-conscious and didn't want his parents to know that his body had changed, that he now had pubic hair. What would they do if they saw him with an erection? It was the sort of thing Pat Dresbach was sure to make fun of. Or punish him for. He hated being exposed to the man in any way.

But not going to nudist camps also had its hazards. Every time they refused, their father was furious and made them stay indoors and do housework while he and his wife went alone.

The boys were halfway up the stairs when somebody called their names. Wayne felt his belly tighten. They had no choice but to turn back and go through the kitchen into the long combination dining room–living room.

Though relieved to see that his parents and the other couple were clothed, Wayne sensed there was still a possibility of trouble. His father's face was flushed, and his eyes were slow to focus, just as they were whenever he had had too much to drink.

A white fur rug was spread in front of the unlit fireplace, and around it were clustered several easy chairs and a sofa. While Shirley sat somewhat apart from the others, her husband had squeezed onto the sofa with the young couple whom he introduced to the boys as Nick and Darlene—no last names. Lee, then Wayne, stepped forward and shook hands.

"Don't they have nice manners," Darlene said. It was something people were always saying.

"They better," Pat growled. "How about bringing us fresh drinks? And don't get your fingers caught in the ice machine, Wayne. That kid's got the coordination of a snake with a broken back."

"You mean they're bartenders?" Nick asked.

As a matter of fact they were. From the time they were ten or eleven, they had been taught to mix drinks. When they lived in Lanham, they were often seen circulating at parties, serving cocktails to people who had come to swim nude in the Dresbach pool. As discreet as professional bartenders, they also knew better than to mention to anybody what they saw at home.

Nor did they normally discuss such things with one another. Perhaps they were afraid of being overheard. Or, since a certain amount of distrust had cropped up between them, maybe each boy feared the other would betray him to his father. But most likely, given their youth and the depths of their bewilderment, they simply didn't know what to say.

So that night as they mixed drinks, they didn't comment on how young Nick and Darlene were—at least twenty years the Dresbachs' juniors. And they didn't mention what an improbable pair they were. While Nick was well dressed and talked, as Wayne remembered, "like a college man," Darlene had the brassy, hard-edged look of a barmaid. Wearing a purple halter and a pair of black short-shorts, she had her hair sculpted into a beehive and her lips smeared bright red, a different shade from the color on her finger- and toenails.

As the boys brought in the drinks, Pat Dresbach was discussing one of his favorite subjects: the way he wanted to die. "I'd like to croak in jail at age ninety-nine, awaiting trial for rape."

Darlene and Nick laughed, but Shirley nodded to the boys, whispering, "Don't talk that way, Pat."

"What the hell are you protecting them from? They gotta learn sometime."

"About sex or death?" Nick asked.

"Both. They need to know the difference."

Again everybody laughed, except Shirley and the boys.

Shirley tried not to grimace or frown. She knew how crude Pat could be and had learned long ago that any display of disapproval merely egged him on. Her face was set in what she imagined was a neutral expression. But with her chin lifted, her gray eyes aimed at some object in the distance, and her lips pressed firmly together, she looked prim, self-contained, and disapproving toward the people around her.

She glanced at Lee and Wayne and believed she had given them a faint, reassuring smile. Although they never spoke of it, she assumed the three of them understood one another and shared a conspiracy against Pat. But even as she smiled—or thought she had—Shirley did not open her lips. Self-conscious

about her false teeth and fearful of her husband, she took the precaution of showing only a narrow range of emotions.

Yet this, too, infuriated Pat who sometimes snarled, "What the
hell are you, constipated? That's why you're so fat. You're full of
shit."

At forty-seven, Shirley had started to lose her figure and put on
weight. Still, Pat liked her to wear a bikini—or nothing at all.

Among Dresbach's many rules, the primary one was that his
children should be neither seen nor heard. Whenever he had
company, he ordered the boys upstairs and expected them to stay
there until morning. For this Shirley was grateful; she thought it
reduced the chances for arguments and ugly scenes. But tonight
Pat told them to stand at attention in front of the sofa, and
Shirley dreaded what she knew was coming.

Although the brothers strongly resembled one another, the
differences between them were emphasized when they stood side
by side. Where Wayne's hair was short and wild, Lee's long
blond locks were combed into a kind of pompadour. Lee's teeth
were large, white, and even, but Wayne's had been chipped when
he fell from a jungle gym. While Lee's shoulders were thrown
back and his head was held high, Wayne's shoulders sloped and
his eyes were lowered.

"Get your hands out of your pockets," Dresbach told Wayne.
"And straighten up."

"It's late," Shirley interrupted timidly. "They have school tomorrow."

Ignoring her, Pat asked Nick and Darlene, "Which one do you
think is older?" Then before they could speak, he answered his
own question. "Wayne is, by eleven months. Can you believe it?
Not only is he smaller than his kid brother, he should be a year
ahead of him at school. But why don't you tell these people what
happened, Wayne?"

"I failed the ninth grade."

"What? Speak up. Can't hear you!"

"I failed the ninth grade."

"Why?"

He glanced at Shirley, then back to his father. "Well, I wanted
to take the general course, but I got stuck in academic and I . . .

well, I . . ." He was gesturing with his hands as he groped for words.

"Quit waving your arms like a goddamn wop. And tell the truth. You flunked because you're lazy."

"That's not it." He pressed his fists to his sides. "I just belong in the general course."

"Why? You want to be a ditchdigger the rest of your life?"

Shirley hoped he wouldn't answer. Once when Pat asked him this question, he had said, "Yes, that's what I'd like to be," and Pat had hit Wayne in the face with his fist, knocking him over a coffee table.

"He'll do better this year," Shirley said.

"Sure he will," said Nick, made noticeably uncomfortable by this domestic tirade.

"I doubt it," Dresbach said. "The trouble is, he's almost as stubborn as he is stupid. I always hoped he'd be a good example for Lee, somebody for him to look up to. But Lee, he's the leader. He's better at school, better at sports, more popular with girls."

As Pat ran through the litany of Wayne's failures, Shirley thought he was goading himself more than he was Wayne. Certainly he showed more emotion, and it seemed to be Wayne's refusal to react that fueled his father's rage. But she knew from experience it was better to take it in silence than to fight back, better to remain passive than to offer Pat an excuse to do what he wanted, which was to cause pain, draw blood.

By now Pat was shouting, "You're nothing but a bastard—an ungrateful little bastard."

"Please don't call him that," Shirley mumbled, but she stayed in her chair off to one side, afraid to come between her husband and her adopted son.

"Why? That's what he is. Nothing but a worthless bastard."

In the silence that followed, the boys stood at attention, like soldiers on punishment detail. Darlene gazed into the fireplace; Nick rattled the ice in his glass; Shirley let her eyes drift toward the ceiling.

"Oh, fuck it all," Dresbach said. "Mix us another round, then get to bed, both of you."

Shirley thought relief was written clearly on her face. In fact, she looked bored.

7

At the top of the stairs Lee's room lay to the right, Wayne's to the left. Switching on the light, Wayne sagged onto the edge of the bed, staring at a second door in his room, the one which led to the catwalk, then to the outside staircase. He was angry, sad, deflated. He felt this way whenever his father hollered at him in front of company, and he couldn't imagine a time when the humiliation would end. As long as they lived in the same house, he believed his father would ridicule him, comparing him unfavorably with Lee.

Fleetingly he considered running away. But he had tried that four times already and had begun to suspect there was no way of escaping his father.

There also seemed no way of escaping that word, "bastard," of all the insults he had to suffer, the one he hated most. Over the years, depending on Pat Dresbach's mood, Wayne had been told wildly different stories about his real parents—that they had been killed in an automobile accident, that they had relinquished Lee and him because they were poor and unstable, that they had offered the boys in payment of a legal bill. But in every account there were two constants: his parents hadn't been married and they didn't want him. Sometimes Dresbach made it sound as if it were Wayne alone—not Lee—they were anxious to get rid of. Only he was the worthless bastard.

Much as he would have liked to learn more about his real parents, he didn't dare ask. He had done that once, and Dresbach had burst out angrily, "Why the hell all this interest in them? Aren't we good enough for you?"

As always, after his father had hollered at him, Wayne couldn't sleep. For years he had hoped he would get used to Dresbach's verbal abuse. He thought if he was patient, if he was willing to put up with the pain, he would eventually lose the capacity to feel or to care. It would be like going barefoot. The first warm day of spring he could hardly bear to tender-foot it along the gravel and crushed-shell road to the pier. But by early summer his feet were calloused and hard as shoe leather.

But it didn't work that way with his emotions. His father's

Life for Death

taunts hurt him more now, not less. Wayne's hide seemed to have gotten thinner, and the bruises and abrasions never healed.

Moving over to his desk, he opened a volume of the Encyclopedia Britannica. This was part of his summer-long punishment, the keystone of his father's program to upgrade his academic performance.

When he flunked the ninth grade, the Dresbachs had had him tested at the Remedial Education Center in Washington, D.C. Then, after the battery of interviews and examinations, they brought him home, marched him up to his room, and laid down the law. In addition to staying indoors all during the vacation, he was to read the encyclopedia every night. Wayne assumed that the Remedial Education Center had recommended this, that because of his low scores, his parents had been told to discipline him for being dumb.

In fact the center had recommended something quite different. Staff diagnostician Louise Lee reported that "Wayne's scores on the oral reading and spelling [tests] are well above grade level. There are indications in his handling of arithmetic problems and the comprehension section of the silent reading test that show need of help in *how* to study. (It should be noted that his performance in arithmetic in the Wechsler-Bellevue was average.)"

To find out whether visual handicaps prevented him from fulfilling his intellectual potential, Miss Lee administered "dominance" and Keystone Visual Survey tests.

"Dominance tests . . . determine whether there is any left-sided tendency or mixture of dominance. Either of these tendencies appears to be a contributing factor to the establishment of left-to-right progression in reading and writing and the making of reversal errors."

Significantly, Miss Lee learned that "Wayne is right-handed and right-footed, but left-eyed."

As for the Keystone Visual Survey, "Wayne's performance on these tests was not satisfactory for usable vision with the right eye for either far or near point, nor for stereopsis."

It was revealed that as a child Wayne had had an operation on his right eye to correct a squint. Subsequently he lost effective use of that eye altogether and depended entirely on his left eye, thus accounting for the dominance problem Miss Lee had discovered and the trouble he had reading numbers.

But she concluded that these physical difficulties, bothersome as they might be, were of secondary importance. "Many inconsistencies and blockings in Wayne's performance . . . indicate need of help in straightening out emotional problems before he can function adequately in an academic situation."

Myra Orleans, the psychologist at the Remedial Education Center, carried Miss Lee's conclusions further, reemphasizing that, although Wayne's intelligence was above average:

> There is evidence in the pattern of his performance and in his uneven functioning that emotional problems are hampering Wayne and impairing his efficiency. His test responses sometimes reflect poor social and practical judgment.
>
> At this time Wayne is functioning below his intellectual potential. He seems very anxious and worried about himself and his capabilities. Although there are strong indications that he would like to both solve his personal problems and perform better academically, he feels helpless and is quite dependent and insecure. Psychiatric evaluation and psychotherapy are recommended.

The Dresbachs never discussed any of this with Wayne—neither his visual impairment nor his need for psychotherapy. Instead, they told him he was lazy and stupid. And of course they kept him in his room reading the encyclopedia.

But what began as a punishment soon became one of the few pleasures in his life. Through reading Wayne found the release, the escape, which running away had not provided. Each evening when his father sent him upstairs, he grumbled as if he couldn't bear to face another book. But once he had retreated to his bedroom with its view of the bay and its slanting dormer ceiling which suggested a cozy tent, he relaxed and felt relatively safe, his one fear being that if his parents learned how much he liked it here, they might put the room off limits. Opening the encyclopedia to his favorite subjects, he would read about nature, animals, exploration, and adventure.

This night, however, he was too upset to concentrate. His eyes ran over the pages, but nothing registered, nothing made sense. Frequently after scenes with his father, regardless of whether Dresbach was hollering at him alone, or at Lee and Shirley as well, Wayne couldn't finish his homework and next day at school couldn't keep his mind on the assignments. His teachers said that this dreamy, distracted quality was one reason he never worked up to his ability.

Leaving the book open, not bothering to switch off the overhead light, Wayne lay on the bed and let his thoughts roam. Actually they were scarcely thoughts, more like flickering, disjointed films which replayed all the most painful experiences of his life. Later, when he tried to describe these haunting memory-films which sent him reeling back through the years, his words were dry and lifeless, and not even the efforts of dozens of psychiatrists could help him unkink the chronology. But for Wayne the memories remained charged with such emotion that even though he spoke in monosyllables and in a monotone, his hands trembled and his palms turned moist with sweat.

He remembered his father's taunts, the petty cruelties, the broken promises. The man was a master at raising the boys' hopes, then dashing them. Frequently Dresbach swore that if they behaved themselves, he would take them to amusement parks or ball games. But then he would deny he had said any such thing.

Most of all, Wayne remembered the arguments, the beatings, the shouting matches between his adoptive parents which degenerated into fistfights. Often he was rousted out of bed late at night, dragged downstairs with Lee, and told that the family was splitting up. Who did the boys want to stay with—their mother or father? And when they invariably chose Shirley, Pat whipped them, punched his wife, smashed glasses, furniture, and windows. At least once a month this scene was repeated so that by 1960, the spring Wayne failed the ninth grade, he told the high school counselor he wouldn't be returning to Southern that fall. His parents were getting a divorce, he said, and his mother planned to move out west with Lee and him. Other times he told people his father would take Lee while his mother kept him.

For a while this daydream sustained him. In a small town

somewhere in the Rocky Mountains, he and Shirley would live alone and they would be happy. He would go to school, but take the general course and in the afternoon he'd work somewhere—maybe in a grocery store—to help pay the bills. That would leave them weekends to ride horses or to hike through the redwood forests he had seen in his encyclopedia. Then in winter they would call on their water-skiing experience and learn to snow ski.

But the appeal of the dream dissipated whenever Wayne remembered that he had already been out west with Shirley. A few summers ago the whole family had driven to Kansas to visit relatives and see where Pat and Shirley had been born.

On the way, while the boys watched the endless white stripe of highway disappear beneath the Chrysler, Shirley told them about her parents, who were approaching eighty—they had been married for sixty years—and who sounded as if they had stepped out of a cheerful TV program about the frontier. Early in the century, her father, Art Shaffer, had worked for the Crystal Ice Company, hauling blocks of ice from Independence to Elk City in a farm wagon. He'd set off from Elk City about one o'clock in the afternoon, pick up his load in Independence, cover it with hay, then drive back in the cool of night. Once, when the river had flooded and he couldn't cross at Clifford's Ford, he had had to detour and come into town on the Sedan road. By the time he reached Elk City, the cakes weighed only fifty pounds.

Pat, however, said nothing about his family, and as soon as they reached the heat-warped, windswept, dusty plains, he didn't want to visit anybody or see anything. For more than a week he stayed in the motel, drunk from morning till night, babbling about his childhood, yelling and slapping at his children.

Fed up with him, Shirley had moved in with her mother and father, but for some reason she didn't bring Wayne and Lee with her. She left them in that room with Dresbach, to weather his binge as best they could. Perhaps she thought he was too far gone to harm them. Maybe she had been pushed and tormented to the point where she could only think of saving herself. But as Wayne lay awake at night, smelling the sour stench of his father's body, watching him hawk up the bitter contents of his belly, then pass out and snuffle and groan through the stiff whiskers of his nose, the boy felt he had been abandoned, set adrift on this strange, rolling ocean of land.

Concerning the nudist camps, Wayne recalled driving with his parents to New Jersey, to a place named "the something Pines. We went there a lot." When Lee and he were kids, they played contentedly with the other children, but as they grew older, they noticed a lot of family friends and business acquaintances there, and it bothered them to see these men and women without clothes.

Then one day at home Wayne discovered a cache of photographs in the bottom drawer of his father's desk. Since there were so many shots of those same family friends, he thought they must have been taken at nudist camps. But along with the familiar faces, he recognized familiar spots—the swimming pool in Lanham, the secluded patio in Franklin Manor, his parents' bedroom, the living room in front of the fireplace. And the people weren't playing volleyball or sunbathing, as they did at camp.

There were close-ups of couples engaged in intercourse, oral sex, sodomy. Sometimes three or four people were sandwiched together. Then long lines of them, more than a dozen men and women, were locked together at the lips, the anus, the loins, their faces contorted, their bodies straining.

Positive that these photos came from his father's new Polaroid camera, Wayne shuffled through them again, fearful he would find one of his mother. Some of the women had their faces averted, and there were several bodies that resembled Shirley's. But Wayne decided it could not be; he didn't believe his mother would do anything like this.

Both fascinated and repelled, he dug deeper into the drawer, then methodically searched the house, uncovering a trove of pornography, most of it professional, some of it amateur. There was, for instance, a sheaf of eight-by-ten glossies—blurred action shots of couples in motel rooms, their angry eyes glazed by flashbulbs. Later Wayne learned that his father used these pictures as evidence in divorce cases. Rumor had it that Dresbach derived special pleasure from taking his own photographs of philandering husbands and wives and, with uncanny frequency, his customers, primarily the women, became family friends who wound up posing in group shots and daisy chains.

Pat Dresbach's legal practice offered an easy way of meeting young, lonely, and vulnerable women, and this, in turn, was a way of ensuring the friendship of powerful men who had specialized appetites. There are those who believe that, far from being a mere dabbler and private collector, he was a pornography dealer. But whatever the extent of his involvement in this trade, Dresbach seems to have used sex for professional gain as well as pleasure.

His own personal preference was for animals. He liked pictures of women being mounted by dogs and donkeys and of young girls forcing into their mouths the tumescent organs of goats and horses. Through his friendship with an airline executive, Dresbach obtained reduced-price fares and sometimes flew to Tijuana for the specialty acts. Then in 1958 he traveled to North Africa to see an elaborate exhibition of zoophilism.

The following summer, Shirley went to Europe with a family friend, Louise Pettit, leaving the boys alone with Pat. As Wayne recalled, "Lee asked her if we could go and she just laughed and said that she had enough trouble with us at home. She stayed [away] a couple of months."

Wayne missed her, he admitted, but didn't really blame her for leaving Lee and him with their father, who had been obstreperous lately and had beaten Shirley the night before she departed. He did say, however, that he soon got tired of all the work they had to do. Now, in addition to their usual chores, they had to cook and clean and, at Pat's insistence, they remained indoors most of the day answering the telephone and taking down business messages.

Then their father started bringing home strange women. When one named Mary Jane moved in, Wayne told Lee he was leaving. Though his younger brother chose not to join him, Wayne removed the outboard motor from one of the family boats and bolted it onto a runabout that belonged to a friend. He and the other boy set off down the bay, south toward Calvert Cliffs, beaching the boat there and hiding the motor. Then they struck out overland, hitchhiking to Shenandoah, Virginia, where his friend had once lived. A hundred and seventy miles from home, Wayne felt happy and as far as he was concerned, he had gone for good—although he had given no thought to how he would support himself.

Within a few days somebody recognized Wayne's friend and called his family. The boy's father drove down to pick them up and brought them back to Franklin Manor, where Dresbach was too drunk to do anything except scream at Wayne.

Perhaps he was also too tired. A woman named Cora had moved in with Mary Jane, and both of them slept in the same bed with Pat. According to Wayne, Cora cussed a lot, but Mary Jane seemed like a nice woman. He said that about her even after his father sobered up and beat him with a razor strap while Mary Jane sat and watched.

The day Shirley returned from Europe, the boys were exuberant, and Pat, too, was in a buoyant mood. No doubt he assumed —quite rightly—that neither Wayne nor Lee would mention the women he had brought into the house.

Together they drove to Washington to pick Shirley up at the airport. Then to celebrate her homecoming, they stopped at a restaurant for dinner. But it took a long time to get a table, and Pat had finished four martinis before they were served. When Shirley asked him to slow down, he told her, "Shut the fuck up," and ordered a bottle of wine. Although she said nothing more, he continued to lash out at her, then at the boys.

Soon other customers were staring at them. Someone must have complained; the manager stepped over and asked Dresbach to quiet down or leave.

Having long since lost his appetite, Wayne wanted to flee this room full of people, all of whom were watching now. But his father wanted to fight.

It was a common occurrence. When he drank, Dresbach got loud, and when he was shouting full pitch, someone always told him to shut up. After that he was as likely to throw a plate as a punch. Once in a bar, Wayne had seen him smash a beer mug through the glass front of a pinball machine. Around Washington and Annapolis there were dozens of clubs and restaurants which had kicked him out and warned him not to return.

Tonight he cursed the manager and the bouncer, too. He said he'd take them both on; he said he'd never come back; he said he'd sue. He was still shouting as they muscled him across the room and out the door. And he shouted all the way home, driving eighty and ninety miles an hour over unbanked country roads while his wife and boys begged him to slow down.

When they reached Franklin Manor, he dragged Shirley from the car and cracked her in the mouth, knocking her to the pavement. On hands and knees, she scuttled across the driveway and dashed into the house, locking the door behind her. But Dresbach broke a window, went in after her, and grabbed her by the hair and was hammering her with his fists when Lee and Wayne tried to pull him away.

"You little bastards, you want some, too?" Turning on the boys, he chased them through the kitchen, walloping them in the back as they ran up the outside staircase. Then at the top he caught Lee, pushed him against the wall, and pummeled him. Wayne grabbed his father by the shoulders and shoved.

For an instant Dresbach teetered. Then he fell backward, his head thudding against each step as he slid to the bottom of the stairwell.

Wayne froze, half-afraid he had killed his father, half-afraid that he hadn't. He expected Dresbach to bound up the stairs, slashing at him like a buzz saw. But Pat stayed where he was, curled on his side, unconscious, a surprisingly small man, scarcely believable as a child- and wife-beater. Though he revived after Lee, Wayne, and Shirley carried him into the bedroom, he didn't protest when they stretched him out fully clothed and pulled a cover up to his neck.

Minutes later, Wayne left the house and wandered for the rest of the night. Once again, he swore he would never go back; he couldn't stand it any longer. But he had no real plan and no money. He wasn't a streetwise hustler, and in 1959 there was no subculture of dopers, pimps, and pushers to welcome runaways from small towns. He made it as far as the nearby community of Shady Side, where the police spotted him the next morning strolling aimlessly along the road. Showing little interest in why he had left home, they drove him back to Franklin Manor.

The same pattern marked the third and fourth times he took

off. He set out with no plan and no hope except to put distance between his father and him. Once he hitchhiked to his old neighborhood in Lanham and met a boy his age who also wanted to run away. They were following some railroad tracks into Washington when a plainclothesman picked them up.

Weeks later he was off again, this time with the idea of heading south to Florida. But that night as he crawled into a parked car to sleep, the police nabbed him, slapped him into a cell at the Upper Marlboro Station, and called his father.

Mr. Dresbach drove over from Franklin Manor and demanded to see his son.

Wayne heard one of the guards say, "I'm not letting you in there with that stick."

"Just gimme the little bastard and I'll take care of him outside."

"The condition you're in, I can't turn him over to you. Sober up and come back tomorrow."

"I'm his father. I'm a lawyer. I'll have your goddamn badge."

"Hold it down, mister, or you'll end up spending the night in the cell next to his."

Although relieved that the police hadn't handed him over, Wayne realized his punishment had only been postponed. Tomorrow or the next day, Pat Dresbach would return and take him away. There was nothing he could do about that and no way to avoid a tongue-lashing and a whipping. Even if he could have brought himself to tell the police what was happening at home, he didn't believe they would protect him.

Several times, when Dresbach was manhandling the boys or her, Shirley had called the cops. But the instant Pat saw a squad car pull into the driveway, he calmed down and composed himself. It was startling—almost frightening, Wayne remembered— to witness this rapid metamorphosis and hear the man's voice, which had been shrill with threats and obscenities, drop into a lower register, taking on the reasonable tones of a successful lawyer.

Yes, he would concede to the puzzled officers, there had been a family spat, and he and his wife had probably lost their tempers, the way married couples sometimes will. But it was nothing serious, certainly nothing to bother them about. He hoped they understood; they must have known how women are. With a wink or a rueful smile, he would allude to the tension, the foul moods, and the nagging he always had to endure at this time of the month.

And sitting there with her hair disheveled, her lips trembling, and her clothes rumpled, Shirley would appear to be the very picture of menstrual hysteria. There was no use trying to persuade these men otherwise; she had soon learned the dangers of doing that. The moment the police left, Dresbach was likely to turn on her again.

Now Shirley no longer risked calling for help. Whenever she was fed up or frightened, she left the house, sometimes staying away for days, letting the boys fend for themselves.

Still, the police had another occasion to visit that big red-brick house on the waterfront. They showed up on a winter morning, with one officer at the wheel of the pink-and-white Chrysler and a second driving a squad car with Dresbach sprawled in the back seat. They said they had found Pat on a deserted road, moaning about his shoulder and how horribly it hurt. He claimed he had somehow been hit by the tailfin of a passing car and had barely had the strength to crawl back into the Chrysler before he collapsed.

Solicitous, deferential, the police took Shirley aside and explained that Pat didn't appear to be badly injured. But he had been drinking. In fact, he was still quite drunk and could not sit up straight at the kitchen table. Recommending coffee, a couple of aspirin, and a lot of rest, the officers took their leave, politely asking Shirley to keep her husband off the road when he was in this condition.

Afterward, slumped in a chair, Dresbach refused to eat or drink anything, refused to go to bed. He was in pain, he hollered. Why didn't somebody help him?

While Lee and Wayne looked on from the kitchen door, Shirley asked if he wanted her to call a doctor.

"To hell with a doctor. You do something."

"But what, Pat?" Like the boys, she was afraid that at any moment his agony would turn to anger and he would strike out at her. She kept her distance.

When Dresbach pitched to his feet, the three of them backed away warily and watched him fumble in a drawer next to the sink. Then, when he grabbed a butcher knife and staggered toward them, they scattered into the dining room. But, waving the knife, he cried, "Don't go. For God's sake, help me."

Losing his balance, he lunged, and the knife dropped to the floor at Shirley's feet.

Quickly she picked it up, and Pat stumbled back to the kitchen table, sat down, and unbuttoned his shirt, exposing a purple bruise on his left shoulder. "Cut it off."

"What are you talking about?" Shirley asked.

"My arm's killing me. Cut it off."

"You're crazy."

"Do what I tell you, goddammit."

Years later Wayne still recalled his father's voice wailing with a depth of misery which could not have been caused solely by that bruised shoulder. It sounded as if Dresbach were pleading with his wife to kill him, and as she stood there tense and expectant, testing the weight of the knife in her hand, she appeared to consider doing just that. With two strides she could have crossed the kitchen and plunged the blade into his bare chest.

But Wayne moved first. Stepping between his parents, he grabbed the knife from Shirley.

"Okay, you do it," Pat said to him. "Come on and cut it off."

Putting the butcher knife back in the drawer, Wayne ran up to his room, his damp hands shaking. Much as he hated the man, he had not been tempted to stab his father. But struck by the rare intensity of her eyes, the pugnacious set of her jaw, he wondered whether his mother might have done it. And he wondered why his father wanted to die.

On nights like this, when Wayne dangled in a web of memories, he often fell asleep on top of the covers, looking straight up at the light. But tonight, as he was drifting off, he heard something strange downstairs—a series of muffled groans, followed by what sounded like slaps. Always concerned for his mother's safety, he stepped out into the hallway and strained in the darkness, trying to distinguish voices. Someone was getting hurt—that was clear—and Wayne decided to see what was the matter.

Creeping down the stairs to where an oriental carpet was draped over the banister, he crouched and continued to listen, still not daring to break his father's rule and spy on the company. But the slapping was louder now, the moaning more resonant. When he heard his mother's voice, he drew back the carpet and gazed into the living room.

On the white fur rug in front of the fireplace, his father lay on his back naked and, while Darlene, also naked, sat astride him, posting like an equestrienne, Dresbach reached up and slapped her face and breasts, leaving the pink imprint of his hand. Far from not liking it, Darlene urged him on, riding him hard, her breath coming in quick rasps.

Wayne swung his eyes away, but wound up staring at his mother. She was on the sofa, stretched out under Nick, who drove up into her while she lay there inert, her arms and legs limp. Wayne thought she had to have been forced, was hurt, and staying motionless out of fright or pain. But then her spine arched and she began groaning and brought both arms and legs up around Nick, hugging his shoulders and hips.

Letting go of the carpet, Wayne sank back against the wall. But he could still hear her groans. Crawling up the stairs and into his room, he closed the door.

He could expect anything from his father. But he had believed that his mother was different, that he could trust her and that she was on his side. Now he thought she was just as bad as Dresbach.

For the second time that night Wayne sat on his bed, staring at the door to the catwalk that led to the outside staircase down to the carport. Or, if he took a brief detour, it would lead to his father's office where five rifles were racked on the wall.

Fall 1960

The school year went much as Wayne had feared it would. Although he made passing grades, this didn't satisfy his parents, and each day after class he had to hurry home while Lee ran off to football practice. On weekends he was allowed out only when he went with Pat and Shirley and sat in the stands cheering for his younger brother. Then as the other kids drove off with their dates to victory parties or dances, he returned to Franklin Manor and climbed the stairs to his room.

Wayne thought it was like being in prison—the confinement, the petty restrictions, the rules enforced under the threat of immediate punishment, the isolation, the silence. Unless he was drunk or angry, Pat seldom had much to say, and at meals the family set about eating as if the goal were to see who could finish and get away first.

Wayne was glad to have his room to hide in. Having mixed his father three or four martinis every night before dinner, he knew how little it would take to ignite the flame that smoldered just beneath the confident, good-natured surface which Dresbach showed the rest of the world. All that fall the arguments and fights raged on between Shirley and Pat, and some mornings no amount of powder could camouflage the bruises and cuts on her face.

On nights when they had company, Dresbach continued to order the boys to stand at attention while he taunted Wayne with Lee's superiority. Then later, when the guests had gone, he dragged them out of bed and subjected them to the inevitable grilling. He and Shirley were getting a divorce, he'd say. Who did they want to stay with? Their answer was always the same, as was his violent reaction.

Fortunately for Wayne, however, 1960 was an election year, and some of Pat's energy was diverted to politics. Like many Americans, he faithfully watched the televised debates between

Richard Nixon and John Kennedy and he encouraged his sons to
sit with him while he explained the issues. This was history, he
said, a subject they should study for its lessons about the future.

One of Kennedy's campaign promises caught Wayne's attention. Appealing to the nation's idealism, the young senator from
Massachusetts swore he would inaugurate a new program called
the Peace Corps which would send volunteers to distant corners
of the globe. There they would teach English, offer technical and
agricultural advice, and—what immediately inflamed Wayne's
imagination—serve as forest rangers. It sounded like a program
expressly designed to rescue him; he envisioned himself in the
mountains of South America or the rain forests of Africa, far
away on his own, respected and loved by the people he was helping.

But, of course, he was fifteen years old and having a hard
time understanding arithmetic. A remote frontier post on another
continent seemed less chimerical to him than the day he would
graduate from high school.

It was this way whenever he attempted to imagine an end to
his misery. Sometimes he was tempted to run away and try to
join the Navy. But then staring into the bathroom mirror,
searching for his first whiskers, Wayne would admit that he had
difficulty passing for his own age; he'd never be able to trick a
recruitment officer. He'd have to wait until he was eighteen, and
he feared he'd never make it.

2

Although by early October the days were still warm and the air,
humming with bees, was laced with the winy scent of wind-fallen
apples, the bay was too cold for swimming and water skiing. At
night, as the temperature dropped and the wind rose, Wayne
stood in the window of his room and watched crisp leaves skitter
over the ground, piling up against the bulkhead in heaps of red,
purple, and gold. He had a fantasy of sneaking out with matches
and setting them afire, signaling the ships in the channel to rescue him. But then rain turned the leaves to soggy mulch.

Despite the wet weather, the Dunns continued coming down
on weekends. They had installed a space heater in their cottage

and in the evening the family gathered around it to eat popcorn and talk. Lee joined them, huddling close to Karen, and a few times Wayne stopped by, too. But to Mary Helen he seemed as changed as the season. He was even quieter now and appeared to be sunk deeply into himself. Since that night on the pier when so much had poured out of him, he had not spoken to her at all about his family. Whenever she asked how he was, he said, "Okay." When she pressed him, "How about at home?" he said, "It's about the same," but wouldn't elaborate.

Although back then Tommy Dunn knew nothing specific about the Dresbachs—his wife had never told him what Wayne had revealed—they had always seemed odd to him. They were unlike any people he had ever met.

Tommy himself was from Cincinnati, Ohio, the third son in a large, poor family which became poorer still—downright destitute, in fact—when his father died. To keep the family together, his mother went to work as a charwoman, and while she was down on her knees scrubbing floors, Tommy was out on the street selling newspapers. He worked the same corner with a burly black boy named Ezzard Charles, who later went on to win the heavyweight championship of the world.

Tommy, too, was a boxer, a lightweight, but he had little opportunity to train. When his mother married a widower who had a lot of children of his own, there were even more mouths to feed, and Tommy had to quit high school and find a full-time job driving a laundry truck.

In a sense, World War II saved him. He joined the Navy, was stationed in Washington, D.C., and assigned to the Naval Exchange laundry. After his discharge, he stayed where he was and eventually advanced to assistant manager, then manager.

For more than thirty years, he was around military people. Most of them were all right, he thought, but he was never like them, never gung-ho on discipline and authority. And he certainly never tried to force his boys to make a career of the service. He hoped they would stay in school as long as they could. Having worked all his life, he wanted something better for them, and having had no real education himself, he realized his disadvantages. He wasn't bitter about it, but he knew his limits. There had always been officers to remind him of his limits.

So he took on a second job at night tending bar and told the kids to stay in school. Of course, he couldn't do as much for them as he'd have liked; there was only so much money to go around. But one thing about running a laundry, you could keep your family in clean clothes. He took pride in the fact that nobody ever saw his kids wear the same shirts or pants day after day.

Short and stocky, Tommy had continued to box in the Navy and he still walked on the balls of his feet, carrying himself with the easy grace of an athlete. His three boys had been interested in sports, and he had encouraged them, but never pushed them the way some Little League parents will. He liked to see them have fun. They didn't have to be stars for him to enjoy watching them.

That was part of the reason he began going to Lee's games; he liked the boy and he liked football. "It was as simple as that," he said.

But there was also the fact that Karen wanted to see Lee's games, and she had no way of getting there unless her father drove her. Sometimes this meant a fifty- or sixty-mile round trip.

"Tell you the truth," Tommy admitted, "I didn't understand it. When our boys were too young to drive and they had dates, I carried them in my car. I figured it was the boy's father's responsibility. But obviously the Dresbachs didn't look at it that way, and it made me damn mad. I mean, we'd see them at the games, we'd be sitting on the same side of the stands, and they knew we were there rooting for their son. But do you think they'd ever sit with us or even say hello? Hell no! It was like we weren't there. And after the game, they'd leave while we waited for Lee to shower and dress. Then we'd drive him home and sometimes turn right around for Washington. If it wasn't for Karen and the fact I liked Lee—really felt sorry for him—there's no way in the world I'd have done that.

"I remember this one game the coach used Lee to shuttle plays to the quarterback. Hell, he was just a freshman and lucky to be playing at all. But suddenly Mr. Dresbach breaks out, shouting, 'Hey, Lee, you're nothing but a waterboy. You hear me, nothing but a messenger boy.' And that was right in front of his teammates and friends. A thing like that can crush a kid. You know, they say Dresbach favored Lee, but I think he was hurt by that family almost as bad as Wayne."

Tommy shook his head. "I don't understand it. How do you explain people who hurt their kids? Why'd the Dresbachs adopt the boys in the first place?"

3

If the Dunns found the Dresbachs baffling and infuriating, it was with good reason. In most ways, Pat and Shirley were contradictory people.

When it suited his purposes, Mr. Dresbach could project the image of a man of substance, a conscientious citizen concerned about political issues and anxious for his adopted sons to avoid "bad company." But he was also a notorious scofflaw who each year got hundreds of dollars worth of traffic citations, then bragged of influential connections who had his tickets fixed. This might explain why he had no qualms about speeding through densely populated areas, driving without a license, hunting without a license, shooting swans and other protected fowl, and getting into drunken brawls.

In the same way that he casually accepted risks that might have ruined his legal career, he also appeared indifferent or blind to the damage he did to the image he had of himself as a connoisseur of class and quality. He drove a Chrysler, but outfitted it with a carriage bell which he rang whenever he passed an attractive woman. Although he claimed to be proud of his wife and told everybody about her famous uncle, he often ridiculed her in public, referring to Shirley as "the worst piece of ass I ever had." While he demanded that Wayne and Lee excel at school, he boasted he had been kicked out of West Point—a boast which turns out not to be true. There's no record that Dresbach ever attended the U.S. Military Academy.

In matters both petty and important, Dresbach insisted on running the boys' lives. He wanted to choose their friends, their clothes, their course of study. But then he told them they didn't need friends, and he refused to help them with their studies or to buy them clothes. He said four pairs of pants and five shirts were quite sufficient for them—this despite his and Shirley's vast wardrobes.

Dresbach's language reminded people of a longshoreman rather than a lawyer, yet he slapped Wayne and Lee for saying "Heck" and "Jeez." Although he claimed he hated roughnecks and hoodlums, he beat the boys ruthlessly and threatened that if they lost a fight at school, they would have him to reckon with when they got home. Once when Wayne had been bloodied by an older fellow, Dresbach called his son a "chickenshit" and a "pussy," then knocked him unconscious.

To his parties Pat invited pornographers, prostitutes, exhibitionists, sadomasochists, and pedophiliacs. But like some hardshell fundamentalist, he warned Wayne and Lee about the dangers of masturbation and insanity, intercourse and disease, women and filth. Above all, he cautioned them to save sex until they were married.

It should come as no surprise that when Wayne started to have problems, Pat professed to see no connection between the boy's behavior and his home life. He ascribed Wayne's academic difficulties to laziness and poor study habits, and his running away to the influence of bad companions and lower-class children.

4

But if it is difficult to fathom Pat Dresbach, it is nearly impossible to penetrate the facade which Shirley presented to the world. Of the few close friends she made, most spoke of her with sympathy, stressing her talents. She was intelligent, they said— "much smarter than Pat"—and had "an artistic nature." She played the piano and the organ, painted landscapes, and once did a portrait of the boys, which many people admired.

Then each spring Shirley closed the piano, put aside her brushes and oils, and worked in her home as a private income-tax consultant. She had "a good head for figures," although, ironically, she had never graduated from high school. Instead she had taken a three-year general business course: the same course she and Pat forbade Wayne to take.

During the busy months before April 15, it was not uncommon for her to earn more money than Pat, and while he expressed great pride in her when he was sober, he could be cruelly derisive when drunk. He complained that she had more interest in numbers than in sex; he said she insulted him publicly, creating an impression that he couldn't support his family. But he never forced her to quit working, some say because he needed the extra income; he wasn't nearly as wealthy as he liked to let on.

What outsiders saw as Shirley's remoteness, her friends attributed to shyness, depression, and a deeply rooted fear of her husband. Dominated by Pat, made to feel ugly and insignificant, she was, they claim, a classic example of what in the 70s would be called a battered wife. The more he beat her, the more he tormented her emotionally and abused her verbally, the more Shirley seemed to think she had failed Pat and deserved to be punished.

That she was disturbed and acutely unhappy, no one denied. Her suicide attempts alone proved this. Still, it isn't easy to understand her behavior. Much as she might give the impression of helplessness, she wasn't without financial resources, and she had a prominent family behind her. She could be imperious with people, and she liked to have her own way. Although she frequently threatened to divorce Dresbach, she said she stayed with him for the children's sake. Since she knew he brutally mistreated the boys, it is hard to follow her reasoning—especially when she had a disconcerting habit of standing by, silent and expressionless, while Pat taunted or thrashed them.

Her friends maintain that she was confused and frightened and didn't know what to do. "Pat had knocked all the confidence out of her." But less sympathetic observers thought she was simply detached. Some missing or warped element in her character seemed to prevent her from connecting with anything or anybody.

One remarkably candid female friend, who was intimate with both of the Dresbachs, remembered how Shirley used to urge women to have sex with Pat. She assured them that she didn't care; she said she and her husband had an arrangement. At first the friend thought that Shirley hoped if Pat had a variety of partners, he wouldn't bother her as much. But then she decided that Shirley didn't have the capacity to be bothered.

Often Pat spread out a white fur rug in the living room in front of his wife, and then while he slapped, bit, scratched, and had his peculiar brand of sex with some stranger, Shirley stayed in her chair, sometimes watching, sometimes reading a book or leafing through the newspaper. Occasionally she closed the book, crawled down on the floor, and made it a threesome. But whatever she chose to do, it all seemed to be the same to her.

There were things she did for Wayne, however, which may indicate she was, in her fashion, trying to help. For instance, after a summer of ignoring the advice of the Remedial Education Center, she took a few tentative steps in the fall of 1960 to obtain psychotherapy for him. Yet, even as she did so, her efforts were tempered by a hardheaded practicality and a brusque dismissal of any implication that she was to blame for his problems.

On September 15, while asking Southern High School to assist her in finding a psychiatrist, she provided information which she must have thought proved she had not been remiss as a mother. Along with the report from the Remedial Education Center, she sent a letter explaining that at the age of five Wayne had had an operation to straighten his right eye, which was turning in. Afterward she drove him to a therapist once a week and made him follow the exercises the doctor prescribed. Wayne wore glasses until he was in the fifth grade, but then Shirley discovered he was removing them before he reached school.

"Last summer before taking him to the [Remedial Education Center], I took him to an ophthamologist who enjoys a good reputation and was quite chagrined when he informed me that Wayne did not use his right eye at all—but that he could get along fine using just one eye and not to be the kind of mother that went around looking for excuses for my son when he was just too lazy to do his schoolwork."

In addition to expressing this suspicion, shared by her husband, that Wayne's difficulties were due to laziness, Shirley revealed other contradictions in her professed eagerness to get counseling for him. On September 28 a teacher placed a memo in the guidance counselor's file at Southern High School.

I contacted Mrs. Dresbach about the delay which will be necessary before Wayne can receive service. I told her that

the waiting list is large and it will probably be several
months before an appointment can be arranged at the Mental Health Clinic.

During my home visit, Mrs. Dresbach revealed that her
husband had previously tried to get professional help for
Wayne. It seems that Mr. Dresbach had utilized the testimony of psychiatrists in his legal work. These people refused
aid on the grounds that young people are too inconsistent in
their patterns.

I suggested that if she felt the problem to be urgent, it
might be advisable to contact Dr. Witold Winiarz [a psychiatrist with a private practice in Annapolis and the husband
of Dr. Elizabeth Winiarz]. She indicated that this might be
a very good idea and would discuss this possibility with her
husband.

Since Shirley was trying to arrange an appointment at the
Anne Arundel County Mental Health Clinic, a public facility,
she appeared eager to avoid the higher cost of sending her
adopted son to a private therapist—even though this would delay
Wayne's treatment for several months. There also has to be some
question whether Dresbach ever made earlier efforts to obtain professional help. It is hard to believe any therapist would,
without a preliminary examination, refuse a child "aid on the
grounds that young people are too inconsistent in their patterns."
But one can imagine Pat asking for free, off-the-cuff advice and
being turned down.

Apparently the Dresbachs never "felt the problem to be urgent" enough to contact Dr. Witold Winiarz or any other psychiatrist in private practice—again, one suspects, because they did
not want to foot the bill.

Yet, while it is easy to condemn Shirley's attitude as the worst
sort of parsimony—the kind of petty cheapness both boys later
complained about—it is also possible that she had gone about
getting a psychiatrist without Pat's approval and desperately did
not want him to find out, as he surely would have if she had had
to cover the costs of a private therapist. Because she knew well
the secrets Wayne might reveal, it isn't idle to speculate that, out
of growing fear or despair, having had her oblique appeals to

friends and to the police ignored, Shirley realized her last hope was that a psychiatrist would discover what was happening and would somehow save Lee and her, as well as Wayne.

Judging by the material in the guidance counselor's files, authorities at Southern High School already recognized something was drastically wrong in the Dresbach household.

> It is felt that Wayne's basic problem is a family one and that there is little relationship between Father and Son. . . . In a conference held with Mr. Dresbach and the Principal, Mr. Dresbach showed indications of favoring the younger child and made some derogatory remarks about Wayne's intelligence. Evidently Wayne has sensed this in his Father and resentment has grown towards him.

Yet while Wayne admitted to the counselor that his father drank heavily and was too strict, he did not add that Dresbach sometimes lost all control and beat his wife, along with the boys. And he never mentioned his parents' nudism, their parties, the women his father brought into the house, or what he had seen that night from his hiding place on the stairs. Perhaps he was too frightened or ashamed to discuss this. Maybe he had a sense— even much later, after the murders—that he should protect his mother's reputation. But in the coming months few things would complicate his already desperate plight more than his inability to present an accurate account of what went on in his home.

5

That autumn one of Wayne's few chances to escape the oppressive atmosphere of the house was to go check on the family boats which were moored in the cove, a brackish estuary that snaked into the salt marshes north of Franklin Manor. Most people dry-docked their boats during the winter, but with duck season due to open November 9, Dresbach left his two runabouts in the water.

Actually, Pat no longer owned both boats. He had given the smaller one to Wayne and Lee, and it was to care for this prized possession that Wayne left the house one afternoon in early October and raced Mac to the cove. Their feet crackled on fallen leaves, sending squirrels skittering in every direction, and the dog darted after them, his deep-pitched barks booming over the water.

At the cove, a man Wayne knew by sight, but not by name—he was one of the summer people—was having trouble hauling out his motor-sailer. The man didn't ask for help; he didn't have to. Leaving his own work, Wayne went over to lend a hand.

They backed a trailer down the ramp and into the water. Then taking off their shoes, they rolled up their pants and waded in up to their knees, guiding the boat onto the cradle. But just as they were making it fast, Mac spotted something and leaped into the cove, splashing Wayne and splattering his trousers with mud.

Like most fifteen-year-old boys, he didn't pay much attention to this until he reached home and Shirley shouted at him for ruining his clothes. He said he was sorry, but explained it wasn't his fault.

His mother took down a willow switch she sometimes used on the boys and told him to turn around.

Wayne refused.

"What did you say?" Shirley demanded, her normally mild gray eyes narrowing in anger.

"I said no." He was nearly as shocked by his defiance as she was. Although he knew from experience that it was more embarrassing than painful to have her swat his butt with the willow switch, he thought she didn't have a right to whip him. Not after what he had seen her doing.

"Turn around or I'll tell your father."

"No."

"You know what he'll do to you."

"I don't care," he said. "Just don't you touch me."

When she lifted the switch as if to slap his face, Wayne raised a hand to protect himself. But Shirley saw this as a menacing gesture and flinched.

"All right, mister, you're making me do it. I'm going to tell him you threatened me."

"I didn't!"

"Don't lie. I just saw you. Get away from me."

Up in his room, waiting for his father to return from work, Wayne was furious rather than frightened. He tried to read to calm himself, but couldn't focus on the words. He stood at the window and stared out at a placid stretch of the bay, yet even that didn't pacify him. He was sick of being blamed, sick of never being believed. Now he'd get a beating, he could count on that, and all because of his mother, who was about to betray him again. She knew it wasn't his fault Mac had splashed him and she surely knew he wouldn't hurt her. Why was she doing this?

When Pat Dresbach got home, he mixed his own martini, put on his captain's hat, and let Wayne wait a bit longer while he listened to Shirley's side of the story. Then he summoned the boy downstairs and didn't sound particularly angry. He didn't look angry either as he stood in the open, carpeted space between the living room and dining room, rocking back and forth on the balls of his feet, sipping his drink.

But Wayne kept his distance.

"What's this your mother tells me?" Dresbach asked in a quiet voice, as if he couldn't make up his mind whom to believe.

"I can explain."

"You better. Because she says you threatened to hit her."

Wayne glanced at Shirley, who stood off to one side, next to the electric organ. Her eyes evaded his. She looked as if she found this all trashy and distasteful.

"What's this explanation?" Pat asked, still calm.

"I didn't threaten to hit her."

"Come closer so I don't have to yell. That's it. Now stand up straight and get your hands out of your pockets."

With no warning, Dresbach tossed his martini glass at Wayne's feet and threw a wild roundhouse right. But Wayne hadn't been fooled. He ducked and shot out a fist that landed flush on his father's Adam's apple. If it had struck any other spot, the punch would have done little damage. But as it was, Pat stumbled backward and fell, clawing at his throat and gasping. His captain's hat rolled off under the dining table.

Shirley rushed to Pat. "Are you all right?"

Wayne, too, came close, ready to hit him again if he tried to stand up. But Dresbach was struggling for air, and that effort or the pain or anger had squeezed tears into his eyes. When he blinked, rivulets of water trickled down his face.

"Police." Pat's voice was a thin hiss, like air seeping from a punctured tire.

"Please—don't bring them here," Shirley said.

"Police," he repeated, but grabbed her wrist. "I'm through fooling with this little bastard. Next time I'm calling the police. You hear me?" he asked Wayne. "You ever raise a hand to me or your mother again, you cause us any more trouble, I'm having you put away. I'm sending you to reform school."

Returning to his room, Wayne was exuberant. Pat's threat meant nothing to him. The main thing was that he had stood up to his parents—and he had won. Again and again he went over it in his mind, reliving the satisfaction of that instant when he had hit his father and knocked him down. From here on out, his life would be different, he vowed. There was no need to be afraid, no need to run away, now that he could defend himself.

For several days, this thought sustained him, soothed him, and it ceased to matter so much that he had to hurry straight home from school and stay in his room. It didn't even bother him when his parents sniped at him, for Wayne believed that if things got too bad, if they pushed him too far, he could strike back.

Predictably, it came to that. Afterward he would not remember what had provoked the argument. It could have been almost any-thing—his marks, his cocky new attitude, or Dresbach's usual belligerence—but it quickly degenerated, and as he and his father hurled insults and obscenities at each other, Shirley screamed for them to stop. When Wayne wouldn't shut up, the shoving started. Then the swinging.

As if he had been waiting for just this chance to get even, Dres-bach threw the first punch and followed it up with a flurry of lefts and rights, driving the boy out of the kitchen, across the din-ing room, and onto that same open, carpeted space. Although shorter and lighter, Pat was wiry, strong, and not reluctant to use his sharp elbows and knees to keep his son from moving in close.

Flailing wildly, Wayne fought back, willing to take two or three punches for every one he landed. But soon his lips were split, his nose bleeding, and his eyes so swollen that he could do little to protect himself as his father bobbed from side to side, flicking jabs at his face.

Shirley kept pleading with them to stop, but Dresbach only

loosened his fists and slapped Wayne open-handed, not hurting him badly now, just stinging him, taunting him.

Wayne lowered his head and lunged, grappling blindly until he got hold of Pat's shirt, and dragged him down to the floor. But when he knelt on Dresbach's chest and chopped at him with both fists, his father broke into laughter. "Are you kidding? Is that as hard as you can hit?"

Sobbing, Wayne sagged, and Dresbach shoved him aside. "Get the hell out of here before I bust your ass."

On hands and knees, Wayne crawled to a chair and pulled himself to his feet, then stumbled up to his room. He was bleeding and exhausted, his hands and face throbbed. But far worse than the pain was his renewed sense of impotence. He had been wrong, he realized. He still couldn't stand up to his parents; he couldn't cope with his father. He felt, he later said, "just like a cork floating on the water. So useless. He always made me feel useless, worthless."

6

The next day, Wayne ran away for the last time. Actually, he didn't run far, and he had no destination. He just drifted around the neighborhood, in despair of escaping.

At midday he was wandering along the main road in Franklin Manor hectically thinking half-aloud, "What I ought to do . . . Now I'll go . . . I need to . . ." But he couldn't complete a single thought. Although it might spin fast or slow, his mind was locked in orbit around Pat Dresbach. Until that central fact changed, Wayne was going nowhere.

When Lena Talbert drove up in her car and offered him a lift, he paused as if teetering between sleep and wakefulness, a nightmare or its memory. Then he nodded and climbed in without a word. Of course she was curious what he was doing out of school; he said he was sick and had been sent home early.

With his puffy, bruised face, he looked injured, not ill, and he acted as though he had been knocked unconscious in an accident. Dropping him off in front of his house, Lena watched him walk stiffly up the driveway and in through the carport door.

But then she wheeled around and headed home, not noticing

that Wayne had sneaked back out the same door and set off up the road. He hitchhiked to another small beach community and told a friend he needed a hiding place.

The boy led him to an attic in the garage where a large steamer trunk stood in the corner. Curling up inside it, Wayne let the boy cover him with burlap bags. Then at last his mind quit whirling and he slept.

He remained there the rest of the week, lying awake late at night while the wind howled and the beamed roof of the garage creaked and groaned. He imagined himself aboard ship, far off at sea, sailing toward the exotic ports he had read about. During the day, he roamed the surrounding woods. This was how he thought he would live if he were a forest ranger—hiking, exploring, watching birds and animals, keeping his own hours, eating whatever his friend managed to sneak out of the house.

On Saturday several other boys he knew from school showed up, and they all agreed they should go squirrel hunting. The trouble was, they didn't have any guns or ammo. But Wayne remembered his parents would be in La Plata today, deep in southern Maryland, watching Lee play football. He suggested they borrow his father's guns and bring them back this afternoon before the family returned.

After phoning ahead to make sure the house was empty, they drove to Franklin Manor in the oldest boy's car and climbed the side staircase to Pat Dresbach's office. The wall rack held four shotguns, one of which belonged to Wayne, and a .22 Remington automatic. Letting the other fellows take the shotguns, he kept the .22 for himself and asked them to wait in the car. He'd be with them in a minute.

Wayne realized he was already in trouble, and when his father found him, it would get a lot worse. But he didn't care. It had been months since he'd been this happy and had had a chance to go off with a bunch of guys. He wanted them to like him, to accept him as one of them. Opening the bottom drawer of the desk, he pulled out the stack of photographs, thinking he'd show them to his friends.

By now there were no surprises. Each face, each body was familiar to him. He had studied them many times, turning the pictures this way and that, searching for his mother in the tangle of limbs. Yet as he flipped through them again, he felt the same intense emotions—a sudden rush of what he didn't know well enough to name desire and the slow churning in his belly which could only be called disgust. He thought this was wrong—as wrong for him to look at these snapshots as it was for people to pose for them. And it was wrong for him to touch himself and not be able to stop.

He stuffed the photographs back into the drawer and ran out to the car.

All that afternoon and well into the evening Wayne tramped through the woods, yet never fired a shot. A .22 is not much good for squirrel hunting—not unless you're an expert marksman, which he was not. But it's doubtful that he would have fired a shotgun either. As already mentioned, he didn't like to kill animals and he especially didn't care to use this .22 which he had only once seen Dresbach shoot.

Four or five years ago, when they still lived in Lanham, the family cat had had a litter of kittens, half a dozen, soft fluffy creatures that fumbled over each other as they burrowed close and suckled at their mother's teats. As Wayne understood it from Shirley, the plan was to wait until the kittens were weaned, then give them to friends.

But one weekend morning his father scooped the kittens into a paper sack, picked up the .22, and headed out the back door. Worried, Wayne went with him.

"What are you doing?" he asked as they crossed the yard, passed the stables, and set off toward a creek at the property line.

"Going to get rid of these fucking things," Dresbach said.

"I thought we were going to give them away."

"I'm tired of waiting. Tired of them whining all night and stinking up the house."

At the creek Dresbach rolled the top of the bag tight, then tossed it into the shallow water. While the kittens screeched and pawed to get out, and Wayne sobbed for him not to do it, his father took aim and emptied the rifle. At that range he couldn't miss. The slugs tore the sack to pieces, and blood poured out in trickles, then in a great rush as the bottom gave way.

Wayne wanted to bury the kittens, but Pat told him not to bother. Dogs and buzzards would take care of them.

By the time the squirrel hunt ended, Wayne knew his parents and Lee would long since have come home and it was too late to return the rifles. He told the boys to drop him at the garage. Then, after selling his own shotgun for ten dollars, he hauled the rest of the arsenal up to his hiding place in the attic and settled into the steamer trunk as the wind brought the smell of salt water to his nostrils, and he cast off the lines that bound him to land.

Next morning, when the police came for him, he didn't resist or make any attempt to run. The officers drove him to the Edgewater Station and as they locked him into a cell, he believed he was prepared for the worst. His nights of smooth sailing, his days of roving the forest, were over. Any minute now his father would arrive and start knocking him around.

But Dresbach didn't show up that day, the day after, or the day after that. Charging Wayne with breaking and entering and larceny, he declared his son incorrigible and asked the cops to hold him in jail. Not content with that, he wanted the boy thrown into solitary confinement without a bed or mattress. That would teach the little bastard a lesson, he said.

7

For a man of Dresbach's unremitting cruelty, leaving Wayne in jail and pressing charges against him must have satisfied some deep, immediate craving. But in his eagerness to hurt the boy, he had outsmarted himself and ensured that the case would not remain a private matter. Soon events gathered a momentum of their own, slipping beyond Pat's control.

In the days before the *Gault* decision guaranteed juveniles the same legal rights as adults, officers like Lieutenant Lloyd Smith had almost a free hand with underage offenders. In some precincts this made for capricious and brutal treatment. Without the protection of *habeas corpus* and strict rules of evidence, without the right to a trial by jury, kids could be incarcerated for years on minor charges or simply stashed in institutions at the request of their parents or guardians.

Fortunately, Lloyd Smith had helped organize Anne Arundel County's first juvenile program, and he was fair. Among his fellow officers and around the courthouse, he had a reputation for being lenient—some said too lenient. But, in Smith's opinion, such criticism revealed a serious misconception of his job, which was not just to apprehend and punish juvenile delinquents. He was more interested in preventing underage offenders from hardening into habitual criminals.

Whenever a kid got into trouble, Smith figured there had to be a problem in the home and he believed that during his investigation it was as important to evaluate that problem as it was to establish guilt. Then once he knew not only *how*, but *why* a crime had been committed, he used his discretion in determining how the case should be handled. Despite his reputation for leniency, Smith was no pushover. His size and galvanic temper could be intimidating, and sometimes he found that a tongue-lashing did a kid more good than a stretch in jail. Since he feared most penal institutions were little more than crime factories which produced a high rate of recidivism, Lloyd Smith exhausted all his options—and himself—before slapping a boy behind bars.

That was why the Dresbach case baffled him. Most parents adamantly maintained their children were innocent, even when they knew they weren't. Like Smith, they didn't want to see a young kid dumped in some snakepit. But here was a wealthy, prominent lawyer who insisted his son was guilty and left him in jail. And on charges that would never stick! How could a boy be convicted of breaking and entering his own home? Of selling his own shotgun? Of borrowing his father's guns to go squirrel hunting? Smith agreed Wayne had been stupid—okay, wrong—to do what he did. But why make it worse by jailing him? And why had the boy run away in the first place?

Robert Ogle, Smith's superior at the Juvenile Probation Department, was also puzzled and asked for more background information. So Smith sat down and had a long talk with Wayne. He warned him he had better straighten out and quit running off. But Smith couldn't decide whether he was getting anywhere. The kid was already scared, and he didn't seem a bad sort at all. In fact, he had this quiet, brittle quality that made you think he was

more likely to be abused than to hurt anybody. When Smith
asked what the trouble was at home, Wayne would say only that
his father drank and was too strict.

After three days the Dresbachs picked up Wayne, but they let
the charges against him stand. Later, however, when they returned for an interview with Robert Ogle, Pat had had a sudden
change of mind and heart. Perhaps he had discovered that if he
continued to press charges, this interview would be just the start
of a series of potentially damaging inquiries into his life. As a
matter of course, there would have to be a full investigation of
the family, followed by a hearing under oath in front of a judge.
Since he knew what he might be asked, and what Lee, Wayne, or
his wife might reveal, Dresbach had good reason to drop the
charges, and one must regard his explanation with great suspicion.

Robert Ogle wrote in a report after the Dresbachs were dead:

> When Mr. and Mrs. Dresbach appeared with Wayne . . .
> Mr. Dresbach explained that he had not intended that his
> son be charged with larceny, that he didn't see how a larceny
> charge could conceivably be made out of the existing facts,
> that he had looked over the law on this and was convinced
> that this was not larceny. He said the gun which Wayne had
> sold for $10 was an old gun that he permitted Wayne to use
> and that Wayne had every reason to believe was his own to
> do with as he pleased. Mr. Dresbach said that he had re-
> ported this matter to the police because he was very much
> upset by the fact that the parents of one of the other boys
> involved in this had harbored Wayne . . . while he was a
> runaway, but he explained that Wayne . . . pretended to call
> home and get permission to stay with them. . . . Mr. Dres-
> bach later talked with these people who verified Wayne's
> statement. In view of having obtained this knowledge, Mr.
> Dresbach . . . said as far as he was concerned the whole mat-
> ter could be considered closed.

But then Ogle laid down what amounted to conditions for
dropping the charges. Although these may have sounded like

mere suggestions, it is obvious how difficult it would have been for Pat and Shirley to refuse:

> In the course of our discussion, this officer called to the attention of the parents the fact that he was aware of a referral to the Mental Hygiene Clinic by [Southern High School] and asked them whether they . . . were sufficiently concerned to want this officer to help them get to the Mental Hygiene Clinic with Wayne at an earlier date than might ordinarily be expected. The parents agreed that they would like Wayne to be seen in [the] Mental Hygiene Clinic and agreed to this officer's expediting this as much as possible.

Then Ogle asked the Dresbachs whether they took the boys to church, and when they admitted that they didn't, he "suggested" that they start doing so.

For reasons known best to herself, Shirley chose St. John's Episcopal Church in Shady Side. Father Paul Dawson remembers meeting her and the boys one Sunday in early November, and Shirley struck him as "toney and stylish." At that time St. John's was struggling financially and there was always rejoicing when a new family joined the congregation. Father Dawson greeted the Dresbachs with genuine warmth and invited the boys to participate in the parish youth group.

For several weeks their attendance at services was perfect, but then, as Thanksgiving approached, it became sporadic, and Mr. Dresbach never did show up. Although Wayne and Lee were unfailingly polite, Father Dawson found the formality of their manners strange and unsettling. There seemed to be something frozen about them, especially about Wayne, who came to the youth group to help make Christmas baskets for the poor, but kept to himself and was quiet and nervous.

Hoping to draw closer to the family and to meet Mr. Dresbach, Father Dawson decided to drop in for an impromptu home visit. In the past he had found this was a good way to break down barriers, to put people at ease and demonstrate that Christianity wasn't something to leave behind in church.

One gloomy December afternoon he drove into Franklin

Manor and noticed 60 or 70 per cent of the houses had been closed for the winter. The sight of so many shuttered cottages did little to relieve the day's bleakness. Still, this was one of the best communities in his parish, and the Dresbach house one of the most impressive.

Father Dawson was far more impressed, however, by the reception he got. Shirley answered the front door and didn't bother to conceal her irritation. He thought he must have come at an inconvenient time and he apologized. But she didn't appear to be busy. Her husband and the boys were out; she had the house to herself. She asked him in, yet gave him to understand that she didn't welcome this intrusion.

The young priest lingered just beyond the cluster of armchairs in front of the fireplace.

"What a nice place," he said. "Especially with the fire going."

The words rattled through the room and he glanced around as if to follow their echo. His eyes moved from the color TV—the first he had seen in the parish—to the organ, to several of Shirley's oil paintings hanging on the wall.

She had taken a seat and finally motioned for him to sit down, too. Coldly courteous, her attitude was at best a kind of *noblesse oblige*. When Father Dawson made a few remarks about the holiday season, then asked if she had any questions about Christmas services at St. John's, Shirley's replies were clipped and condescending.

After several more awkward exchanges, he left thinking if this was the way she wanted it, if she didn't welcome any contact with him outside of church, that was fine. He wouldn't bother her— he wouldn't bother himself about the Dresbachs—ever again.

Months later he remembered this angry, ignominious retreat when he heard on radio that Shirley and Pat had been murdered. He was overcome then with regret and thought that he should have tried harder to get through to her, should have told her he was available if she ever needed him.

But, of course, it is doubtful that Shirley would have admitted that she had brought the boys to church only at the insistence of the Juvenile Protection Bureau, that she was obeying the letter —not the spirit—of the conditions Robert Ogle had laid down.

8

Even with Ogle expediting matters, it took several weeks to arrange an interview at the Anne Arundel County Mental Health
Clinic. Meanwhile Pat and Wayne went duck hunting.

In another family, this might have signaled a truce. It might
have indicated the father was anxious to reassure his son that
past troubles would not prevent them from being friends again.
But Wayne had never regarded hunting as a treat and, after all
that had happened recently, he dreaded spending a day alone
with his father—especially since Pat would have a gun in his
hands.

That December morning dawned chilly and damp, with
shrouds of mist hovering over the marshes. The ground squelched
under their feet as they walked to the cove, carrying shotguns
over their shoulders. Wayne thought how odd it was that after
his days in jail, terrible as they had been, he had not felt as safe
anyplace else—not even in his room. There was a simplicity, a
security, to being locked up. Though his cell had been noisy and
evil-smelling, he had soon learned what to expect and could count
on how the police and other prisoners would act. At home, however, he enjoyed no such luxury and he found himself tense, alert,
waiting for something to go wrong and for him to be blamed.

Today's hunting trip had him in an extreme state of nerv-
ousness. He couldn't understand why Pat had suggested it. All
week his father had been in an ugly mood, and as upset as
Wayne was about his impending interview with a psychiatrist,
Dresbach seemed to be even more on edge.

While Wayne made the boat ready, Pat warmed himself with
a flask of Bourbon and shouted orders. Then although already
showing the effects of the liquor, he insisted on steering and sent
Wayne up to the bow where he sat watching his father brush
dangerously close to the shore of the cove.

Just as they reached the bay, they spotted a grebe bobbing on
choppy waves, unperturbed by the oncoming boat.

"Nail it!" Dresbach shouted.

Having seen his father shoot swans, Wayne knew it would do
no good to tell him a grebe wasn't a game bird, that it was pro-

tected by $150 in state and federal fines. "The water's too rough," Wayne said. "I can't get a clean shot."

"The hell with the gun. Hit it with an oar." Dresbach sped directly at the bird.

Staying in the water, the grebe skittered off on a zigzag course, while Wayne stood up and swung the heavy oar.

"Goddammit, don't you have eyes? Hit it!"

Jerking the tiller left and right, Dresbach followed the darting bird. But as Wayne flailed at it again and again, he lost the oar, then his balance, and toppled into the paralyzingly cold water.

Drenched, his winter coat and pants started to drag him under. He rolled onto his back and considered kicking off his boots, but was afraid he'd be punished for losing them. With all this weight on him, he knew he couldn't swim far and doubted he could stay afloat long. As he treaded water, he felt his arms and legs cramp. Battling against panic, he thought, He's going to let me drown. He brought me out today to kill me.

But at last his father circled back and was laughing as he cut the engine and came alongside. "You are one sad-sack son-of-a-bitch. I don't believe you could beat your own meat if it wasn't hooked onto you."

Wayne had no sooner hauled himself up into the boat than Pat started the engine and set off again for the duck blind, a scrapwood shack that stood on pilings a mile or so offshore.

"Aren't you going to take me back?" Wayne asked.

"We've wasted enough time."

"I'm freezing."

"You'll survive."

"Please, just drop me in front of the house. I'll run in and change and hurry right back out."

"Nah, your mother sees you like that, she'll raise hell and make you stay home."

When they reached open water, the full force of the wind hit them and Wayne's shivering increased to uncontrollable shakes. Curling up on the bottom of the boat, he begged his father to let him change clothes. But Dresbach wasn't listening. He opened another flask and nursed it throughout the day as Wayne huddled in a corner of the duck blind, lying on the splintery, unpainted boards.

He couldn't comprehend why he had been made to come, why he was kept here. His father seldom spoke to him and paid him little attention. But for Pat it seemed that his son's presence—no, it was more his pain—fulfilled some urgent need.

By the time they returned to the cove that evening, Wayne barely had the strength to stand up and walk to the house. Dresbach told him to pluck and clean the birds, but he staggered into the kitchen, fumbling off his wet clothes with blue, cramped fingers.

When Shirley saw that Wayne was soaked, she started screaming, just as she had done the day Mac had splashed him. But then he explained how he had fallen overboard, and she turned and shouted at Pat.

He would have none of that. He smacked her in the mouth and shut her up.

By morning Wayne had come down with acute bronchitis. For the rest of his life he would suffer from weak lungs, a chronic cough, and respiratory ailments.

9

On December 14, 1960, Wayne accompanied his parents to the Mental Hygiene Clinic in Annapolis, where they were interviewed by Dr. Elizabeth Winiarz. A native of Lodz, Poland, Elizabeth Winiarz had earned her medical degree and practiced there as a pediatrician before immigrating to the United States shortly after World War II. She completed her training as a child psychiatrist at the University of Maryland and had been working for the state health department for more than a decade. Yet she still spoke with a heavy accent, and her sentences broke into unusual stress patterns.

Calling Pat and Shirley into her office, she explained that she would talk to them first, then to Wayne alone. Now, with the Dresbachs dead and Dr. Winiarz incapacitated by a stroke, the only record of that conversation is Dr. Winiarz's report, an elliptical, cautious, sometimes awkwardly written document, which nevertheless contains fascinating insights—perhaps more fascinating than she was in a position to realize.

Mr. Dresbach . . . assumed the leading role during the interview, trying to give information. He is of small stature, a nervous type person, seemed quite ambitious in his own achievements as well as in his expectations of both sons, who he explained had been adopted. . . . During the interview he could not remember details or exact dates or names and these were the points when his wife filled in, giving more correct data. . . . She was quieter, less complaining about Wayne, more interested in knowing about Wayne than his father, yet she too did not show any particular concern or warmth or a worrisome feeling about this boy's future. It was more fact giving and wondering for the reason why this boy was so different from his younger brother and why he would not want to conform.

The Dresbachs then offered a dubious account of how they had adopted Wayne and Lee. In his law practice, they said, Pat had represented their real parents. He characterized their father as "a bum, an unstable, unreliable person who . . . had not worked steadily, had no achievements whatsoever." Although the man admitted fathering the boys, he had never married their mother and had left the responsibility of raising them up to her.

The mother was "a good looking young girl, with [a] college education, who did not want to marry the father of her children, but she too must have been quite unstable emotionally because later on in life she still had dealings with Mr. Dresbach about some divorces with men she had married after giving up these children."

Dresbach confessed that the adoption had not gone through an agency, but he maintained that the boys' real parents never knew he had raised them in his home. Pat didn't attempt to explain how this was possible in light of the fact that he had subsequently represented their mother. Much later there would be evidence that the woman not only knew where her sons were, but had visited the Dresbachs.

Pat proceeded to say the boys had always been affectionate, especially Wayne who, as a child, was more outgoing and more interested than Lee in other people. He had also shown an early protective instinct toward his younger brother.

With tears in his eyes the father said that he remembers how one night he went to see how the boys were in their beds. He covered Wayne whose blanket had fallen off. Wayne, sleepy as he was, said, "Cover Lee, too, please." Mr. Dresbach says that the boy still will share anything he has or give to his brother Lee, although the two of them fight each other a great deal and are entirely different in character. Lee is ambitious, striving, on the honor list in school whereas Wayne —Dresbach added, forgetting the generosity, kindness and brotherly love he had just mentioned—"does not seem to care about anything or anybody."

After a brief summary of Wayne's academic difficulties, his visual handicap, and his tendency to run away from home, Pat said he couldn't understand why Wayne chose "as his friends boys with either a speech handicap . . . or belonging to the lowest social class. Both parents complained that the boy would never confide in them, would not show any affection, and when problems would come about, he would show no feeling of guilt [or] sorrow, but his reaction would be one of indifference."

Finally, in an appalling piece of misrepresentation, Pat offered a self-serving account of the times Wayne had run away. Stressing the worry and inconvenience these occasions had caused him, he mentioned nothing about his drinking, his unruly temper, the beatings he inflicted upon the boys and his wife, or about Shirley's and his bizarre sex lives.

Dr. Winiarz asked the Dresbachs to wait in the other room while she spoke to Wayne, who had been laboring feverishly to anticipate what the doctor might ask him and what he dared tell her. As desperate as he was to get away from his father, he did not regard this interview as a natural avenue of escape. It had never occurred to him that he might just spill everything he knew, and thereby be rescued. For one thing, he had no precise idea of a psychiatrist's function and, after his interviews with the school counselor, with officers at the Juvenile Probation Bureau, and with the psychologist and diagnostician at the Remedial Education Center, he had no reason to think that some outside authority would step in and save him.

For another thing, he was frightened. He knew what his father would do if he revealed anything approaching the full truth of what was happening at home. And Wayne couldn't believe his father wouldn't have ways of finding out what he said.

Finally, even if he had been confident of Dr. Winiarz's sympathy and willing to risk Dresbach's anger, Wayne would have had grave difficulty expressing himself. As always, his mind was a tumultuous cage full of words and emotions. But nothing emerged from it unmangled; few things of great importance got out at all. Regardless of the subject, his voice was flat, devoid of feelings, and when there was a question about sexual matters, he fell mute.

That day with Dr. Winiarz, his problems were compounded by the fact that he often could not understand her. Her vocabulary confused him almost as much as her accent. He would have asked her to explain certain words, but he was afraid she'd give his parents a bad report if he bothered her with "a lot of dumb questions."

And so Wayne's interview was distinguished more by what he left unsaid than by what he could bring himself to discuss. Still, his silences, his evasions, and his fidgety manner spoke to Dr. Winiarz.

She wrote that he was "blond, blue-eyed, quite husky. He was well dressed, appeared a rather tense and nervous boy. . . . He had bitten fingernails and his speech was rather abrupt and fast . . . he appeared immature for his age and this also was confirmed by the way of expressing himself [in] a rambling and unclear fashion."

He told her that winters in Franklin Manor were lonely and dull and there was nothing to do, even when his parents didn't restrict him to the house. On weekdays he was forbidden to watch television, and on weekends his father forced him to do household chores or go hiking and hunting with him. The family, Wayne said, seldom went anywhere together, seldom had any fun.

Yet, in explaining why he ran away, he was no more candid than his father. He accepted all the blame and said he was restless and just wanted to flee the isolation and monotony. Although he admitted that his father and mother drank, sometimes to excess, and were too strict with him, he revealed little about the dramatic events of the last few months, downplaying, for instance, the days he had spent in jail and not mentioning his recent bout with bronchitis.

Dr. Winiarz worked hard to get him to discuss his feelings:

> I tried to find out whether he had any attachments to his folks and I asked with whom he could easier discuss personal problems if something did not go right. Would it be mother or father? He thought for quite some time and said, "I think mother." After a while I asked him whether he could tell me to whom out of all [the] people he knew, friends or relatives or teachers or other professional people, he would feel closest, in other words most care for. Again he thought for quite some time and he said, "I think the young pastor in our Episcopal church where I go for services on Sunday." On second place he said, "My shop teacher. I think they are both wonderful men." This . . . sounded as if he were not attached to his parents and his dealings with them are like with strangers. During this first interview I did not touch the topic of adoption. It was not time to talk about that, but it only proved that his relationship with them was not like with true parents. Neither did I get the feeling that his adoptive parents had a true feeling of management as loving parents would feel with a problem child.

What was all the more remarkable about Wayne's declaration of closeness to Father Dawson was that he had seen the priest just half a dozen times and had scarcely spoken to him.

Although neither the Dresbachs nor Wayne had volunteered any intimate details about their sordid and chaotic home life, Dr. Winiarz's conclusions were accurate and her recommendations emphatic:

> My impression during this interview was that this boy seems to be acting out neurotically . . . the standards of the parents' expectations are rather high and . . . he could not cope. . . . He is very restless, has a slight visual handicap, he knows he is adopted, he did not seem to be very happy or

congenial with his parents. . . . To my thinking at the present time the boy would need psychotherapy and the parents need intensive case work. In addition . . . [Wayne] would most probably be better off and happier in a boarding school than to continue in rivalry with his brother and a poor relationship with his parents in [his] present school setting taking a general course which the father belittles in a very open and derogatory way. I have arranged for psychological testing, the measurement of his intellectual endowment as well as projective testing. On Dec. 22, at 1 P.M., Mrs. Dresbach will . . . come along with Wayne.

By midweek, however, an arctic cold front moved through Maryland, dumping one of the heaviest snowfalls of the winter. Roads in many rural areas were impassable and would remain that way for the rest of the month. Somehow Shirley and Wayne made it to Annapolis, but Dr. Winiarz's report for 12/22/60 read:

Could not be tested. Mrs. Hirsh couldn't come—bad weather —psychologist did not arrive.

As school recessed for Christmas, Wayne was depressed and apprehensive. Over the holidays he knew he would have to spend more time than normal with his parents, and that prospect filled him with dread. He hoped they wouldn't have much company. His father had taken to calling him "a sickie" and said if Wayne wasn't crazy, then why was he seeing a psychiatrist?

He knew better than to argue, especially at this time of year when Pat drank so heavily. He didn't think there was anything wrong with him, but he doubted he could convince Dr. Winiarz or anyone else. And it had occurred to him recently that, if his father found out he was, as Dresbach put it, "broadcasting family business," it might not mean just another beating. It might mean something much worse.

Already his father had threatened to send him to reform school if he caused more trouble. Now Wayne wondered what was to prevent Dresbach from claiming he was insane and shunting him into an asylum. Recalling those occasions when Shirley had apal to the police for help, he knew how skillful Pat was at twisting the truth, at turning a person's words against him. Wayne wouldn't stand a chance.

During the holidays, he went over his problems again and again, feverishly searching for an answer. He had tried to live up to his parents' demands. He had tried to run away. Finally he had tried to fight back. And at every turn he had failed. He had no idea what to do next. He felt like an animal in a trap, delirious with pain and confusion, chewing at his wounds, willing to gnaw off his own leg to get free.

By Christmas Eve Wayne had reached a dead end. Anxiety-stricken and exhausted, he could no longer go through the motions which the season demanded. Although he had helped decorate St. John's with holly wreaths and pine boughs, and he cared deeply for Father Dawson, he did not see how religion had anything to do with his life. He told the Dresbachs he wouldn't attend midnight services with them; it didn't matter how hard they beat him.

Surprisingly, his father didn't attempt to make him go, perhaps because this gave Pat an excuse for not going either. But he did make Wayne sit up with him while he killed a fifth of Bourbon and berated his son for being so much trouble, such an ingrate, such an embarrassment to the family. When Dresbach passed out, Wayne sneaked off to bed.

December 29, 1960, Dr. Winiarz's report read:

> Was not tested, icy road—psychologist did not arrive. Interviewed mother—later Wayne—mother talked in a rather detached way saying parents could never reach him. He kisses them . . . goodnight but never talks about personal problems. Parents had to search for him with the help of the police each time he took off. He has nothing to explain upon return, answers in monosyllables "yes, no, I don't know, O.K." . . . Wayne impressed me again as emotionally unstable, bitten nails, sits like on hot coal, talks in a rush, acts out impulsively. He denied any problems. . . . Superficially friendly and cooperative yet guarded as to personal matters, hard to get good rapport with.

It is interesting to note that this was the meeting which Dr. Winiarz later characterized as cheerful. The newspapers quoted her as saying that Wayne "and his mother were in a good humor. . . . They talked about how wonderful Christmas had been." But there was no mention of this good humor in her official report, just as there was no mention in the newspapers of Dr. Winiarz's unflattering opinion of the Dresbachs.

On January 5, 1961, the day of Wayne's next scheduled interview, he was back in school. The roads were clear, and Shirley was supposed to pick him up at Southern High and drive him to Dr. Winiarz's office. But for some reason, after having twice made the trip through snow and ice, Shirley didn't show up. She left Wayne waiting in the school lobby from 10 A.M. until noon, when he gave up and went to lunch. She never bothered to explain why she hadn't come.

Dr. Winiarz's report for 1/5/61 offers no explanation either:

> Special worker, Mrs. Foley, called [Dresbach] home at 10 A.M. to confirm presence of psychologist. Nobody answered. Dresbachs did not come in today.

Perhaps Shirley forgot. Perhaps she was miffed and wanted to repay the psychologist for missing the two previous appointments. Whatever the reason, this was another—and final—inconsistency on the part of a woman whose life had been full of them.

Less than forty-eight hours later, Shirley and Pat were dead.

Winter 1961

1

As fall passed into winter, football season ended, and Lee took up basketball. Some people said that even as a freshman, he was good enough for the varsity. But he chose to stay on the junior varsity and get more experience. On Friday night, January 6, both the JV and varsity teams had games against Frederick Sasscer in Upper Marlboro.

Though his father was furious at Wayne for missing yesterday's appointment with Dr. Winiarz—Dresbach complained that this therapy was costing him a fortune—he told Wayne to get out of the house and go and watch his younger brother's game. But the two boys didn't travel to Upper Marlboro together. Lee left from school on the team bus. Generally Wayne would have gone with his parents, but since they were entertaining company that night, he rode on a bus packed with other students.

Dallas Talbert attended the game, and he spoke to Wayne at half-time. "He and I used to have this private joke," Dallas remembers. "Whenever I saw him, I'd ask, 'What are you in the doghouse for this time, Wayne?' But that night he appeared to be out of the doghouse and enjoying himself. It never occurred to me to ask if he needed a ride home."

The Dunns did offer him a ride, but he said he'd rather go back on the bus with his classmates. "I think he felt he'd be in the way," Tommy said. "Not that there wasn't room in our car. Just, you know, he probably thought he'd be horning in on Karen and Lee. I sure wish we had insisted."

But the Dunns didn't insist, and while Lee went straight home with them and was dropped on his doorstep by 11 P.M., Wayne's bus took a circuitous route. First it stopped at Wayson's Corner Restaurant, where all the kids had hamburgers and Cokes. Then it proceeded toward Southern High, pausing every few minutes to let off people who lived along the road. Finally, after it reached the school, Wayne had to hitch a ride to the entrance of Franklin Manor and walk a mile and a half home.

It was nearly midnight as he approached the house and noticed a third car in the driveway. It belonged to C. J. Pettit, a friend of Pat's. Since that night in early September when he had seen his parents swapping with Nick and Darlene, Wayne had worried what he might find whenever he passed through the living room at odd hours. At the very least, he feared he might be made to stand at attention while his father mocked and ridiculed him in front of company; more than anything now, he hated being called crazy. So it wasn't until after Mr. and Mrs. Pettit left that he went in and told his parents he was home.

With one glance, he knew there would be trouble. While Shirley sipped at a tom collins, Pat worked on a glass of Canadian Club. They were both drunk, sitting listlessly in front of the fireplace.

"Where the hell have you been?" Dresbach demanded.

"At the game."

"Don't gimme that shit. Lee's been home more than an hour. Why weren't you with him?"

"You know I can't ride on the team bus with him." Unsure whether Lee had permission to date Karen tonight and reluctant to involve the Dunns, Wayne didn't mention that Lee had gotten a lift right to the front door. Even under oath, both boys would maintain the fiction that Lee had ridden home on the team bus.

"Quit lying," Shirley said. "Just once, don't give us a hard time. Haven't you caused enough trouble?"

"I'm telling the truth. Call Lee and ask him."

"We're not going to wake him up just so he can lie for you." Groggy as both of them were, they seemed to be hollering at him out of habit, as if trying to stir in Wayne an emotion of which they were incapable.

"It's no lie. Ask anybody who was on the bus."

"You get in this late," Dresbach shouted, "and you expect us to believe you came straight home. We'd have to be as nuts as you to swallow that."

"Lemme explain. You see, my bus stopped at Wayson's Corner and—"

"So you didn't come straight home."

"What I'm saying is, everybody wanted to stop and get something to eat. I didn't have any choice."

"Bullshit! You've been off screwing around with your hoodlum friends."

"Please, you gotta believe me."

"Oh, Wayne," his mother wearily sighed and shoved her long brown hair away from her face. "Every time we turn around, you're in trouble. How can we trust you?"

He looked at her a long while, thinking of all that he might have told her about trust and betrayal. Yesterday, as he waited for her in the school lobby, he had wondered whether there was anybody in his life he could count on, anybody who cared about him. He decided there was no one.

When the Dresbachs finished yelling at him, Wayne trudged up the stairs and lay in bed, gazing at the ceiling, just as he had done that night in September, just as he had done so many times since. All the nights, all the torments, of his life seemed to have been telescoped into this one room, into this one petty argument with his parents.

Whatever he tried, it turned out wrong. Whatever he said, they accused him of lying. Whatever he accomplished, it couldn't compare with what Lee had done. No matter where he ran, they found him and beat him. Then, when he fought back, they threatened him with reform school.

It seemed to him they were playing some hideous trick, trying to destroy him, trying to drive him crazy with their unfairness. They told him to get out of the house and go to the game, then screamed at him for being late when it wasn't his fault. They wouldn't let him play sports, but thought he should ride on the team bus with Lee.

It made him dizzy and sick to think of these things and to feel he couldn't move a muscle to help himself. At every step, every gesture, he had to be careful or his father would scream at him for being clumsy, for waving his hands "like a wop."

As Wayne lay there immobile, letting all his most painful memory-films play, he didn't believe anything could be worse than what he had been through, what he was going through, what he would have to endure tomorrow, the next day and the next. Not even prison could be worse. Not even death. He might as well be dead, he decided, if he didn't do something to save himself.

It was then that he thought of killing his father. He had no real plan, no delusion that he could get away with it. As had been the case whenever he ran away from home, he didn't consider how he would live afterward. His mind could function only so far in advance, only to that instant when he would pull the trigger and all his agony would end.

2

What Wayne did next is a matter of conjecture. As both he and Lee told various and conflicting versions of the murders, their accounts of when the Dresbachs were killed, where they were shot, and what Lee's reaction had been, would change from day to day. Years later, Wayne explained that once he had signed the confession, he expected to spend the rest of his life in jail or to be executed, so he hadn't cared what he said, no matter how self-incriminating. His only hope was to protect Lee and to avoid discussing painful subjects.

What follows is for the first time the full story, according to Wayne. It is based on personal interviews, police and psychiatric reports, and testimony at his trial.

Saturday morning, January 7, after a deep, dreamless sleep, Wayne woke about 8 A.M. His rage was undiminished, his resolve unchanged. After walking through Lee's empty room to the bathroom, he descended the staircase and heard his parents mumbling in their bedroom.

Still in his nightclothes, he crossed the living and dining rooms to the kitchen, where Lee sat at the table reading the newspaper and eating a bowl of cold spaghetti for breakfast. Without stopping or speaking to his brother, Wayne went up the half-flight of stairs to his father's office and grabbed a rifle from the wall rack.

It would have been more logical—certainly more brutally efficient—to use a shotgun. But perhaps he recalled that day when the kick of the twelve-gauge had slammed him against a tree trunk and sent a sudden burn of pain sizzling through his body.

Instead, he grabbed the .22 Remington Automatic, with which his father had killed the litter of kittens.

Then he climbed the stairs to the top floor and opened the action of the rifle as he hurried through the catwalk from the north end of the house to his bedroom. Noticing that the .22 was not fully loaded, he went back down to the living room and crossed to the kitchen. By now, after he had done a complete circuit of the house, his heart was thudding, his blood hammered at his temples, his brain was a swarming hive of non-thought.

Lee was still at the kitchen table. Wayne opened a cabinet, fumbled with a box of ammunition, and kept pressing bullets into the rifle until it wouldn't hold any more.

"I'm going to shoot Father," he said.

Lee didn't respond.

"I got in late last night," Wayne said. "I explained why, but they wouldn't listen. They kept yelling at me. I can't take it anymore. I'm going to kill him."

Still Lee said nothing, and when Wayne left the kitchen, his brother went back to reading the newspaper.

Wayne stationed himself in the living room between a green armchair and the color television set, next to the wall, not far from the hallway which led to his parents' bedroom. For several minutes he stood there, holding the loaded rifle and thinking—or, rather, trying to think. Afterward, he could not explain why he waited, why he hadn't rushed into the bedroom and shot Pat there. Perhaps he was afraid he'd hit his mother. Subconsciously he might have hoped someone or something would stop him.

On the conscious level, however, he was aware only of the pulse of his blood, the acid-heat of his anger. He felt somebody was robbing him; somebody was stealing his last, his most precious, possession. Unless he fought back, he was finished. He would become the nothing that his father said he was.

He heard the bedroom door open. Then he saw Pat Dresbach step through the hallway, putting on a thermal undershirt. From the waist down, he was naked, his penis flapping between his legs as he walked. Wayne shouldered the rifle. When his father was crossing the dining room, he squeezed the trigger. Then he fired again and again, brass shells clinking at his feet.

The first shot smacked into the side of Dresbach's right buttock, passing through it and out the left buttock. The second shot crushed the right side of his jaw and spun him around to face his son. Wayne hit him a third time, in the chest, and saw his father reel and fall, crawl into the kitchen, bleeding badly, and shout "Shirley!" before he collapsed on the tile floor.

Rushing across the room, Wayne hovered over his father. Lee had left the table and also moved near Dresbach. According to Wayne, Lee then said, "Shoot him again."

From a range of no more than a few feet now, Wayne fired three more times. One slug tore into his father's left arm; the next two smashed into the small of his back and coursed up through the body into his chest. After that, Dresbach didn't move, didn't make another sound.

Wayne looked at Lee, then turned away. He was sick at his stomach and unsteady on his feet; yet his anger hadn't died. It was the rage that sickened him—not the shooting, not the blood. Somehow, even though stunned by the enormity of what he had done, he felt it hadn't been enough.

He stumbled into the other room and when he reached the open space between the dining area and the living room, he saw Shirley standing in the hallway. She was naked, her body still warm with sleep, her belly creased by surgical scars just above the delta of dark hair. As she gazed at him, her gray eyes wide and expectant, she appeared frozen, like a doe in a spotlight. She didn't speak, didn't try to flee. She simply raised her right arm, perhaps appealing to him, perhaps in a futile attempt to protect herself.

Without thinking Wayne squeezed off a burst of four rounds. One ripped through Shirley's arm and into her chest. The second also punctured her chest. Then he lost control and the next two shots flew wild, one slamming into a closet door, another shattering a mirror on the wall. She staggered into the bedroom and fell with blood bubbling at her nose and mouth.

Wayne went upstairs, and while he was in his bedroom, changing into his school clothes, Lee appeared.

"Where are you going?" Lee's voice sounded surprisingly calm. But then it startled Wayne to realize that after what he had done —and despite the commotion in his belly—he too could speak calmly. He told Lee he didn't know where he would go.

"Why don't you tie me up?" Lee asked.

"What for?"

Lee was silent a moment, then said, "Shoot me, too."

Although his brother's voice still sounded normal, Wayne was beginning to wonder about him. It had never occurred to him to kill Lee. Even with the rifle in his hands, after acting out automatically against Shirley, he felt no urge to shoot him. As he reasoned, "Lee and I never got along all that hot, but I knew he was my kin"—his only known blood relative—"and he hadn't been doing to me all the things they had."

After putting on his shoes, Wayne picked up the .22 and pushed by Lee, saying, "Gimme half an hour's head start."

Wayne moved with a strange sort of weightlessness that reminded him of swimming. Buoyant, inhaling air in rhythmic gulps, he glided over the surface of things, not thinking, barely registering impressions. He no longer felt sick to his stomach; he no longer felt anything at all.

Downstairs, Wayne searched for the keys to his mother's car, but they weren't in their accustomed place on the mantelpiece. Careful not to glance at his father, he checked the kitchen counter and, not finding the keys there either, he climbed the steps to Pat's office, where the smooth, gliding sensation evaporated. Lee stood there at an ironing board, pressing a pair of pants.

"What the hell are you doing?" Wayne asked.

"Ironing my pants."

"I see that. But why?"

"Because I'm going to see Karen."

Deeply bewildered, Wayne went back downstairs and out the carport door to the driveway. Mac bounded from the garage, frisking and barking, ready to play. But Wayne waved him away.

He slipped the .22 under the front seat of his mother's car. Then, from his father's car, he fetched a spare set of keys. He decided to take Shirley's Chrysler because his father's had a bad muffler. It is impossible to say why this mattered to him since his plan was to drive to the main highway, step on the gas, and ram into a tree. Wayne figured that would be enough to kill him.

When he hit an open stretch of road, he floored the accelerator and soon had the Chrysler up to ninety miles an hour. The thick trunks of maples and oaks passed in a blur several feet from the right front fender. All he had to do now was give the steering wheel a yank. But somehow he had lost his momentum, lost all thought of what he meant to do. He never consciously decided not to commit suicide. He never decided to do anything. He just drove.

Eventually he found himself at Southern High School and, seeing cars parked near the gymnasium, he stopped and went in. There was a church-league basketball game in progress, and some of his classmates were watching. Wayne chatted with them, never mentioning what he had done. Afterward, they said he had seemed "happy and gay."

As he left, Denny Zang and Cub Scotten went with him, and when they saw he had a car, they asked for a ride, although they knew he was too young to have a license. He told them his parents were in Washington, then drove the boys down to Moreland's gas station, where they bought bubble gum and bottles of soda pop.

When they came back out to the Chrysler, Wayne spotted Officer Joseph Grzesiak's squad car, but didn't seem upset. He simply told Denny, who was eighteen, to take the wheel. It was as if his one worry were being caught driving without a license. Even as Grzesiak swooped down to arrest him, Wayne remained calm and unperturbed.

3

That evening, after he had confessed, Wayne was transferred to Spring Grove Hospital and arrived at 5:15 P.M. in the custody of two policemen. According to Dr. Hong, who admitted him, Wayne displayed little emotion and "could not give any reason why he shot his parents. When asked how he felt at that moment, he said he got somewhat upset. When asked how he is feeling [now] he answered that he is feeling fine. . . . He is alert, responsive, but his affect seemed to be shallow."

Unaware of Wayne's I.Q., and without any clinical evidence to substantiate his opinion, Dr. Hong wrote: "He may well have [a] mental deficiency. Mr. Dresbach was supposed to be on E Ward because he is a juvenile, but after [the] interview with this patient it was found that he killed his mother and father, so we decided to send this patient to Hall 4, North Main Building," a more secure area.

Attendants confiscated his belt and shoelaces, then locked him in a room where the "calm," "unemotional," fifteen-year-old boy lay awake all night, crying. Whenever he heard anyone in the corridor, however, he turned his face to the pillow to muffle his sobs, and when an attendant stopped to ask how he was, he said, "Fine."

Punctuating the lesson with insults and slaps, Pat Dresbach had taught him that men don't cry; men don't show their feelings. Although Wayne rejected most of what his father said, that rule was encoded on his brain. He vowed that no one in this hospital would see him acting like a sissy.

He would also never discuss his feelings with the hospital personnel. But then, what he felt that first night would have been beyond description even for someone older and far more articulate than Wayne. He had never experienced such a sense of guilt and yearning, a palpable hunger, for death. He had thought nothing could be worse than the life the Dresbachs had forced him to lead. Now he knew better. This was worse; this was as bad as you could get. For years his father had accused him of being a worthless bastard. Now he believed he had done just the thing that proved Pat was right.

Less than forty-eight hours later, although Wayne had created "no management problem" and displayed no hostile tendencies, the doctors at Spring Grove decided not to take chances. They transferred him to Clifton T. Perkins, which was more like a prison than a hospital. His first and most lasting impression of the place was of a babbling, ambulatory patient who had a bullet in his head which could not be removed by surgery.

Despite this, and other grotesqueries he was exposed to, Wayne's adjustment was rapid. Shunted from the prison of his home into a maximum security ward, he saw the new rules and routines as a mere intensification of his problems with the Dresbachs, a continuation of what had come to seem his perpetual punishment for an unknown crime which he must have committed long before he killed his parents.

But, of course, there were radical changes. From here on, every agency and institution that dealt with him operated according to principles which were narrowly conceived and rigorously applied. There would be no more missed appointments, no more postponements because of bad weather. Schedules and procedures were as rigid as the iron bars on the windows. Wayne was interviewed and underwent examinations; information was gathered, memos promptly written, reports filed, and action taken.

This was in glaring contrast to the performance of the agencies which should have protected Wayne before his arrest. Like all states, Maryland has laws concerning adoptions and child abuse. But the Dresbachs easily evaded them.

The public school system supposedly has counselors on the alert for students with learning disabilities, physical handicaps, and emotional difficulties. Wayne suffered all three, and from the records it is obvious that authorities at Southern High School realized the blame for his academic failures lay with his family. Yet there is no indication that they did much more than offer to put Wayne on the waiting list for the Mental Health Clinic.

On several occasions, the Anne Arundel Police Department and the Juvenile Probation Department had had dealings with the Dresbachs. Wayne had run away five times and had complained to the police, just as he had to the school counselor, that his parents drank to excess and were too strict with him. Yet the police never investigated and, until Pat declared Wayne incorrigible and charged him with a felony, they didn't think of correlating their information with Southern High School's.

While it is true that nobody outside the family knew the full horror of what was happening, and while it is also true that Wayne was never very communicative, it would not have required much probing—a few phone calls, a conversation with one or two neighbors and with some of Wayne's classmates—to learn, if not the entire story, then perhaps enough of it to prevent a tragedy. But considering the lethargy of most bureaucracies, it isn't surprising that only after the murders did society's machinery start to move with relentless speed—although still with haphazard efficiency.

At 3 P.M. on January 9, Wayne entered Clifton T. Perkins and, according to the admitting physician, Dr. Ramon A. Salas, he "coolly and calmly" narrated an account of the killings, answering every question, but volunteering no information on his own. Although polite and cooperative, "he remained much unconcerned about everything and when asked why he committed the crime he just answered, 'I don't know, I guess I was mad.'"

In this initial report, there was one reference to Lee: ". . . his brother, who saw the incident, was too late [to prevent it], hit him in the arm and ran upstairs."

Having heard this skeletal, misleading summary of events, Dr. Salas promptly recorded his impression of the patient: "Personality Trait Disturbance, Passive-Aggressive Personality, Aggressive type."

Next day Dr. Jacob Morgenstern, superintendent of the hospital, arrived at Ward 3 and found Wayne on the porch with another patient.

"Where's your parents?" the patient asked Wayne.

"I guess my father's in hell and my mother's in heaven."

Leading Wayne into his office, Dr. Morgenstern explained the purpose of these examinations and said that some of the material might be sent to the court. He added, according to his record of the meeting, that it was up to Wayne "to cooperate in giving information and that he would not be forced to give any information other than on a voluntary basis." But Wayne wasn't aware that he had a legal right to remain silent and that anything he said could be used against him.

During the preliminary conversation, Wayne prowled the room, picking things up off the floor. He found a piece of thread and played with it nervously as the interview progressed.

Dr. Morgenstern observed in his report that Wayne "was clean and well-kept. His manners were those of a polite youngster and he paid a great deal of attention to the questions. He appeared not to be concerned at all, especially considering the seriousness of the offense and his present situation."

It is not clear why Wayne impressed the doctor as "not concerned at all" when he was, at the same time, paying "a great deal of attention to the questions" and had just been pacing restlessly around the room. Certainly a lawyer would have stressed to Wayne how serious his situation was. But he still didn't have one and he wasn't in the best frame of mind to comprehend his predicament.

After answering quite a few questions, the boy interrupted and asked one: "Are you German?"

Like Dr. Winiarz, Dr. Hong, and Dr. Salas, Jacob Morgenstern had an accent. Compounding Wayne's sense of dislocation, it seemed that he had been transported to a world of foreigners. In the next few weeks he would also be examined by Drs. Prado, Hernandez, Guerrero, and Oropollo.

The patient struck Dr. Morgenstern as "oriented in all spheres." Yet to anybody aware of what he had gone through in the last few years, his responses sounded like those of an amnesiac. When asked why he ran away so often, he said, "I don't know exactly. There was a reason. Every time there was a reason." Although he discussed his father's drinking, he didn't mention the beatings, the verbal cruelties, the times Dresbach brought strange women into the house, or what he had seen of his parents' sex lives. Even his version of recent events was vague and full of hesitations.

When asked to explain why he killed his parents, Wayne politely said, "Do I have to repeat the same thing I already told Dr. Salas?"

"Not if you don't feel like it."

"I don't want to be mean or anything like that."

"Does it bother you to talk about it?"

"Yes, I get a stomach ache."

"Why?"

"I don't know."

"Could you give a description of yourself? What kind of person you are?"

In one of the most poignant moments of the interview, Wayne answered like any other earnest, middle-class child raised in the 50s. "I just try to get along with everybody. I try to be nice to everybody, to be polite, neat, clean. I don't like to hear boys cussing all the time. I stay away from guys like that. Usually I tell the truth, except for some little white lies."

"What do you think is going to happen to you?"

He shoved his hands under his thighs, sitting on them. "I don't know. Probably I'll stay here or go to some other place until I'm twenty-one."

"Why do you feel that will be the case?"

"I don't know. After I'm twenty-one, I'll probably go to some other place. Jail or something. I don't know."

In conclusion Dr. Morgenstern wrote: "He believes that he is a normal child, that he is not different from anybody, the only thing [is] it might take him longer to do arithmetic, which he does not like. . . ."

"When the interview was finished, the patient, in a very polite way, asked whether he could ask for something. He explained he had a sort of musical instrument, made out of a wooden block with some drums, which he would like to have in order to pass his time in practicing music. He was told that this will be referred to the Rehabilitation and Recreation Department."

4

While at Clifton T. Perkins, Wayne had one visitor. Father Paul Dawson drove up every week and struggled to stay in touch with the boy. In the beginning, he urged him to discuss his feelings. Then, failing that, he labored to get him to talk about anything. But whereas Wayne was evasive or vague with the doctors, he was almost pathologically quiet with the young priest, who often left these meetings in a state of nervous exhaustion, his thin face drawn with tension.

Most people told Father Dawson he was wasting his time. A fellow Episcopalian priest, a man who had taken a degree in psychiatry as well as in divinity, advised him that it was hopeless. He was letting his heart rule his head. Kids like Wayne, he said—killers, psychopaths, mental defectives—didn't recover; institutionalization only made them worse. The boy's life was over.

But Father Dawson wouldn't accept what seemed inevitable to other people. He thought he knew what caused them to recoil. Wayne's crime was close to nightmare, close to some primal image of adolescent rage and sexual confusion. It was too horrifying to contemplate, for it reminded everybody of the secret anger and violence in their own hearts.

The case had the dimensions, the profound impact, of Greek

myth, Father Dawson believed. *Oedipus Rex*, perhaps. The actions were obscene, taking place offstage while their tragic consequences were played out in public. But whereas Oedipus had blinded himself in recognition of the enormity of his crime, Wayne seemed to have bitten off his tongue.

Still Father Dawson could not stop trying. He felt accountable and believed that if there was nothing in his ministry that applied to this boy, then it was pointless to remain a priest. On a purely human level, he also sensed Wayne's loneliness, his longing to express himself, to reach out for contact with another human being.

The priest soon realized, however, that it was futile to cite biblical parables or to make religious allusions. Wayne had had no spiritual training whatsoever. Finally he confessed that the Dresbachs were not Episcopalians and that he had no idea why Shirley had chosen to bring him to St. John's Church. He and Lee had never even been baptized.

Father Dawson was stunned. Why, he wondered, had Harry Woodring requested a requiem mass? Why had Lee received communion?

Then abruptly this link between the priest and boy snapped, and Wayne's isolation was complete. Another snowstorm paralyzed the state, dropping almost twenty inches on parts of Maryland. It was days before plowing crews cleared city streets, then started work on county roads. Meanwhile Father Dawson was trapped in Shady Side.

For Wayne the snow-covered fields surrounding the hospital were broken into interlocking geometrical patterns by the bars on the windows and the chicken wire imbedded in thick glass. In years past he would have been eager to go sledding or ice skating. But since shooting his parents, he had not slept more than a few hours a night, and he was listless and haunted by daydreams, by fantasies of being rescued.

He had begun to believe his real parents would soon appear. Having read about the murders and seen his picture in the papers, they would come and ask for him. They would explain why they had abandoned him. They would explain that the Dresbachs had stolen him. They would explain to the police what kind of people Pat and Shirley were. They would explain . . .

But, of course, no one came. No one explained.

5

While the heavy snow kept Father Dawson from visiting, the tests continued and Wayne plodded through each one with the same stolid indifference. Rorschach test, block test, neurological test, word-pair test—no matter what the exam or the results, he maintained he had no mental problems.

On January 25 he met a second time with Ramon Salas, and by now the doctor had received copies of the police reports, Dr. Winiarz's files, and other pertinent documents. This might explain why Salas was able to elicit from Wayne more specific information about his home life and the murders. But there were still important omissions.

Although Wayne now admitted his father often beat him, his brother, and his mother, he mentioned nothing about Dresbach's more baroque acts of sadism, his collection of pornography, or the women he brought into the house. He also said nothing about the scene he had witnessed from the staircase that night in September. In fact, at no point in his conversations with any of the doctors did he suggest that Shirley's behavior influenced his actions.

When Dr. Salas inquired about his sex education, Wayne said Pat had told him the facts of life. But as the doctor tried to determine what these "facts" were, Wayne became flustered and ". . . refused to elaborate on their conversation . . . he denied ever having sexual relations or masturbation." Later in the interview, he vowed he would never marry "because that brings too many troubles. . . . He would prefer to remain single and travel a lot if he ever gets out of this situation. He refused to elaborate further when asked about what kind of problems . . . marriage might bring."

As for his account of the morning of January 7, he began going to greater lengths to shield Lee from any possible blame. According to his new version, Lee knew nothing about his intentions and was in no position to intervene. Lee had been asleep, was awakened by the shots, and dashed downstairs too late to do anything except shout "Stop!" and hit Wayne on the arm. Afterward he ran back upstairs, presumably to hide.

This story coincided with Lee's statement to the police even less than it did with Wayne's confession.

In his summary, Dr. Salas recapitulated the unhappiness, the harassment, and physical abuse Wayne had suffered from Dresbach whose "alleged excessive drinking . . . probably made him an individual with [a] severe psychopathology of his own." This, along with the blatant favoritism shown toward Lee, had produced in "the patient an overwhelming anxiety manifested in restlessness, fingernail biting, running away from home, and [a] profound feeling of hopelessness and inferiority."

Then ironically, in view of Wayne's wish to protect Lee, Dr. Salas added:

> Now may I say for the benefit of further dynamic formulation that the killing of the parents was not the only trigger point, but also there seems to be some symbolic unconscious wish of destroying the brother and with him all the challenge that had made the patient's life miserable. [Once Wayne killed them] the brother would not have parents to provide for him and to praise him. At the same time the brother would not be able to go to school and be smarter, so after all the patient would be important.

Why Dr. Salas believed Lee would not be able to go to school after the Dresbachs' deaths is difficult to say. But as for the rest of his speculation, Wayne responded that by killing his parents he felt he was helping his brother, not hurting him. After all, Lee, too, had received rough treatment at their hands. "Besides," Wayne later said, "if I really wanted to destroy him, I had the chance. I had the gun, but I didn't use it. Not on him, anyway."

The final entries on Dr. Salas' report were:

Predisposition: Passive Aggressive Personality
Impairment: Severe
Prognosis: Guarded

He decided to save his case recommendation for the next day's staff conference.

6

Wayne knew the authorities had sent him to Clifton T. Perkins "to study me, to see whether there is something wrong with me, if I am insane." But no one had explained that he wasn't there for treatment.

Even the Dunns, the Talberts, and Father Dawson failed to recognize the significance of this observation period. Assuming that the boy would be dealt with in Juvenile Court, they believed that Judge Benjamin Michaelson was waiting for a psychiatric evaluation before he decided what sort of therapy Wayne should receive.

In reality, however, Judge Michaelson was simply waiting for the doctors at Perkins to decide whether Wayne had been sane at the time of the murders, was capable of assisting in his own defense, and therefore was competent to stand trial. Considering the stringency of the state's law on insanity, there could not have been much doubt about the ultimate decision.

At that time Maryland, like most states, based its insanity test solely upon the defendant's ability to distinguish between right and wrong. Known as the M'Naghten Rule, this narrow, archaic, nonclinical definition of mental competence allowed for very little subtlety of interpretation or flexibility of application. The prevailing Maryland case on the point was *Spencer* vs. *State,* tried in 1887, in which the Court of Appeals reiterated the primacy of the right and wrong test and rejected a plea of irresistible impulse. The Court had also denied pleas of temporary insanity and diminished responsibility which were frequently brought with success in nearby Washington, D.C. under the Durham Rule. As many people were to remark, if Wayne had shot his parents in Pat's Washington office, he would most likely never have come to trial.

On July 1, 1970, Maryland supposedly made its insanity test more liberal. But when asked in 1978 what it now took to get an accused murderer declared mentally incompetent, a psychologist at the Patuxent Institute for Defective Delinquents conceded that this was a moot question, a matter of political pressures and public opinion as much as of clinical analysis. "Sometimes you know the community, not to mention the jury, just won't buy an insanity plea regardless of what a psychiatrist says. If it's a sensational, gruesome crime he's committed, the defendant has to be swinging from a chandelier and eating his own feces before anybody'll believe he's incompetent."

On January 26 the staff conference started before Wayne arrived. Fifteen psychiatrists, psychologists, and neurologists answered the roll call, then listened to Ramon Salas present his observations about patient ⚹228. Afterward Dr. Salas called for other reports.

The only one of potential significance was delivered by Dr. Morgenstern, who explained that Wayne's electroencephalograph test had turned up a grossly abnormal 14-6 pattern with diffuse spiking activity. This appeared to indicate that the patient fell into the convulsive disorder category and that he might well have experienced bizarre sensations—i.e., sudden dizziness, flushing, shivering, or blushing—unprovoked by external stimulation. The 14-6 pattern with spike activity, often observed in patients with a history of violence, can be a symptom of deep-line brain damage.

At this point Wayne was called in and went through a question and answer session which reveals as much about the doctors' methodology as it does the boy's state of mind.

Q. These are all members of the hospital staff, Wayne, and we have been going over the material that we have gathered together about you since you have been here. Do you understand why you are here—could you tell us why you think you are here?
A. For observation.
Q. Do you think you need to be observed?
A. Well, for what I did I think people think I need to be. I don't think I am insane.
Q. Do you think that killing your mother and father makes this necessary?

A. Yes.

Q. Tell me, how do you feel about doing this?

A. Not too good!

Q. Tell me more about how you feel?

A. Kind of sorry, lonesome, etc.

Q. For whom are you lonesome?

A. My brother, my mother and father.

Q. Why do you miss your mother and father?

A. I don't know. I don't hear them talking all the time and I don't have them around.

Q. How did you get along with them?

A. Not too well sometimes and pretty good other times.

Q. What did you have trouble about?

A. Whenever I brought home a bad grade card.

Q. What would happen?

A. They would get mad.

Q. Who?

A. My father—not my mother so much.

Q. What would your father be likely to say on such occasions?

A. He just tried to tell me to do better. I can't explain it.

Q. Did he ever get angry enough to strike you?

A. Yes.

Q. How often?

A. Last year I failed the 9th grade and every time I brought home a report card he would.

Q. How were your grades in comparison with your brother's?

A. This year he has got all B's and I have all C's and one B.

Q. Were his grades constantly better than yours?

A. Yes.

Q. How did you feel?

A. I guess he was doing better than I was.

Q. Did your folks express any feelings [about the] differences in your grades?

A. They just asked me why I didn't do better. They felt I should do better than Lee.

Q. Did this ever make you angry?

A. Not angry, just a little mad.

Q. Tell us briefly, what happened just before the incident

and describe the incident of the shooting of your mother and father.

A. I went to a basketball game. My bus came home slower than the team bus which my brother was on. I got home about an hour later than my brother. I told them what happened but they didn't believe me. They got mad and started fussing and I went to bed. I got up the next morning, went to the office, got the .22 and when my father came out, I shot him and when mother came out I shot her.

Q. How did you feel then?

A. Confused I guess—scared.

Q. Why were you frightened?

A. By just doing it.

Q. What scared you?

A. Just doing it.

Q. Did you think about what would happen when you did this?

A. Not then.

Q. Have you thought about it since?

A. Yes.

Q. What were your thoughts?

A. I will probably get a place in Hagerstown [at a state penal institution for juveniles].

Q. How long?

A. I don't know.

Q. You don't seem to think that shooting your mother and father was too serious.

A. Well, it was.

Q. How serious do you think it is?

A. I don't know how to explain but it is really serious.

Q. Anything more serious that you can think of?

A. No.

Q. What do you think will happen to your brother now?

A. Now he is living with neighbors, I guess. I don't know.

Q. Where will he go after that?

A. Out to Kansas, I guess, to live with our grandparents.

Q. How did you feel about being adopted?

A. I didn't think much about it. Sometimes I wondered where my real mother and father was.

Q. Did you make any effort to find them?
A. Nothing more than thinking about it.
Q. Is there anything else you might want to tell us that might be helpful to us in making a decision about you?
A. None that I can think of.

It is hard to imagine that anybody facing murder charges could be less forceful in his own defense. One can understand why the doctors concluded that Wayne was not displaying the appropriate "affect" of concern and regret. But once one recognizes how determined he was to avoid discussing certain painful subjects—especially sex and his ambiguous emotions toward Shirley—there is a perverse logic to his self-incriminating answers. Under the best circumstances, Wayne had always found it difficult to express himself. Now, under the worst possible circumstances, he had conscious—as well as unconscious—motives for keeping his feelings and certain vital information hidden.

Of course, the doctors did not know this. But close attention to the details of his interviews, a cursory review of the documents at their disposal, and a bit of double-checking should have shown that he was being far less than candid. If this had roused their suspicions and led to more resourceful questioning, the doctors might have discovered the full horror of the Dresbachs' home life. Or short of that, somebody might at least have remarked that, regardless of whether Wayne was legally sane, his refusal to provide more than a sketchy outline of events seriously diminished his capacity to assist in his defense. But that day at the staff conference the discussion was limited to psychological categories and to the patient's fitness to stand trial, as strictly defined by Maryland law.

Dr. Hernandez mentioned . . . that Dr. Salas seems to give a complete picture of this patient in his case work-up . . . as to the diagnosis, Dr. Hernandez feels the patient could not be called Passive Aggressive personality; however, he feels the patient could have an emotional inadequacy. In Dr. Hernandez's opinion Wayne was competent to stand trial.

Dr. Guerrero stated that the patient impressed him as a schizophrenic, also that Mr. Oropollo brought out some

schizophrenia in the psychological. Mr. Oropollo stated that
the patient's schizophrenic process may underlie this. He also
thinks the patient can stand trial.

Dr. Prado . . . is of the opinion that the patient was responsible at the time of the crime. He also stated that the
EEG [electroencephalograph] findings were not correlated
with the clinical findings as they should be in order to give
proper significance as to the diagnosis of convulsive disorder.

Dr. Morgenstern feels that the most striking feature in this
patient is the way in which he talks about unpleasant things,
such as the shooting of his parents, in a "matter of fact" way.
This could be a schizophrenic feature but . . . Dr. Morgenstern stated that he has seen this blandness in other young-
sters with character disorders. The EEG pattern suggests
brain pathology which we failed to substantiate by neurological examination. How much of this pathology should be
considered in evaluat[ing] a patient's responsibility is a factor
which is difficult to discuss at this time. . . . As to the future
management of this patient, Dr. Morgenstern feels it is more
likely that the patient's incarceration at the Reformatory
might be adding to his already pronounced character disorder. . . .

Dr. Hamilton feels that the patient has been exposed to a
great deal of trauma in his life and thus has established a
pattern of reacting to it by his bland front. There is a great
deal of neurotic conflict and his character disorder is beneath
this. Dr. Hamilton feels that the way in which this patient
reacts to stress is a very pathological thing. He also feels the
patient is able to stand trial.

Recommendation: A letter will be written to the court stating that it is the staff's opinion that the patient was responsible at the time of the alleged offenses and is able to stand
trial.

7

While Wayne underwent evaluation at Clifton T. Perkins
prison hospital, Lloyd Smith pursued his investigation. Following
up on rumors about the Dresbachs, he learned that Pat wasn't

welcome at many nudist camps. It seems he had this aggravating habit of taking photographs.

When Smith mentioned this to Lena Talbert, she remembered the camera which the police had asked her to hold. Wondering what was on the film, she had it developed.

The snapshots, taken on the Dresbachs' patio, featured several nude women in what Lena would only describe as "revolting poses. That stuff was just plain sick. I called Lieutenant Smith and got that garbage right out of my house."

Another neighbor of the Dresbachs telephoned the Dunns and in a halting, flustered manner said he had once seen Pat in a sleazy bar in North Beach, trying to pick up men. He appeared to be particularly interested in rough trade—sailors and oystermen and truck drivers. The neighbor had assumed Dresbach was a homosexual, but then Pat had stepped over to his table and casually explained that he liked to take photographs of strangers having sex with Shirley.

"I think he expected me to volunteer," the incredulous man told the Dunns. "I got the hell out of there."

When the Dunns urged him to repeat this story to the police, the man said, "And have them put me on the stand? Not on your life." He wasn't about to get up in front of a courtroom full of people and testify about "those things."

As the Dunns were to discover, this squeamish sentiment was quite common in Franklin Manor and surrounding communities. Some people could not bring themselves to believe what Pat and Shirley had been doing. Others believed it—in fact, they had long known what was going on—but they couldn't bring themselves to talk about it, at least not for the record.

At that time, just ten years before the advent of *Penthouse* and *Hustler* and *Deep Throat*, *Lady Chatterly's Lover* was still banned from Maryland libraries and bookstores, and more mundane aspects of human sexuality were considered unfit topics for reading, much less for conversation. So, in a sense, there simply wasn't an accepted vocabulary which would have permitted people to discuss the Dresbachs in public. Sensational rumors about Pat and Shirley rippled through the county, but in the official records the words "pornography" and "promiscuity" were forced to carry more freight then they could bear as they were substituted for the colloquial equivalents of anal intercourse, sadism, cunnilingus, fellatio, incest, and zoophilism.

To comprehend the Dresbach case, therefore, it is crucial to keep in mind that while Wayne was pathetically inarticulate, he was not alone in his inability to talk about what had happened in his house. Lee, for example, displayed even greater hesitancy to discuss the highly charged sexual atmosphere.

On January 26, the same day as the staff conference at Perkins, Robert Ogle of the Juvenile Protection Bureau came to the Talberts' to interview him, and after some prodding Lee admitted "their father would go about the home nude from time to time but their mother would not. When I asked him how he and Wayne felt about their father doing this, he said emphatically, 'We didn't appreciate it.'" He didn't elaborate on this or anything else, however, and it seemed to have slipped his mind that Shirley frequently walked around without clothes and that she was nude the morning she died.

But after this momentary lapse, Lee's powers of recall improved, and he dropped a bombshell, informing Ogle "that the Monday before the offense, Wayne had told him he was going to shoot both of the parents."

This claim contradicted—and in effect condemned—his brother on two critical counts. It was taken by the prosecutor as conclusive evidence that Wayne had premeditated the murders for five days and had planned all along to kill Shirley as well as Pat. Wayne would deny this repeatedly, but the damage had been done.

Given all the gossip about sex, Tommy Dunn thought people were in danger of ignoring the other things that had gone on in the Dresbach house. To his mind, it was much worse that Pat had been beating the boys with his fists from the time they were ten and eleven years old. Tommy was the first to admit he was no angel. There were times when he fell into foul tempers, and he had had his share of shouting and shoving matches and even occasional fights. But he had never—*never!*—raised a hand in anger at any of his kids, and the idea of hitting them with his fists or a belt buckle or a stick and drawing blood . . . well, that sickened him.

When he married Mary Helen, she had had two sons by a previous marriage. They were just toddlers, and Tommy had treated them as if they were his own children. Or, to be honest about it, he'd always tried to treat them a bit better. He knew what it was to have a stepfather, and he didn't want them growing up to hate him.

Once when Mike had misbehaved and Mary Helen had asked Tommy to spank him, he had marched the boy upstairs and had a long talk with him. He told him how much he had hurt his mother, how much he had disappointed them both. That wasn't the way they had raised him, that wasn't what the nuns at school had taught him. Then as he saw tears spill from Mike's eyes, Tommy gave him a light, almost friendly swat on the seat of his pants and said, "Now you better pretend to cry or your mother's going to come up here and get mad at both of us."

Tommy could understand a man's disciplining his kids. But to do what Dresbach had done—to slap them around, blacken their eyes and bloody their lips, to knock them down when he got really mad, then to taunt them and make fun of them in front of company—Tommy just couldn't imagine anything more cruel. And he couldn't believe that a jury wouldn't agree with him.

8

To tourists, Annapolis consists almost entirely of the Naval Academy and the city's historical center, a sort of miniature Williamsburg where people still live and work along bumpy brick streets, in colonial houses and clapboard cottages. During the day the ancient maple and oak trees pulse with a shrill rabble of starlings and sparrows; after dark, crickets and frogs take up the chorus. In the harbor, luxury yachts dock beside fishing boats and skipjacks, the broad-beamed flat-bottomed sailing craft favored by oystermen. Expensive seafood restaurants stand cheek by prickly jowl with raw bars and carry-out crab joints. And in warm weather, when the Severn is at low tide, the pungent odor of shucked oysters and discarded crab shells drifts uphill to the Governor's mansion and the State Capitol building.

But in early February of 1961, when Wayne was transferred from Clifton T. Perkins to Annapolis, he saw none of the views favored by photographers. Instead, he was dumped in the town jail, an antique and crumbling building which has long since been demolished and replaced by a modern facility. Back then it stood in a blighted area where winos and indigents vomited in gutters and slept on doorsteps. In cold weather, some of them might have dreamed of "three hots and a cot," but nobody who had done time in that jail would ever be desperate enough to want to go back. Segregated into two tiers, with blacks on the bottom floor and whites upstairs, it made few other discriminations. The drunk and the disorderly, the child molester and the adolescent offender, the shoplifter and the murderer were all penned together as they awaited trial.

"It was the worst place I've ever been," Mary Helen remembered. "The worst place I hope I'll ever be. Tommy and I kept saying we wanted to see Wayne and finally, when the police realized none of his family cared a good goddamn about him, they let us and the Talberts and a few other people visit him on Sunday mornings. Sometimes it was all I could do to drag myself down there. But I knew if it was depressing for us, it must have been unbearable for Wayne."

The visiting room was a narrow hallway with a row of windows on one wall. Gray-green paint scaled off the ceiling, and under the fluorescent bulbs everybody's face had a sickly, jaundiced color.

"We'd all line up at those windows," Mary Helen said, "and talk through the bars. You'd be standing hip-to-hip with the person at the next window, and there would be women and kids crying and men screaming back in the cells and sometimes you couldn't be sure what you were saying or hearing. And the smell . . . I can't describe it, but if you've ever been in a jail, maybe you know what I mean."

The smell is like no other. It is not just ancient ground-in dirt or newly splashed disinfectant or vomit and sweat and urine. It is some nameless secretion which humans seem to give off when they are miserable and terrified and herded into a tight spot that bristles with violence.

"The first time we saw Wayne," Mary Helen said, "he looked dead. Everything about him—his eyes, his skin, his hair—was lifeless, and he just stood there. He didn't know what to say. Neither did we. So I reached through the bars and pulled him close and kissed him. I can't say he responded much, but he didn't push me away either, and somehow we got through the hour. It was never easy, not even with all my kids there, each one talking for a few minutes, but we came back every Sunday. Afterward I'd cry all the way home, wondering what I'd do if one of my kids was in that place. Then I realized I'd do just what I was doing. Wayne had become one of my kids."

The Talberts, too, were appalled by conditions in the Annapolis jail, and Lena went to the county sheriff and told him he had to do something. "I said he couldn't throw a little boy in with hardened criminals. No matter what Wayne was accused of doing, he was fifteen years old. That's what griped me. In the very beginning when they hadn't decided yet whether to try him as an adult, they were already treating him like one. Actually they were treating him a lot worse. Any adult would have known enough to demand a lawyer."

After a lecture from Lena, the sheriff ordered Wayne segregated from the rest of the prisoners. He was locked into an enclosed room usually reserved for women. While this shielded him from "harmful influences"—a euphemism for homosexual rape—it amounted to solitary confinement, a punishment generally dealt out to the most dangerous and unruly inmates. After a week of this isolation, Wayne pleaded to be let out, at least for a few hours a day. The request was granted.

On Sundays, as a special privilege, his visitors were permitted to come upstairs to his room. "That was quite an experience," Mary Helen recalled. "An ordeal really. At first I thought it'd be better to see him alone, not looking through bars. But it was worse. There were fewer reasons for him not to talk and fewer excuses for us not to find something to say. He still seemed kind of numb. You know, dazed. He didn't react one way or the other. He'd answer your questions, and that was it.

"Sometimes we'd bring Lee with us, and that was no help, because then both boys would sit there like cigar-store Indians. The whole hour would pass and they wouldn't have said ten words to each other.

"I didn't understand it. Lee was never at a loss for words any other time, and I didn't see why he couldn't try harder with Wayne. Finally I told him so. I'll never forget what he said. Over the years he repeated it again and again when I jumped on him for not helping Wayne more. 'You weren't there,' he'd say. 'You didn't see what he did to my parents.'

"That slowed me down a while and made me think what a terrible thing it must have been for Lee to go through. But when I learned what the Dresbachs were really like—Lee himself told me a lot of things they did to him—I realized if anybody ought to have understood *what* Wayne did, and *why*, Lee should have. It's an awful thing to say, but there's no getting around it. He had damn good reason to be thankful Wayne shot them. There's no telling what those people meant to do to the boys."

9

Among Wayne's visitors there was one who surprised him. Occasionally C. J. Pettit, a friend of his parents, the last person outside the family to see them alive, came to the jail with Lee. When Wayne heard that Mr. Pettit had petitioned to be made administrator of the Dresbach estate and guardian of both boys, he was still more surprised. He had never known Pettit was all that close to his parents and he had expected a relative from Kansas to look after things.

But Pettit maintained in his petition:

> the only other next of kin of H. Malone Dresbach is his aunt, Florence Ramsey of Hutchinson, Kansas. She filed her renunciation to administer the estate in favor of your petitioner and it is her desire that the said Charles J. Pettit administer this estate and act as guardian for the said minor children of H. Malone Dresbach, and that H. Nathaniel Blaustein act as his attorney in both instances. The said Charles J. Pettit has for many years past been a close friend of both H. Malone Dresbach and his wife, Shirley Dresbach, and he is thoroughly familiar with their personal affairs; and H. Nathaniel Blaustein has been associated with the said H. Malone Dresbach in the practice of law and is likewise familiar with many of his personal affairs.
>
> . . . the next of kin of said Shirley Dresbach are her par-

ents, Arthur Shaffer and his wife of Independence, Kansas, who are eighty or more years of age and unable to serve in any capacity in either of these estates; and the Honorable Harry Woodring of Topeka, Kansas, a former Secretary of War, an uncle of the said Shirley Dresbach, and they too filed their renunciations. . . .

While Shirley's parents were obviously too old to assume responsibility for Wayne and Lee, there was no attempt to explain why Florence Ramsey, Harry Woodring, or some other relative didn't volunteer. There was also no explanation for Pettit's failure to mention that Harold Malone Dresbach's mother, Anna, was alive and residing in Palm Springs, California. Pettit had good reason to know this since, as administrator of the estate, he sent Anna Dresbach a monthly check, then covered the cost of her funeral in 1967, as part of an agreement which Dresbach had reached with his mother when she relinquished all rights to her husband's estate.

But in a case shot through with unanswered questions, this was just one more among many.

10

For such a small, pleasant, self-effacing woman, Lena Talbert worked indefatigably on Wayne's behalf and never lacked courage. Nothing demonstrated her pluckiness more dramatically than the fact that she took it upon herself to speak to Judge Benjamin Michaelson when he was said to be deliberating whether to try the boy as a juvenile or an adult.

Whatever else one might think of Judge Michaelson, he is an imposing man, even now in his eighties; and no matter what else people in Anne Arundel County choose to say about him, they all agree that there will never be another judge like him. This is a reflection of changes in Maryland politics and demographic patterns as much as it is an estimate of Michaelson's formidable reputation.

In 1961 many Maryland districts had one dominating, senior, circuit court judge. The Fifth District, for example, had Benjamin Michaelson. Or, to put it the way many people did, Judge Michaelson *had* the district. While nobody doubted his integrity or his knowledge of the law, his almost absolute authority made for a situation that could easily be abused, even when the judge believed he was acting solely in the public interest.

As one well-known Annapolis lawyer described him, "Ben Michaelson was hard-working, strict, and super-smart. It was a challenge to take a case to his court, and I liked that. But given his position, given the way things operated back then, he wound up trying to exercise a lot more prerogatives than any circuit judge should have. He was autocratic and quirky and a real stickler about scheduling. If he decided it was a one-day case, that's all you got, period. Not that he ever had a very crowded docket. That's just how he liked to run things.

"He was an absolute bear on lawyers. He'd lecture you and badger you and he wouldn't stand for any bad conduct or antics in the courtroom. But the funny thing was, he himself would blurt out the most incredibly injudicious comments in front of the jury, especially during opening arguments and summations, which weren't recorded back in those days. You could protest all you wanted, but what good would it do? His comments weren't on the transcript and it was pointless to appeal. And if you bitched too much, you had to be ready for him to fight back. He was no patsy. When he got mad, he'd turn purple and let his glasses drop down off his nose and hang from one ear and he'd just stare at you. It was the damnedest performance you ever saw. And believe me, it intimidated a lot of people."

A tall, scowling man, with a floss of white hair covering a pink skull, Judge Michaelson had a list of pet peeves and apparently arrogated to himself cases that were misdemeanors and should have been heard by a magistrate. For instance, he felt there was a direct link between juvenile delinquency and the sale of liquor to minors, and he insisted on hearing all such cases in Circuit Court.

He was also reputed to have an elephantine memory. Cases, precedents, laws, and the faces of small-time offenders were etched in his mind forever. There is a story still told around the Annapolis courthouse about the time Judge Michaelson took his son, Benjamin, Jr., to an Orioles baseball game in Baltimore and spotted a crowd of teen-agers misbehaving in the bleachers. Pointing them out to his son, he said that he remembered them from Juvenile Court and quoted the charges against them and the sentences he had handed down.

But as much pride as he took in his own good memory, the judge enjoyed even more the way local people remembered him. Seldom a day went by, he said, that someone didn't stop him on the street and thank him for a favor he had done years ago. Often it was a mother or father, still grateful that Michaelson had straightened out their wayward son before it was too late. Or occasionally, the judge said, it was the boy, himself, admitting that he might have slipped off the deep end if the judge hadn't grabbed him by the scruff of the neck, so to speak, and shoved him onto the right path. Such encounters convinced Benjamin Michaelson that his years on the bench had not been wasted.

The day Lena Talbert came to talk to him, however, Michaelson's vaunted memory seemed to have deserted him. Pleading for Wayne, Lena said, "He's just a little boy, a child. Haven't you seen him?"

The judge replied that he hadn't, forgetting that evening in January when Wayne had been brought to his house in shackles.

"Well, he's small. He doesn't look fifteen."

Michaelson reminded her that the boy had committed a heinous crime—double homicide with strong evidence of premeditation.

"But he didn't have any real choice," Lena said. "He was pushed into it. Don't you know about his parents—the kinds of things they subjected him to?"

Allowing that he had heard rumors, the judge explained that he had to decide whether anything the Dresbachs had done to the boy—things that could be proved—justified a plea of self-defense.

When she repeated that Wayne hadn't had any choice, that he had been driven to it, Judge Michaelson answered that if he was insane, that would certainly affect his deliberations. But, it seemed to him, even under the worst circumstances, Wayne had better alternatives than shooting his parents. Why hadn't he just run away?

For a moment, Lena was speechless. His question frightened and flabbergasted her. Hadn't Judge Michaelson read the newspapers? During the course of his deliberations, hadn't he spoken with Lloyd Smith or Robert Ogle? Surely he should have known that Wayne had run away five times.

Although Lena wasn't aware of it then, Michaelson had signed several documents concerning the larceny charge which Mr. Dresbach had brought against Wayne the last time he ran away. He should indeed have known about the boy's futile efforts to escape his father.

When Lena could bring herself to speak again, she began reciting a list of the Dresbachs' offenses—the nudism, the pornography, the promiscuity, the drinking, the beatings—but she had a sense that Michaelson wasn't listening, that he had already made up his mind.

11

From the start, there was never much chance Wayne would be tried as a juvenile. In Maryland, at that time, it was virtually automatic for an underage offender to have his juvenile status waived if he was older than fourteen and the charge was murder or some other "heinous crime."

Today, the law is significantly different. Although a juvenile charged with murder is immediately remanded to the Circuit Court, he can appeal for a hearing to be waived back to Juvenile Court. During this hearing, the presiding judge takes testimony from character witnesses and others, then applies five criteria in reaching a decision: (1) the defendant's age, (2) his mental and physical condition, (3) his amenability to treatment in the juvenile system, (4) the nature of his offense, and (5) the public safety.

Afterward, if the judge has ruled that the defendant should be tried as an adult, he usually disqualifies himself from further involvement since he is likely to have reviewed evidence based on hearsay and conjecture which would not be admissible at a trial. In 1961, however, Benjamin Michaelson apparently felt no obligation to step down. After he announced that Wayne would be indicted for murder in the first degree, he continued to preside over the case.

The Talberts and the Dunns, who knew little about law, were infuriated by Michaelson's decision, and they wondered about his impartiality. But Father Dawson, also no expert on jurisprudence, reserved his opinion and still hoped there could be a moral and humane solution.

Calling on Judge Michaelson in his chambers, Father Dawson attempted to establish some general grounds for agreement. He said he appreciated the judge's dilemma. There were, of course, precedents that had to be followed, legal formalities and rituals that had to be observed. But while society—not to mention the Maryland legal system—could not condone the killings and had to hold a trial, he hoped the judge would concur that the most important question was what would happen to Wayne after the jury reached its verdict. The boy was fifteen. If found guilty, he had a whole lifetime to rehabilitate himself. It didn't make sense to hand down a long prison sentence and risk destroying him. Wasn't it more reasonable to send him to a special institution where he could continue his education and receive therapy?

Father Dawson said he knew of a number of church schools which welcomed problem children who had had histories of antisocial behavior and, in some instances, criminal records. If Wayne were convicted, would the judge consider placing him in such a school rather than in prison?

Michaelson's response seemed one of bemused condescension. While he said he was pleased that the priest and other members of the community had taken an interest in this case, he explained that they lacked his long, sad experience and had no idea how hard it was to rehabilitate a boy like Wayne. Still, he didn't say no; in fact, in an equivocal way he appeared to offer some encouragement. At least that's how Father Dawson interpreted his answer.

Hurrying home, he drew up a list of close to a hundred church-affiliated boys' schools and sent off letters describing Wayne's background and his present plight. Each one ended with an impassioned plea.

He has been a model prisoner . . . he has responded in a
most heartening way to my attempts to minister to him. I
am convinced that were he given an opportunity . . . in a
Christian environment in which he could know deep Christian love and nourishment, and at the same time, receive
some expert counsel or therapy, he could be completely rehabilitated and would prove to be a fine and responsible citizen. My contention is that he was provoked unmercifully to
do what he did.

I have made contact with just about all the authorities involved in his case and it appears that suggestions from my
side may carry some weight. . . . Could you inform me as to
whether there is any chance that you could handle such a
problem—and if you can't, could you give me some advice as
to where I could turn?

12

On March 3, Albert Goodman filed an order to enter his appearance as attorney for Ralph Wayne Dresbach. For the last two
months, Goodman, like many people in Maryland, had been
aware of the case and, because of the extraordinary nature of the
crime, he had paid more than passing attention to the news stories. When Nathaniel Blaustein called from Washington and
asked him to defend Wayne, he accepted the challenge. But after
reviewing the police and psychiatric reports, he must have realized how steeply the odds were stacked against his client.

Since Albert Goodman later came in for some *sotto voce* criticism, it is only fair to review the problems that confronted him as
he prepared a defense.

Within hours after the killings, Wayne had confessed, offering
no excuses. Still without legal counsel, he had been examined by
more than a dozen psychiatrists, psychologists, and neurologists,
all of whom had heard him repeat variations on this confession
and not one of whom had expressed the opinion that he was insane as defined by the M'Naghten Rule.

Insofar as it could be evaluated, public opinion seemed to be
running against Wayne. Newspapers in Washington and

throughout the state had scarcely alluded to the rumors about the Dresbachs. Instead, they portrayed Wayne as cold and unfeeling. An adopted boy whose origins were shrouded in mystery, he was made to appear the living embodiment of *The Bad Seed*, a sensational novel, then a successful film of the late 50s, about a psychopathic child who plots and executes the murders of friends and family with chilling lucidity.

As already mentioned, bail was out of the question, as was an appeal of the waiver of Wayne's juvenile status. What was worse, there was no possibility of plea bargaining. Considering the defendant's age, his emotional instability, and the squalor of his home life, one might have expected a quiet courthouse discussion between the State's attorney and the attorney for the defense, followed by an announcement that the boy had pleaded guilty to second degree murder or manslaughter. But at that time in Maryland, plea bargaining didn't exist officially. Although in urban areas with crowded dockets some cases were disposed of after informal, off-the-record negotiations, this wasn't true in Annapolis where Judge Benjamin Michaelson, that stickler on scheduling, seldom had a backlog of work.

Of course, one way of avoiding Michaelson, along with all the prejudicial pretrial publicity, would have been to request a change of venue. In cases involving capital offenses, such requests were almost automatically granted. But Goodman had decided that he wanted to stay in Annapolis. He said he had a surer sense there of community values and the kind of jury he would get. Local people also knew his reputation, and he knew them.

Among those he knew well were Benjamin Michaelson, Sr. and the prosecuting attorney, Osborne Duvall, Jr. whom Goodman had helped train during his own tenure as State's attorney. To complete the circle, Judge Michaelson's son, Benjamin Jr., was a lawyer and at one point had worked in Goodman's office.

Goodman's worst problem, however, was one he couldn't have anticipated and didn't know how to cope with. His client would scarcely talk to him. At times, he appeared to be in a fugue state. Huddled on his bunk, his mouth half open, his eyes glazed, he stared at Goodman as if he had seen a ghost.

In a sense, Wayne had. For his lawyer looked like his father risen from the dead. The resemblance astounded and frightened him. Like Dresbach, Albert Goodman was short and wiry and had a receding hairline that exposed a high, tanned forehead.

Goodman also spoke like his father. Not that he hollered threats or obscenities, but he often used legal terms which Wayne couldn't follow. He knew he should have asked questions, but his questions had led to many humiliations in the past and he didn't want to appear as stupid and helpless as he felt.

There was another thing that kept Wayne silent, wary. He thought he had heard Goodman refer to his father as Pat, the nickname used by Dresbach's closest friends. At once, he inferred that his lawyer had been on intimate terms with his parents and would never believe anything he said against them. And since Wayne knew Goodman had been hired by family friends, he feared that he would tell them whatever he said—especially if it put them in a bad light. This man wasn't here to defend him, Wayne decided. He was out to protect the Dresbachs and their acquaintances.

Years later, Albert Goodman conceded that he had known Harold Dresbach a little—as a lawyer, though, not as a friend. He remembered nothing about the nickname and was adamant that he had not learned about Pat's and Shirley's personal lives until he read the reports of the Juvenile Probation Bureau. As Goodman interpreted it, Wayne's failure to communicate was just further evidence of how deeply disturbed the boy was.

Thus Goodman's first thought was to try to find several psychiatrists who would contradict the opinion of the doctors at Clifton T. Perkins and swear that Wayne was legally insane and therefore not responsible for his actions.

If this failed, Goodman would have to fall back on a second line of defense, which depended upon two flawed arguments whose combined weight might nevertheless sway a jury's sympathies. He would contend that, while Wayne might not be insane according to the M'Naghten Rule, the boy was clearly sick, emotionally unbalanced, and incapable of true premeditation. What is more, Goodman would maintain that Wayne's mental problems were due to the abuse he had suffered from his adoptive parents, who had raised him in a depraved environment. In short, he would attempt to put Pat and Shirley Dresbach on trial and demonstrate that they had driven their child close to a complete breakdown, in which extreme state of mind he had killed them.

13

When he first entered the Annapolis jail, Wayne had regarded it as "a bad dream, unreal," and he missed his friends, his dog Mac, and his room under the eaves where he had read late into the night and watched ships sail down the channel and out to sea. Now he lay in his bunk, gazing at a steel wall pitted with rust, and dreamed of being in his boat, exhilarated by the speed and the cool sting of the salt spray. His legs ached from inactivity. He longed to go hiking in the woods, looking for arrowheads, or walking along the shore searching for fossilized shark's teeth.

But after a few months, he stopped daydreaming and stopped fantasizing that his real parents would show up and save him. It was his old life and his Sunday visits that came to seem "unreal." Much as he looked forward to them as a break in the monotony, he felt uneasy around people from outside. They knew so little about him and the life he was forced to lead behind bars, and there was so much he couldn't say—especially not to Lee.

He had made efforts to break through to his brother. Once, very tentatively, he had even tried to talk about Pat and Shirley. He asked where they were buried and hoped this would lead to other subjects. But Lee drew back, flustered and angry, and refused to answer. Minutes later, he left, just as he would do whenever Wayne mentioned their parents.

Another time when Wayne asked how Mac was, Lee said he had no idea. "But aren't you looking after him?" Wayne demanded. Lee confessed he wasn't; he had too much else to do. There was his schoolwork and basketball and dates with Karen and . . . well, finally, he and C.J. had decided to give the dog away.

After that Wayne asked nothing of his brother. Occasionally he found himself wondering about his personal belongings. What had happened to his books, his clothes, his clock radio, cornet, fishing rods, and baseball mitts? But he said nothing. He knew he had to resign himself to the loss of everything.

Gradually then he was sucked up into the airless, self-perpetuating system of jailhouse gossip, wisdom, fear, and honor. His sense of reality, already skewed, and his sense of self, always distorted by his father's cruelty, were now shaped by convicts; and he had to bend to their rules just as surely as he had to obey the guards.

Cigarettes served as money here, and he could buy liquor—bonded or homebrewed—pills—uppers or downers—and favors and preferential treatment. Everything was available except women, but there was no scarcity of sex. Although his room afforded him some protection, Wayne got out several hours a day and he heard what the other cons called him. He was a "pretty boy." Small, fair, smooth-faced, a perfect "catcher," as opposed to the bigger, more aggressive "pitchers," he soon learned which men and which dim corridors to avoid.

But everybody warned him that it wouldn't be so easy in the state pen, or wherever he went next. He had better make up his mind, they said, what he meant to do. Already he had been beaten up badly by a man who was trying to steal his wristwatch, and he realized that if you couldn't protect yourself, no one else would. Certainly not the guards.

He decided he would pump iron, put on weight, and take care of himself. But the more experienced cons said there was always somebody bigger and tougher. Or somebody who had a taste for muscle boys. Or somebody who just wanted to bust your ass. The exercise room in many prisons crackles with barely suppressed violence and, rather than burning off hostility, weightlifting seems to bring it to a boiling point, particularly as the blacks work out in one corner and the whites in the other, glaring across the space between them, strutting, flexing, striking poses, every gesture a potential warning or provocation.

The best thing for a boy his size, some guys said, was to face facts and get married. Become some big con's punk. "What you do," they told him, "is when you get to the pen, you go up to the biggest, meanest mother in the yard and promise if he'll protect you, you'll fuck for him and nobody else. Believe me, that's better than having the whole cell block cracking on you."

One weekday afternoon, Wayne had a surprise visit. The principal of Southern High School had gotten special permission to bring some classmates and friends to see Wayne, and after several minutes of uncomfortable silence, then a few shy questions, the boys filled the room with boisterous talk and laughter. They might have been just a gang of kids, gripped by spring fever, cutting up in history class.

But all the talk and laughter died when Wayne took a pack of Camels from his breast pocket, tamped one on his thumbnail, lit up and inhaled. The boys eyed the principal uneasily.

For the rest of these ninth graders, smoking was strictly forbidden, and although they sneaked an occasional cigarette, they would never light up in front of an adult. But here was Wayne puffing away, then starting another Camel off the butt of the first.

After four months in jail, his fingers were stained with nicotine, and he was smoking more than a pack a day. In retrospect, it was a small, laughable thing, but at the time, this seemed the most accurate measure of the differences between Wayne and his classmates; he smoked in front of the principal, and the principal said nothing.

Soon there would be more dramatic signs—indelible marks—to underscore the differences. One day in May, when the weather had warmed and the steel walls of his room shimmered like a griddle, he stripped off his shirt, sat on his bunk, and knotted his left fist while an older prisoner sterilized a sewing needle with a lit match. Then the man dipped the needle into a vial of liquid and jabbed it into Wayne's shoulder and held it there until a tiny blue speck appeared under his skin. Slowly he repeated this process, needling dots of india ink into Wayne's shoulder and connecting them to form the letters W.D.

Careful not to wince, not to betray any fear, Wayne turned his right shoulder and let the man tattoo a star on his deltoid muscle. Then, exposing the soft underside of his right forearm, he braced himself as the man blotted the sweat and started something more ambitious.

After an hour, the needle felt blunt, and it took more pressure to push in the tip. The holes it made looked bigger and the ink seemed to blur, although Wayne thought that might have been his imagination or the misting of his eyes. He stayed quiet and still, moving only to take in his mouth the cigarettes a friend lit for him.

Quite a few men were in the room now. Some of them joked and said the sweat that plastered his trousers to his legs was pee. But most of them remained silent, showing their respect for what he was going through—a painful rite of passage.

As the amateur tattooer made his last jab, he sighed like a schoolboy putting a period at the end of a long difficult test question. Then he drew back to admire his work. Legible even if it was a little fuzzy around the edges, the word *Wayne* was scrawled across the pale flesh.

Years afterward when anybody asked him about the tattoos, Wayne, with characteristic self-deprecation, said that they had been done when he was too young and dumb to know any better. But if pressed, he would confess that there had been a reason. He knew if he hoped to survive among the other prisoners, he had to prove that he was tough, he could take it. And he wanted to show he was one of them. Although he hadn't been convicted of anything yet, he had begun to look like a con.

14

On April 5, Albert Goodman filed a petition to have Wayne moved for a day to the courthouse in Baltimore where he was examined by a psychologist, a psychiatrist, and a physician specializing in electroencephalography. Hired by the defense, these doctors were scheduled to examine him again in early May. But significant events intervened.

Because of overcrowding in the jail, another prisoner had been put into the room with Wayne. Tall, rangy, and muscular, Kenny was awaiting trial on charges of armed robbery. But, from the moment he arrived, he made it clear he had no intention of letting a jury decide his fate.

Pumping Wayne for information, Kenny learned that the door to the room was opened at noon when the guard brought lunch, then for a few hours in late afternoon, and again briefly at dinnertime. After that it was locked for twelve hours until breakfast. The guards had never varied the schedule and had never shaken the place down.

"Great," Kenny said, grinning. He went to a window and tested the bars, measuring their circumference and the distance between them. Then he stepped out of his shoes and removed several hacksaw blades from the insoles.

"Don't say a fucking word about this," he warned Wayne, and set to work. Notching the first bar about an inch above the windowsill, he held both ends of the blade and sawed back and forth with smooth short strokes that filed off a fine gray powder.

Within minutes, Kenny was dripping sweat and looked as though he would break long before the bar did. But he kept at it while Wayne sat on his bunk and watched, the rasp of the saw barely audible even at this distance.

At 11:50 Kenny swept the filings into the palm of his hand and flushed them down the toilet. By the time the guard showed up with lunch, he had toweled off and was standing in front of the window smoking a cigarette.

Work continued throughout the afternoon, the evening, and well into the night. When the lights blinked out, Kenny quit for a few minutes as if afraid that darkness had improved the guards' ears. But when he heard nothing outside the room, he figured no one could hear him either and resumed sawing. Although his fingers ached and his arms had gone rubbery, he made some progress by rocking his shoulders, his entire upper torso, from side to side, dragging the blade across the bar.

The next day, when Kenny cut through the bottom of the first bar, Wayne started to wonder whether he would make it. And if he did, what should *he* do? He stepped over to the window and glanced at the walled courtyard three stories below.

"How are you going to get down there?"

"Climb. I'm a human fly." Kenny was notching another bar.

Wayne craned his neck and saw a drainpipe within arm's length of the window; behind the drainpipe, brick ledges jutted out every few rows. If a man sat on the windowsill, leaned left, and got a good handhold on the pipe, he could, with luck, swing his feet over onto a ledge. After that, if the pipe wasn't rusty and the bricks didn't crumble, it wouldn't be any problem to climb down to the courtyard. But trouble would be waiting there.

"A German shepherd patrols the yard after dark," Wayne said.

"I ain't afraid of any damn dog. They're scared of me."

"Still, how are you going to get out of the courtyard?"

Kenny pointed to the building whose back formed one wall of the yard. A storm cellar door led into its basement. "I had this checked out. That's a barber shop. A little mom-and-pop place that opens right onto the street."

"The door's got a padlock on it."

"Right, and I been tearing loose locks like that since I was your age. Ain't no way they can stop me. Not unless you squeal." Kenny pressed the jagged edge of the blade against Wayne's throat.

"I won't. I swear."

"What you oughta do, you oughta come with me."

"You'd let me?"

"Why not? We'll steal a car and go to Florida. I got friends there."

"I'll think it over."

"Yeah, you do that. And while you're thinking, what about spelling me? My arms are about half dead."

After an instant's hesitation, Wayne took the blade and began sawing. But he hadn't made up his mind. There were a lot of angles to consider. The only thing he knew for sure was that he wouldn't squeal. He had been in jail long enough to realize the danger of doing that. If Kenny didn't cut him, someone else would.

Still, if he didn't tip off the guards, they'd probably punish him. But punish him how, he wondered. He was already awaiting trial for double murder in the first degree. What did he have to lose? He decided there was nothing more anybody in authority could do to him. In a way, he was invulnerable.

The thought gave him no cause for elation. For if he was invulnerable, he felt it was only because his life had lost all value. Whether he stayed or went with Kenny, was good or bad, lived or died, didn't matter to anyone.

Over the weekend, they worked around the clock, sleeping in shifts, stopping only for meals and for the Dunns' visit Sunday morning. Despite his fatigue, Wayne came to regard this as a game: a combination physical endurance test and schoolboy prank in which he would trick the guards.

Monday night, after lights-out, the game ended. One by one, Kenny removed the bars, laying them on a bunk. Then he took several fresh rolls of toilet paper and soaked them in the sink until they weighed more than a pound apiece. Carrying them to the window, he hissed at the German shepherd and the dog trotted over to the wall, gazing upward, mouth open, long tongue lolling.

Kenny hurled a wad of the wet paper, missed the dog, and hit the courtyard with the force of a brick. Standing its ground, the German shepherd was growling when the second roll landed smack on its head. It fell without a sound, its legs splayed wide.

"Let's go," Kenny said. Slipping one of the sawed-off bars under the waistband of his pants, he hoisted himself up onto the windowsill, reached his long arm to the left, and got a grip on the drainpipe. He gave it a shake, testing its strength, swiveled sideways and stuck out his foot, groping for the ledge. Then he eased off the windowsill. After that, it was as simple as climbing down a ladder.

In the yard below, the dog had tottered to its feet and was whining. Kenny slapped its snout with the iron bar and knocked it out again.

Though Wayne tried to do exactly what Kenny had done, he was trembling and had a hard time scrambling up onto the windowsill. He was terrified by the height and the yawning darkness of the courtyard. For a moment he couldn't move. Then he felt himself teetering dizzily. He reached for the drainpipe, but couldn't be sure of his grip. His palms were clammy; the metal slippery. Finally he lunged and slid down the pipe like a linesman down a telegraph pole. When he hit bottom, his knuckles, ankles, and knees had been scraped raw.

"Over here," Kenny whispered.

Using the bar as a lever, he snapped off the lock and opened the door to the storm cellar. They shut it behind them, descending into a deeper darkness where they barked their shins on odds and ends of junk and bumped into the furnace, setting off an enormous reverberation in the heating ducts. At last they found the stairs and went up to the barber shop, where the front window let in the dull yellow glow of a street lamp.

After checking the cash register—it was empty—Kenny crawled

to the window and glanced one direction, then the other. When he saw nobody, he stood up and strolled out the front door with Wayne at his heels.

Kenny slid behind the steering wheel of the first car they came to and had it hot-wired by the time Wayne got in on the other side.

"Awright, awright, just take it easy. There's no rush," Kenny kept saying to himself, even as he rumbled over the brick streets and squealed around corners, bouncing off curbs.

Wayne, himself, would not—could not—have slowed down. As his blood raced, his breathing came in short, quick gasps. He wouldn't feel safe until they were out of Annapolis, out of the state.

But when they reached Route 50, Kenny headed north.

"Thought we were going to Florida," Wayne said.

"We are. But first I gotta see a friend in Baltimore. You can't go anywhere without cash."

Wayne didn't like the idea of stopping, and especially not of seeing somebody. He didn't like being in Baltimore, either. He had been there only once before and that time he had been delivered in shackles to the courthouse for his psychiatric examinations. He knew nothing about the city, and after four months in jail, he found that the traffic, the flickering lights, the crowds milling outside of bars and burlesque houses compounded his sense of dislocation.

But Kenny knew right where he was going and when he reached a large, leafy park, he pulled to the curb and kept the motor running.

"Tell you what, Wayne. You wait here and I'll be back to pick you up after I see my friend."

"What do you mean?"

"I mean what I said. I can't come crashing in on the man with somebody he's never met before."

"I'll wait in the car."

"You'll wait where I told you. You want me to toss you out on your ass? Now, let's not argue. Go over there and sit on that bench. I'll be right back."

Wayne waited an hour, then another, before it occurred to him Kenny wasn't coming back. Still, he couldn't bring himself to leave the bench. He didn't know where he was. He had no money —not even a dime for the telephone—and there was no one to call anyway. So he stayed there, shivering in the cool, spring air, sitting on his hands to stop them from shaking. He was reminded of all the times he had run away—the first rush of excitement, the certainty that he'd never be caught, the sense of freedom and power at being on his own. Then, inevitably, the letdown when he realized he wouldn't make it. He had failed again.

Presently a man strolled out of the park and asked if he had a match. Wayne said no. The man then offered him a cigarette and produced a lighter and said it was foolish of him to forget he didn't need a match. These days he was forgetting things all the time. Like tonight, dinner had slipped his mind. He was hungry. Was Wayne? Would he like to go somewhere and get a sandwich?

Suddenly three squad cars screeched to a halt in front of the bench, and half a dozen cops scrambled out, guns drawn. The man started screaming, "Don't hit me, don't hit me." But they brushed him aside and grabbed Wayne.

When they found out he wasn't armed and saw how small he was, the police couldn't stop laughing. There had to have been some screw-up, they said. This kid didn't look old enough to bust a window, much less ice his mother and father.

But when the state troopers hauled Wayne back to Annapolis in handcuffs and leg irons, the guards there weren't amused. For the rest of the night, they badgered him for information about Kenny. Who gave him the hacksaw blades? Where was he headed? Did he have a gun?

Wayne wouldn't answer. Although Kenny had ditched him, Wayne wouldn't betray him and wasn't especially angry. He understood why Kenny had had to do it. Who'd want to make a run for it with a double murderer? A kid, at that?

"Awright, smartass," one cop said, "you make us look bad, you hold out on us, we'll stick it all on you. We're talking about escape, breaking and entering, auto theft. You're going to be in jail till your dick shrivels and drops off."

"Jail! Fuck jail!" another cop shouted, grabbing Wayne and slamming him against the wall. "He's a killer. I'm going to see that this little cocksucker fries. You hear me? You're getting the chair."

Then they threw him into the hole, a three-by-seven cage enclosed in a shell of concrete. The cryptlike room contained a blanket, a lumpy mattress on the floor, and a commode in the corner. Nothing else. The lone source of light was a narrow window set so high on the wall it showed only a pale blue oblong of sky.

15

While Wayne languished in solitary confinement, Father Dawson alone was allowed in to see him, and he got out only for further psychiatric examinations. The day after his escape, three doctors hired by the defense arrived at the Annapolis jail.

Dr. Leonard H. Ainsworth administered a battery of eight tests, then drafted a psychological evaluation which he would discuss in depth at the trial.

Dr. Charles N. Luttrell of the Johns Hopkins Hospital interviewed Wayne and submitted a "Neurology Consultation Note." Since Dr. Luttrell was not called upon to testify, it is worth noting two items from his report.

Wayne finally admitted that his father brought women into the house while Shirley was away. Then, in recapitulating the events immediately preceding the murders, he said he got the .22 automatic rifle, "went into the kitchen where his brother was seated at the table drinking orange juice and told his brother that he was going to kill his father, that morning. He stated that his brother said, 'Yeah!'"

If Dr. Luttrell saw any significance in these revelations, he did not indicate it in his report. Perhaps he didn't realize he had stumbled onto previously unexplored territory. But one would have expected Albert Goodman to be intrigued by Wayne's contention that his younger brother knew in advance what he meant to do and seemed to agree with it.

Under *Impression*, Dr. Luttrell wrote: "Sociopathic personality disorder with anti-social reactions."

By far the longest interviews were conducted by Dr. Manfred S. Guttmacher, whose professional reputation was such that after his death a prize was named for him and awarded each year by

the American Psychiatric Association to the outstanding contribution to the literature of forensic psychiatry. Author of four
books and several dozen articles, a staff member at seven hospi-
tals, and, years later, a consultant at Jack Ruby's trial, Dr. Guttmacher established with Wayne a rapport which many others
found impossible, and he elicited a long list of the boy's likes
and dislikes, aspirations and fears.

> . . . he said he wanted to be a forest ranger. He likes the out-
> doors and the woods and being around animals. He is very
> fond of pets and dogs. . . . He is fond of swimming. He
> once dove off a forty foot board while he was visiting in Ten-
> nessee. When asked whether he was frightened of anything,
> he said that he is . . . scared of bad report cards. . . . He
> volunteered that he likes the rain, he likes the smell of it. He
> then says that Lee was scared of the dark and thunder and
> lightning, but that he was not. He says his father's driving
> used to frighten him . . . according to the patient, he would
> drive around ninety miles an hour. He said he was also
> frightened of driving with him when he was drunk. . . . The
> patient denies using marijuana and other drugs. He can't
> stand even the smell of any alcoholic drinks. . . . He does
> not gamble. His favorite game is baseball.

Of his mother Wayne said, "Of course, she was nicer [than
father]. She was nicer looking and had a nicer character." She
smiled a lot and was generally good-humored. Although he could
not—or would not—account for why he had killed her, he did say
that "she loved one [of us boys] more than the other" and he left
no doubt that Lee was her favorite.

Wayne had no trouble now discussing the times his parents
had taken Lee and him to nudist camps and he told of one occasion when, while Shirley was in Europe, Pat wanted the boys to
go with him alone.

"The patient was asked whether his father would run around
with women when he was drinking or do things of that kind, and
the patient replied, 'No, but when he was drunk he'd talk about
all the whorehouses he'd been to.'" Wayne then said that Pat
had brought women home when his mother was away. Perhaps he

saw a distinction between "running around" with women and bringing them home.

But on certain subjects Wayne was still evasive. When "asked whether the boys were ever exposed to any sexual activity on the part of the parents," he said no.

Dr. Guttmacher concluded that Wayne's running away "resulted from an unconscious fear of his own powerful and hostile impulses and was an instinctive effort on his part to prevent the very type of tragedy that did occur. . . . His hatred of his adopting father was so intense that violence toward him is not surprising in retrospect." But when Dr. Guttmacher asked whether he ran away from home for "fear that if he remained there he might resort to violence against his parents," Wayne said that, quite to the contrary, he ran away because he feared his father would hurt him.

Dr. Guttmacher wrote: "It is . . . impossible to reach any rational explanation for the killing of his mother. This has a perseverative quality—when he had once started shooting he could not control his destructive urges."

But one must remember that Wayne felt his mother favored Lee, and Dr. Ainsworth had noted in his report—and would testify at the trial—"the patient views authority figures, both male and female, as remote, rather forbidding people who lack warmth and spontaneity. This view of authority figures is characteristic of children who have suffered an early severe maternal deprivation experience. Such a deprivation experience very frequently leaves the child emotionally and intellectually impaired. A distinctly diminished impulse-control system also appears as a part of this syndrome."

Of course, what Wayne hadn't mentioned was what he had seen that night when he peered through the banister rails at his parents in the living room. Had Dr. Guttmacher known about this scene and the emotions it had roused, he might well have wondered whether the boy would have shot Shirley if she had not appeared at precisely the moment she did and if she had not been nude.

To flesh out his information on Wayne, Dr. Guttmacher interviewed Lee and heard essentially the same story about Pat Dresbach's strictness, his drinking, and his sadism. Although he was as hesitant as his brother to dwell on sexual matters, Lee recalled "that when his father was drunk he would say that he went out with a whole lot of women and most of them were much better than his mother."

Lee also offered a new version of the morning of the murders: "I got up first. I went downstairs and then I went upstairs just to talk to [Wayne], to ask him what time he got home the night before. I remember he said he had an argument with my father that night. He was mad at him . . . and he said he was going to shoot my mother and father." The examiner then asked him what were Wayne's actual words at the time. He said he did not recall the words. The informant was then told that the examiner had gained the impression that the patient had planned to shoot the father but not the mother and he was asked whether he was certain that [Wayne] said that he was going to shoot his mother and his father. Lee says that he was certain about this. When the examiner asked the informant what his reaction was to this statement, he said, "I thought he was kidding. I went downstairs and ate my breakfast and read the paper. I saw him coming down then and standing there with the gun, but I still thought he was kidding. I didn't even think he would stay there until my father came out. Then I heard the gun. Wayne went upstairs. I went up too. I asked where he was going. He said he didn't know. I believe he only had on a teeshirt. He put on another shirt and he went out."

This statement contradicted all of Lee's earlier accounts. He no longer claimed to have hit his brother or shouted for him to stop shooting. And, for the first time, he maintained that he had spoken to Wayne upstairs before the murders, then had seen him descend the staircase with the rifle and wait for his father to emerge from the bedroom.

Although Lee didn't specify whether—or when—he stopped watching, he implied he hadn't witnessed the killings. He just "heard the gun." And he didn't say what Wayne and he talked about afterward or what he did once his brother drove away.

These seemingly petty inconsistencies or failures of memory were of potentially momentous importance in a case of this magnitude. Whatever the explanation for them, they suggested that Lee might not be an altogether reliable witness.

Finally Dr. Guttmacher interviewed Nathaniel Blaustein, who had shared an office suite with Pat Dresbach for fifteen months. One would have expected Guttmacher to speak with C. J. Pettit, Wayne's guardian, who had known the family much longer and had claimed in his court petition to be familiar with their personal affairs. But, judging by the public documents nobody ever asked Pettit for information, and apparently he volunteered none.

Mr. Blaustein, himself, didn't have much to say. He told Guttmacher that Pat Dresbach "seemed to be easygoing, full of life. I think he liked the women." Shirley struck him as a very fine person. As for Wayne, Blaustein had not seen him more than half a dozen times before "the tragedy" and, like Lee, he "seemed to be perfectly normal . . . and well behaved." When Wayne started running away, however, and borrowed his father's guns, Blaustein "advised Mr. Dresbach it was time for more or less drastic action." Whether he was aware that Dresbach took the "drastic action" of leaving his adopted son in jail and charging him with larceny, Mr. Blaustein didn't say.

Dr. Manfred S. Guttmacher had now gathered enough material to evaluate Wayne's mental competence and offer his learned opinion at the trial. In addition to Dr. Guttmacher, Dr. Ainsworth, and Dr. Curtis Marshall, a specialist in electroencephalography, Albert Goodman intended to call just one witness: Lloyd Smith. The salient point of his defense was revealed in the amended pleas which he filed for Wayne on May 15:

1. That he is not guilty as alleged.
2. And for a second plea, that he was insane or lunatic at the time of the commission of the alleged crime.
3. And for a third plea, that he was insane or lunatic at the time of the commission of the alleged crime and that he is insane or lunatic now.

Autumn 1978

While Wayne was in jail that spring, awaiting trial, I was in DeMatha Catholic High School, waiting to graduate. With details large and small, I could contrast our lives at that point, underscoring the differences between us, emphasizing the ironies which seem to enthrall people whenever they describe what they were doing the day Pearl Harbor was attacked or John Kennedy was assassinated.

For instance, while Wayne was at Clifton T. Perkins Hospital, undergoing psychiatric evaluation, I took the Scholastic Aptitude Test and said I wanted the results sent to Harvard, Bowdoin, and Bates colleges.

Soon after he was transferred to the Annapolis jail, I experienced a personal trauma which had more impact on me than Wayne's predicament. A career-long second stringer, I sat on the bench and in agony watched my previously unbeaten high school basketball team lose the city championship. Afterward, I refused to go home. To escape our shame and disappointment, several teammates, including one boy who had broken both arms in the game, drove with me to Franklin Manor and spent a cold, sleepless night in my parents' cottage.

The night Wayne escaped from jail was the night of my senior prom. The day he was interviewed by Dr. Manfred Guttmacher, I was inducted into the National Honor Society. The afternoon Albert Goodman filed his amended pleas, I arrived home from school to learn I had won a scholarship to Bates College. Then, not long before Wayne's trial, I sat in a stifling gymnasium, which smelled of floor polish and rubberized wrestling mats, and listened to the Archbishop of Washington deliver a platitudinous graduation address, wishing us all good luck and God's blessings in the future.

On the surface, then, my life might appear to embody the predictable milestones of American youth, milestones which are generally seen as glowing with happiness—and which Wayne was fated to miss. But, in a sense, I missed them, too, and was struck by what I saw as the similarities, not the differences, between us. For, simultaneous with the Dresbach murders, something had happened to me and my family. Or perhaps it had been happening all along and the murders just brought it into sharp and painful relief. I have said that this marked the end of my youth. But it felt more like the end of everything.

So I didn't go to the senior prom. If I had had a choice, I wouldn't have gone to my graduation either. As it was, I was so abstracted from events, so absorbed in a tumult of personal obsessions, that when my name was called and I came forward to receive my diploma from the Archbishop, I forgot to kneel and kiss his ring. Instead, I gave his outstretched hand a curt shake, as if we had just closed some minor business transaction.

Although they always loomed somewhere at the fringes of my consciousness, it was not specifically—or exclusively—the Dresbach killings which obsessed me. It was more what I saw as their indirect results. With Wayne and Lee two more unknowns had been introduced into the already complex equation of my family, and thereafter it was impossible to say which changes they brought about, which ones they exaggerated, and which ones were unconnected, save by coincidence, with their advent in our lives.

Suddenly I was seized by a realization—scarcely original, yet unique in my experience—of life's random flux, its frightening indifference. I knew now things would not necessarily get better for me and that my ambitions might very well be thwarted. Nothing drove this home harder than the way my dreamy, unrealistic plans for college were blasted.

Without discussing matters with my parents, I had taken it for granted I would go away to college and, since I secretly harbored aspirations of becoming a writer, I decided to bestow myself upon Harvard, which I knew had produced an extraordinary number of famous novelists. After having a copy of my unremarkable high school transcript sent to Cambridge, I filled out the application form longhand, in my dreadful, cramped scrawl, and mailed it off, too.

To be on the safe side, I also applied to Bowdoin and Bates. I had never come near either school, had never met anyone who had been there, and had no idea if they had a history of turning out novelists. But I knew they were located in Maine, and I had a vague notion that it would be nice to spend several years in cold, snowy New England, far from Washington's slushy winters.

Not surprisingly, Harvard rejected my application. (I say "not surprisingly" although this surprised, and bitterly disappointed, me.) But then Bates offered a partial scholarship. While it covered my tuition, I would have to pay room and board, and bear the cost of transportation, books, and supplies. The college financial office estimated this might amount to $2,000 a year—much more than I could earn with a summer job. But I blithely assumed my parents would pay the balance.

In my ignorance of practical exigencies, my failure to plan for the future, and my reluctance to discuss matters with adults, I was not all that different from Wayne. And it occurs to me that much of his behavior, both before and after the killings, cannot be fathomed except in the context of that painful limbo of American adolescence with its alternating illusions of power and complete impotence, of unrealistic privilege and equally unrealistic repression.

But the way our illusions died was radically different. One day in late spring my mother called me outside and we sat on the lawn near the swings and sliding board, where she could watch the nursery children she cared for. She kept her eyes on them while she explained that there was no money to send me away to college. I would have to live at home and commute to the University of Maryland. Since I didn't own a car, I would have to hitchhike, just as I had done in high school.

She said she was sorry. She had intended to tell me before, back when I started sending off applications, but so much had happened recently there just hadn't been time—by which she meant that she could not bear any more upsets and had been unable to face this scene until she absolutely had to. Given all she had gone through—was going through—who could blame her?

I did. I knew that the shock of the murders and the responsibilities she had accepted for Wayne and Lee were not the only things troubling her. Although she had not told me or anyone else that she was losing the sight in her left eye, I sensed something was wrong, sensed her reluctance to let go of me. Still I blamed her. I objected, I argued, and when that didn't work, I sulked.

Indulging in an orgy of self-pity, furious at life's unfairness, I sulked all that spring and summer. Then, in autumn, I registered at the University of Maryland, but held myself aloof. I refused to wear a freshman beanie, went to no mixers or dances, joined no clubs, and never rushed a fraternity (which I couldn't have afforded in the unlikely event I had been accepted). Although I attended all home football games, I went alone and always brought a book—*The Stranger, Notes from the Underground, Nausea,* etc.—which I ostentatiously read during time-outs, half-time, and dull stretches of action.

In class I sat as far from the professor and other students as possible, as if to declare that I wasn't really there. To my knowledge, no one noticed my histrionic contempt. Maryland was a huge university, and for all anybody knew or cared, I *wasn't* there. Often I stood in the dank, dimly lit basement of the Arts and Sciences building, eating a rancid lunch dispensed by a vending machine, and had no trouble imagining myself invisible. Eventually I took to scribbling my student number—03212—instead of my name on tests and term papers.

But I didn't feel invisible, I didn't feel like a faceless integer. I felt like a fool, a clod learning one of the basic lessons of American higher education—learning to be ashamed not of my ignorance, but of my clothes, the way I spoke, my neighborhood, my family.

In my senior year, when I was inducted into Phi Beta Kappa, I decided it was time to make a public gesture. Since I didn't consider myself part of the university, I said I had no interest in any honor or award it might bestow upon me. But my faculty advisor wearily informed me that it didn't matter whether I accepted or declined. Since I had the right grade-point average, my name would be automatically inscribed on the rolls of Phi Beta Kappa.

In those days, it was always in the evening, after the last class, that I thought of Wayne Dresbach and felt a close sense of kinship with him. Especially in foul weather, when I stood drenched on the muddy shoulder of the highway, my books wrapped in newspapers, and tried to flag down a ride, I saw myself as an outcast—to passing drivers I must have looked like a derelict or madman—and I imagined Wayne and I were alike. He was unhappy, and so was I, and that seemed one powerful bond between us. But I believed we had much more than our misery in common. There were also deep confusions of personal identity.

Unlike most adolescents, I never entertained fantasies that I was adopted, perhaps because there was a ready explanation for why I felt like an outsider in my family. When I was a baby, my parents were divorced. Later they remarried, and each had two more children. My father then moved with his new wife, his son, and daughter to New Mexico, and I rarely saw them again. I remained with my mother, and after my older brother, Pat, joined the Air Force, I found myself alone, a Mewshaw among Dunns.

In America, where so many marriages end in divorce, this was far from an unusual experience. Still, it distressed me to think that Tommy Dunn, whom I loved as a father, was no relative of mine, that Karen and Kris were my half-sister and half-brother, and that I had another half-brother and half-sister whom I scarcely knew at all.

To upset me further, since my parents were Catholics, the divorce meant automatic excommunication. They lived, the nuns at school had reminded me, in a constant state of mortal sin and were in danger of eternal damnation. In an early foreshadowing of my anxiety and sense of helplessness over Wayne, I thought I should do something to save them, yet had no idea how to go about it.

What disturbed me most, however, was my name. At home and in the neighborhood I was known as Mike Dunn; at the parish school I was Michael Mewshaw, the name on my birth and baptismal certificates. Since some of my neighborhood playmates were also my classmates, they naturally wondered why my last name was different from my parents'. But I couldn't bring myself to tell the truth. I said Mewshaw was my maiden name, a mysterious term I must have read in a novel.

By the time I was in my teens, I had divided people into two neat compartments—those who knew me as Mewshaw and those who thought my name was Dunn—and I lived in dread that those in one compartment would blunder into the other and begin asking embarrassing questions. Although this seldom happened, something worse did. Eventually I discovered that I hadn't divided people so much as I had divided myself. In fact, I had done such a thorough job of fragmenting my identity that even years later when I returned to Maryland to do research for this book, I found myself suffering an uncomfortable twinge every time I was introduced, for I still ran into people who didn't know me until I dropped my real name and said I was Mike Dunn.

In the beginning, then, the more I learned about Wayne, the more I identified with him. Despite the vastly different dimensions of our problems, I believed I had experienced a minor chord of the major emotions which had formed him. Like Wayne, I felt I did not know where I came from, who I was, or where I belonged.

But, incapable of coping with these uncertainties, I proceeded as if it were more urgent to comprehend Wayne than it was to confront the ambiguities of my own life. It wasn't until later that I realized I could not do one thing without doing the other; I could not grope into Wayne's past without grappling with my own. I could not understand him until I understood myself and admitted that, much as I empathized with him, Wayne had an identity altogether different from mine and altogether different from the image of him that had once answered my needs.

Blank pages, blank spaces in the past—to me they have come to seem much the same. As a writer, I realize, I am always struggling to get to the bottom of a mystery I am constantly in the process of creating.

Summer 1961

1

Over the last two decades, public perceptions—and often misconceptions—about the American legal system cannot fail to have been shaped by the large number of dramatic cases given extensive coverage by the news media. During the 60s, starting with John Kennedy's death, there was an almost unbroken skein of trials involving political assassins, conspirators of the Left and Right, civil rights leaders, union heads, and mass murderers. Then in the 70s, as dozens of Watergate cases dominated the headlines, the lessons of those earlier trials were refined and widely disseminated. Baroque plea bargains and complex defense strategies became common knowledge, and at cocktail parties one was as likely to hear heated debates about fine points of law as about the local football team.

As the nation came to regard the courts as its salvation, as well as its highest form of theater, many people followed legal proceedings with the care and discrimination of critics. To merit their attention, a case had to advance the art of jurisprudence and promise titillating revelations about elected officials or well-known personalities. As in most art forms, imagination and technical virtuosity were also highly prized. Courthouse aficionados routinely expected lawyers to use computers, psychiatrists, dialogue coaches, and wardrobe advisers as they mounted defenses which shattered precedents and created new opportunities for torts or class-action suits. More than anything, however, the public favored cases in which the trial cost millions and lasted for months, and the defense attorney was as famous and flamboyant as his client. For example, Patty Hearst represented by F. Lee Bailey, or the Chicago Seven defended by William Kunstler, or T. Cullen Davis represented by Racehorse Haynes.

On the face of it, the Dresbach trial had all the elements of a major piece of legal theater. It involved a spectacular crime—not just double murder, but patricide and matricide by an adopted child whose mental condition was said to be filigreed with fascinating kinks and crevices. Wealthy, prominent people were potential witnesses, and because of Pat Dresbach's political activities on the state level and Harry Woodring's national reputation, there were possibilities which should have intrigued muckraking reporters. The scent of sexual scandal was strong, especially in those tantalizing hints that Pat might have been a pornography dealer and a procurer for business, political, and military figures in the Washington area.

But soon after the killings, there were signs that this might not develop into a trial which would appeal to spectators with jaded palates. First, Wayne had been left for two months without a lawyer, and during that period, no relative or friend had attempted to take his case to the public. Despite rumors about the Dresbachs, no reporter or TV commentator had so much as suggested that there were extenuating circumstances which might have explained the boy's motives or diminished his guilt.

Second, Wayne's guardians had seen fit to hire a local lawyer; and however impeccable Albert Goodman's reputation might be in Annapolis, no one ever mistook him for Melvin Belli, Edward Bennett Williams or F. Lee Bailey. Or to be more precise, as well as fair, Goodman was never provided with the resources to mount the sort of byzantine, time-consuming defense one has come to expect in cases involving the children of politically and socially prominent parents. He and his assistant, Theodore Bloom, were paid a total fee of $1,500—substantially less than Nathaniel Blaustein received for advising C. J. Pettit in his role as guardian.

So, despite its immense importance for Wayne, the trial fell short of high drama. According to spectators, it was a rambling, humdrum affair, full of false starts and frustrating dead ends. Wayne himself had a hard time following the proceedings, and in this he was not alone. The transcript reveals no great flights of oratory, no clash of wits, no theatrical parry and thrust between prosecution and defense. In fact, while the testimony of witnesses is almost always clear, the lawyers' questions and objections, and the judge's rulings, are frequently devoid of basic elements of logic, syntax, and grammar.

Yet if it lacked the glossy showmanship of some celebrated trials—not to mention the entertainment value of those cases we see smoothly unraveling in the movies and on TV—the Dresbach trial was perhaps a more accurate picture of the kind of justice most Americans received in 1961.

2

Early on the day of the trial, Friday, June 30, Father Dawson and Lena Talbert drove to the Annapolis courthouse. Mary Helen Dunn had intended to go with them, but Wayne begged her not to. Recently they had grown quite close, and he told her he didn't want her to hear what he had done. Mary Helen explained that she had already read about it in the newspapers. Anyway, she said, nothing could destroy her feeling for him. Nothing at all. But he insisted it would be better—he would feel freer to talk—if she stayed away. So she waited at home and planned to drive down to the beach that evening to get a progress report. Like most people, she assumed the trial would last days, perhaps weeks.

Dallas Talbert certainly thought so. He went to work half a day, figuring things wouldn't really get started till that afternoon. He left Washington after lunch and while driving to Annapolis, suspected he was wasting his time. He had a hunch they'd still be choosing jurors. When he got there, he just couldn't believe it. Wayne was on the stand, finishing his testimony.

Expecting jury selection to be prolonged and complicated, many out-of-state lawyers have been surprised by the dispatch with which Maryland trials move. They arrive with long lists of questions and computerized profiles of the ideal juror, only to discover that the *voir dire* process tends to be brisk and straightforward. Each side has four peremptory challenges and, in most districts, prospective jurors are not queried directly by the defense attorney. Instead, the judge reviews the questions, determines their relevance, then poses them himself. This virtually eliminates any possibility of a lawyer's shaping the jury he wants, and it prevents him from gaining insight, however limited, into the people who will decide his client's fate. According to some attorneys, it also impanels far too many prejudiced or otherwise unqualified jurors.

In 1961, in murder trials, there was yet another problem that plagued defense attorneys. Judge Benjamin Michaelson had the right to exclude anyone who expressed conscientious scruples against capital punishment. Albert Goodman objected "that Court is undertaking to select the jury for the State and for the Defense." But Michaelson overruled the objection, and what is known as "a hanging jury" was impaneled, even though the State's attorney, Osborne Duvall, had announced that, in view of Wayne's age, he would not ask for the death penalty.

Then, immediately, Judge Michaelson raised still another difficulty for the defense.

> *Duvall:* The State calls for trial No. 5576 and No. 5577, State vs. Ralph Wayne Dresbach. I understand from counsel that they're willing to try these cases together.
> *Judge Michaelson:* I don't know whether it's a good idea, Mr. State's Attorney, to try these two cases together.
> *Goodman:* The defendant, if Your Honor pleases, has no objection to consolidating the cases.
> *Judge Michaelson:* Have you got some authority to support that?

Surprised by the question, Goodman groped to formulate a reply.

> *Goodman:* I have no objection, if Your Honor pleases. As counsel for the defendant I wasn't aware of any authority, or that there was any need for authority. I thought, by agreement, between the State's Attorney and the Defense Counsel, consolidation is, where the facts are the same, would expedite matters, and make for quick disposition.
> *Judge Michaelson:* Expediting matters is one thing. It isn't a question of expediting, it's a question of the rights of the parties involved.

Afterward, both Goodman and Bloom confessed themselves baffled by Michaelson's ruling that the cases should be tried separately and that this would somehow protect "the rights of the parties involved." It was quite common to try such cases together. Furthermore, Wayne's rights could scarcely have been enhanced by the threat of two trials for murders which were committed within moments of one another. If he was found not guilty of the first charge, he could then be brought to trial for the second.

Perhaps spotting this advantage, Osborne Duvall chose to proceed at once with case No. 5576, the murder of Harold Malone Dresbach.

The State's first witness was Owen Dove, the police officer who took the photographs at the scene of the crime. These photos established the layout of the lower floor of the house and the location of the bodies. Dove testified that he, along with Officers Werner and White, had arrived in Franklin Manor sometime between 10:10 and 10:20 A.M. Goodman objected to the introduction of pictures of blood splotches on the dining room carpet and kitchen floor, but asked no questions.

While the next witness was called, Osborne Duvall went to the table where his assistant, John Blondell, sat. Picking up a sheaf of papers, he reviewed his notes and as he did so, he tore off the corner of a page, popped it into his mouth, and chewed ruminatively. It was something he often did when preparing a case, and to the people closest to him, it seemed he was always preparing a case. Since the State's attorney's office was understaffed, Duvall was chronically overworked and spent most evenings and Saturdays doing research, while his wife and three sons waited for him at home. In eighteen years, he had taken one vacation.

He was a conscientious man, as meticulous about his personal appearance as he was about his professional responsibilities. Short and slight, almost frail, he wore silver-rimmed glasses and was smaller than the teen-age boy he was prosecuting. Yet, at forty, he gave the impression of being older in many ways than anyone else in the courtroom. Even as a child he had been grave, studious, and more mature than his schoolmates. A descendant of French Huguenots who had immigrated to Maryland in the 1730s, Duvall had been brought up by two maiden aunts who kept house for his father, and they had imbued him with the manners and moral standards of an earlier, more genteel age.

As a boy, he played no sports and had to avoid vigorous physical activity; he suffered from *osteogenesis imperfecti* or acute brittleness of the bones. Instead he concentrated on his studies.

He went to St. John's College in Annapolis, then to the University of Maryland Law School. As an adult, he still had no hobbies, no outside interests, and did little socializing except for an occasional business lunch. Raised by his aunts to respect his elders and all authority figures, he was a stern disciplinarian with his own sons and, according to those who knew him well, he had little sympathy for children who rebelled against strict parents. A stickler for detail who excluded his personal feelings from the cases he prosecuted, he was a firm believer in enforcing the law—all laws, even those he thought were bad and should be changed.

His favorite saying was "The law is a jealous mistress." It was for Osborne Duvall. Shortly after the Dresbach trial, he would leave his wife and three sons.

The next witness was Lee Dresbach, who had turned fifteen in April and now lived with the McCracken family in Lanham. In answer to Duvall's questions, he described going to the basketball game the night of January 6 and arriving home on a different bus an hour before his older brother.

Duvall: When is the next time you saw Wayne?

Lee: The next morning, Saturday morning.

Duvall: And about what time was it and where did you see him?

Lee: Saw him in the kitchen around 8:30.

Duvall: And did you have a conversation with him at that time?

Lee: Yes sir.

Duvall: And would you relate that conversation to the Court and Jury, please?

Lee: He said he was going to shoot my mother and father.

Duvall: Did he say anything else at that time?

Lee: Yes sir, he said he had an argument with my father the night before.

Duvall: And did you make any reply to that?

Lee: I asked him why.

Duvall: What was his answer?

Lee: He said because he got home late.

Duvall: Was there any other conversation between you and Wayne at that time about this?

Lee: No sir.

Duvall: Now, after that conversation about 8:30 in the morning in the kitchen, what, if anything, did you do?

Lee: Read the paper.

Duvall: Where did you read the paper?

Lee: In the kitchen.

Duvall: I see. Was Wayne there also?

Lee: No sir.

Duvall: Do you know where he went?

Lee: No sir.

Duvall: When was the next time that you saw Wayne?

Lee: After he shot my father.

Duvall: And do you have any idea what time that was?

Lee: No sir.

Duvall: Could you tell the Court and Jury how long, approximately, it had been after you had had this conversation in the kitchen, which you have just related?

Lee: Not more than 10 minutes.

Duvall: Beg your pardon?

Lee: Not more than 10 minutes.

Duvall: Where were you at the time the shooting occurred?

Lee: In the kitchen.

Duvall: Now, where was Wayne when you next saw him after this conversation?

Lee: In the living room.

Duvall: Where, just where in the living room?

Lee: Right in between the living room and dining room, just getting ready to go upstairs.

Duvall: And did he have anything unusual with him?

Lee: Yes sir.

Duvall: What did he have?

Lee: A gun.

Duvall: What gun was it?

Lee: .22 rifle.

Duvall: And whose gun was it, do you know?

Lee: My father's.

Duvall: And where was that gun kept?

Lee: Upstairs in his office.

Duvall interrupted this train of questioning and had Lee describe the layout of the Dresbach house, both downstairs and upstairs. He seemed determined to establish that Wayne could have reached his father's office and gotten the rifle without going through the kitchen and, therefore, without Lee's having seen him carrying the .22 until after the shooting.

Duvall: Now, you've testified that after your conversation with Wayne you next saw him in the living room after your father had been shot?
Lee: Yes sir.
Duvall: Did you have any conversation with him at that time?
Lee: No sir.
Duvall: What, if anything, did you do?
Lee: He went upstairs and I went upstairs after him.
Duvall: And did you have any conversation with him then?
Lee: I asked him where he was going.
Duvall: What, if any, response, did he give you?
Lee: He said he didn't know.
Duvall: Then what occurred, if anything?
Lee: He took the car.

Duvall: Did you see the gun after you say you saw him with it in the living room?
Lee: No sir.
Duvall: After the shooting?
Lee: No sir.
Duvall: You didn't see that gun at any time later?
Lee: No sir.
Duvall: I'll ask you to try to think whether or not at the time the shots were fired if you made any statement to Wayne? Do you have any recollection of it?
Lee: No sir.
Duvall: Now, before January 7th had you had any conversation with Wayne about your parents, particularly, your father?
Lee: Yes sir.
Duvall: Do you remember when that occurred?

Lee: No sir.

Duvall: Do you know approximately how many days or months before January 7th it occurred?

Lee: No sir.

Duvall: Do you recall when or what season of the year it was that it occurred?

Lee: Fall—winter.

Duvall: Which winter?

Lee: It was after January.

Duvall: You mean last winter or after January of '61?

Lee: '61.

Duvall: This would be within a week of the time then, between January 1 and the 7th, the time of the shooting?

Lee: I believe so.

Duvall: Beg your pardon?

Lee: I believe so.

Duvall: Would you tell the Court and the Jury what conversation that was you had with Wayne?

Lee: He just said he was going to shoot my mother and father.

Duvall: And did you converse with him at length, or in any degree at that time?

Lee: No sir.

Duvall: At that time, sometime between January 1 and January 7th, did he say why he was going to shoot your mother and father?

Lee: No sir.

With this, Osborne Duvall turned the witness over to the attorney for the defense. One would have expected Albert Goodman to be coiled to pounce. Since in almost every answer Lee contradicted something he had said in his deposition to the police or in subsequent interviews, the problem for Goodman might have been deciding where to sink his teeth and draw first blood.

Lee had just sworn that after Wayne told him what he was going to do, Lee had asked why, but had said nothing more. Wayne, however, had told Dr. Luttrell—Goodman had the report in his files—that when Lee heard he was going to kill Pat Dresbach, Lee had said, "Yeah!"

It is also important to recall that in his interview with Dr. Guttmacher—an interview which Goodman had in his files—Lee said that the morning of the murders he had gone upstairs to talk to Wayne and had learned of his intentions. Then later he had watched Wayne walk downstairs with the rifle in his hands and wait for his father to emerge from the bedroom. But now Lee was claiming that he had never seen the weapon until *after* the shootings.

In his deposition to the police—a copy of which was in Goodman's files—Lee had sworn that when his wounded father crawled into the kitchen, he went to the door, shouted for Wayne to stop shooting, and was close enough to hit him in the arm. Now, under oath, he testified that Wayne had been all the way across the dining room, in the living room, much too far away to strike.

And despite Duvall's prompting—". . . try to think whether or not at the time the shots were fired if you made any statement to Wayne"—Lee maintained that he had said nothing. Not "Stop." And certainly not "Shoot him again," which is what Wayne remembered him saying.

Furthermore, Lee had firmly established the time frame, saying that his father had been shot no later than 8:40 A.M. Since Officer Owen Dove had sworn that the police had not arrived until sometime between 10:10 and 10:20 A.M. and since the official records showed that Lee hadn't called Edgewater until 9:58 A.M., there was more than an hour unaccounted for.

Goodman might well have asked what transpired during that interval. While Lee spoke in his police deposition of hitting his brother, then going back to help his father, he also said, "I never did see my mother." Did he not know she had been shot? Did he at no time go into the bedroom to check on her? And when he went upstairs after Wayne, wasn't he afraid of being harmed? Why didn't he flee the house then? Or, since Wayne was out of earshot, why didn't he take that opportunity to telephone the police, the rescue squad, or a neighbor? Was it conceivable that the first and only thing he said to Wayne after the murders was, where are you going? And since according to his testimony, he did not see Wayne with the gun after he went upstairs, why didn't Lee, who was bigger and stronger, try to overpower his brother? Or if he was still too shocked and frightened to restrain his brother or to summon help, why didn't he take action immediately after Wayne left the house?

Of course, all these questions depended upon Goodman's alertness to the discrepancies in Lee's story, and unfortunately, the lawyer did not notice most of them. When asked about this in 1978, Goodman admitted he had never recognized that more than an hour elapsed between the killings and Lee's call to the Edgewater Station. But he said he didn't see that this or any of the contradictions between Lee's trial testimony and his earlier statements constituted a matter of much importance. They seemed to him evidence of nothing more than a young and nervous boy's flawed memory.

But the point was that Lee, flawed memory or not, was producing damaging testimony against his older brother. If, for whatever reason, that testimony was unreliable, Goodman had to make this clear to the jury. If he hoped to win his insanity plea, he needed, at the very least, to challenge Lee's claim that Wayne had told him a week in advance that he intended to shoot his father and his mother. For this made it sound as though Wayne had acted less on impulse and more according to a coldly premeditated plan. Since Wayne denied this and swore he had never consciously considered killing his mother, Goodman had to cast doubt on Lee's memory, his credibility, his version of events— an easy enough order, one would have thought, given the inconsistencies of his statements and the shakiness of some of his responses.

But Goodman's cross-examination commenced with requests for general information. He established that Wayne had failed the ninth grade because his parents forced him to take the academic course, that his father berated him in front of company, that Dresbach had been drinking the night before his death and had refused to believe Wayne's explanation of why he had come home later than Lee. Only then did Goodman touch upon the most dangerous element of Lee's testimony, and the line of questioning was curious indeed. It seemed to concede the truth of an accusation which Wayne had denied before the trial and would deny twice more under oath.

Goodman: When he told you several [days] or a week before the actual shooting that he was going to shoot his mother and father, you didn't have any faith in that, did you?
Lee: No sir.

If it had somehow escaped the jury's attention that the attorney for the defense was as much as admitting that his client had spoken earlier of murder plans for both parents, Goodman reminded them by reframing his question.

Goodman: A week before the actual shooting, when you say Wayne commented that he was going to shoot his mother and father, just what did he tell you they had been doing to him?
Lee: He had just been arguing with my father about his grades.

This led to a discussion of the frequency with which Dresbach criticized and punished Wayne.

Goodman: Over how long a period of time had your father been doing that to Wayne?
Lee: Since about the 7th grade.
Goodman: How else did your father treat Wayne?
Duvall: Objection.
Goodman: Did he beat him at any time?
Duvall: Objection.
Judge Michaelson: Court doesn't see what relevancy that has unless you fix it as to time.
Goodman: All right, sir. After you moved down to Anne Arundel County, I believe that was 1959, wasn't it, about 2 or 3 years ago?
Lee: Yes sir.
Goodman: Did your father drink very much?
Lee: Yes sir.
Goodman: When?
Lee: All the time, mostly on weekends. Two or three times my mother threatened to leave because he'd gotten drunk. And before she was going to Europe he got drunk the night

before and she had to drive herself to the airport, and the
night she got back he got drunk and beat her up.

Goodman: Beat your mother up?

Lee: Yes sir.

Goodman: While your mother was in Europe what did your
father do with you children at home?

Duvall: Objection.

Judge Michaelson: Court will have to keep this thing
confined. I mean, we can't narrate the whole domestic picture here, a lot of incidental things that create difficulties in
the home unless it relates to the issue. Court is going to sustain the objection to any matters, specific matters that may
have occurred between the father and mother, and the father
and the children that is unrelated to the issue.

Goodman: What complaint did your father make to Wayne
about any of his other conduct since you came to Anne
Arundel County in 1959?

Duvall: Object on two grounds, one, remoteness; two, the
issue of self-defense has not been placed in this case by counsel for the defendant in his opening statement to the Jury.

Goodman: If Your Honor pleases, we're not claiming self-
defense, we're claiming state of mind. The state of mind can
be determined.

Judge Michaelson: It should relate to time somewhat close to
the time this thing occurred.

This would not be the last time Duvall would object, and
Michaelson would sustain his objection, to the introduction of
testimony about events not directly related to the killings. It
wasn't enough to show that Wayne had been mercilessly tormented and abused. It seemed Goodman had to concentrate on
the torment and abuse in the weeks preceding the crime, prove
that they had somehow affected Wayne's sanity, and provoked
him to murder.

Clearly this was a logical impossibility. People don't go insane
in a matter of weeks, and no one can plot the course of an emotional breakdown on a calendar. There are indications that
Michaelson understood this and was willing to allow the defense
some latitude to develop its case. But Goodman's questions were

often vague, as if he had no idea where things fit into the mosaic he should have been constructing. When he asked questions such as "What complaint did your father make to Wayne about any of his other conduct since you came to Anne Arundel County in 1959?" he should not have been surprised that Duvall objected.

Goodman: How many times has Wayne run away from home?
Lee: About 4 or 5.
Goodman: Why did he run away?
Lee: Because my father was always running him down in front of people, making him do things that he didn't think he should do.
Goodman: What didn't Wayne want to do?
Lee: One time Wayne was cutting the grass and he missed one little spot and when my father came home he made him cut the whole grass over again.
Goodman: Made him cut the whole lawn over again?
Lee: Yes sir, and he made us go to the duck blind when we didn't want to, and made us go to nudist camps.

By mentioning the Dresbachs' nudism, Lee, the State's witness, had presented Goodman with an opportunity to begin to explore the entire gamut of Pat and Shirley's sexual behavior, which might otherwise have been ruled inadmissible. But, curiously, he chose to dwell on other matters.

Goodman: Made you both go to the duck blind? What else did he make Wayne do that Wayne objected to?
Duvall: May it please the Court, I'll object again. This gives a wide latitude to point of time. Court has indicated that this testimony has to relate within bounds to the occasion when the shooting occurred.
Judge Michaelson: Objection sustained.
Goodman: My question, Lee, is just before, within the course of a few weeks of the shooting, what else did your father complain to Wayne about?
Lee: I don't remember.

Goodman: What about the window-breaking episode, the croquet ball?
Lee: That was when we lived in Lanham.

Goodman had violated an ancient courthouse adage—never ask a question to which you don't know the answer. But at that point he seemed to have forgotten incidents that had occurred just before the murders and instead brought up events from three or four years ago. Then he skittered from subject to subject, rarely following through with questions.

Goodman: Was Wayne completely dressed when he shot his parents on the 7th of January?
Lee: Yes sir.
Goodman: I didn't hear you.
Lee: Yes sir.
Goodman: Had all his clothes on?
Lee: Yes sir.

Lee's interview with Guttmacher, and several other documents, indicated Wayne had been in his nightclothes and had gotten dressed after the shootings. This was a potentially important issue. If Wayne was in such a state of mind that he hadn't dressed that morning, Goodman might have argued that the boy was acting out spontaneously and that there hadn't been sufficient premeditation to justify a first-degree murder charge. But Goodman didn't pause to correct the impression Lee had created.

Goodman: And when he told you that he was going to shoot his parents, why didn't you stop him, Lee?
Lee: I didn't believe him.
Goodman: You did not believe him?
Lee: No sir.

This, too, might have been a productive line of questioning—one which a lawyer could push to the limit. Why hadn't Lee believed Wayne? Why hadn't he taken the precaution of warning his parents? Why hadn't he urged Wayne not to do it? What

were Lee's feelings toward his father? Did he think Wayne was
doing the right thing?

But Goodman changed the subject:

> *Goodman:* Over how long a period of time had your father
> been drinking heavily?
> *Lee:* Long as I can remember. Two or three times he'd
> stopped and then he started over again.
> *Goodman:* How many times had he tried to drive your
> mother away from home?
> *Duvall:* Objection.
> *Judge Michaelson:* Sustained.
> *Goodman:* Since you got to Anne Arundel County?
> *Duvall:* Objection.
> *Judge Michaelson:* Sustained.
> *Goodman:* Had he tried to drive your mother out of the
> house shortly before he was shot by Wayne?
> *Duvall:* Objection.
> *Judge Michaelson:* Sustained. Court can't see the relevancy
> of that.
> *Goodman:* All right, we won't press that any further, Your
> Honor. Thank you very much, Lee.

Osborne Duvall's redirect examination emphasized the prosecution's contention that Dresbach had not mistreated Wayne in the
weeks before his death.

> *Duvall:* Wayne didn't cut this grass in December or January,
> just before the shooting, did he? The time you mentioned
> your father made him cut the grass over because he missed a
> spot?
> *Lee:* No sir.
> *Duvall:* Was it last summer?
> *Lee:* The last part of last summer.
> *Duvall:* The last part of last summer?
> *Lee:* 1960.
> *Duvall:* And when was it, the occasion that you mentioned
> your father making you boys, two boys go to the duck blind
> when you didn't want it?

Lee: Last duck-hunting season.
Duvall: Was it this last year or 60–61 season?
Lee: 60–61.
Duvall: About how long before January 7th was it that he forced or required you to go the duck blind, you and Wayne to go to the duck blind?
Lee: I don't know, I don't know when duck season is in.
Duvall: Before Christmas?
Lee: I don't know when duck-hunting season is in.
Duvall: You don't know when it was?
Lee: No sir.
Duvall: That's all, thank you.

Unwittingly, Duvall had left himself in a dangerously exposed position. While the prosecutor was trying to demonstrate that this duck-hunting episode had taken place in the remote past, his witness had said that it had happened during the recent '60–'61 season. Yet Lee still could not recall the date with certainty. He couldn't even remember whether it was before or after Christmas. Goodman might have jumped on this and shown the jury just how poor Lee's memory was, just how vague were his recollections of dates and events.

Instead, he returned to the question of the Dresbachs' nudism.

Goodman: When did [your father] make you go to the nudist camps? Have you been going to the nudist camps in recent years since you got down to Anne Arundel County?
Lee: Not us.
Goodman: Who did?
Lee: My mother and father.
Goodman: That's all, thank you.

Since this scarcely exhausted the subject, Goodman's brevity is hard to fathom. He might have mentioned that Wayne had told Dr. Guttmacher that his father had tried to take Lee and him to a nudist camp while their mother was in Europe, the summer of 1959, and that during interviews at Clifton T. Perkins the boy had discussed more recent nudist activities. Both brothers had admitted that their parents went around the house without clothes—Lee said only his father did—and, of course, the day they were killed Shirley was naked and Pat was wearing nothing but an undershirt. After establishing these facts, Goodman might have pursued questions about the Dresbachs' sex lives and the pornographic pictures and devices found in their house. But he let the opportunity pass.

The State's next witness was Officer Joseph Grzesiak, who described how he had apprehended Wayne, confiscated the .22, and heard the boy confess to the killings.

Osborne Duvall then called Lieutenant Ashley Vick to the stand, fixed his time of arrival at the Dresbach house at 10:20, and asked him what he had done after the bodies were removed.

Lieutenant Vick said he had found five expended .22 cartridges —four in the living room between the television and the chair, and one in the kitchen. Then he had returned to Edgewater, taken custody of Wayne, and recorded his confession.

After Duvall entered the confession into evidence and had it read aloud to the jury, he questioned Lieutenant Vick on redirect examination.

> *Duvall:* And what did you do when you went to the Dresbach home the second time, Lieutenant?
> *Lt. Vick:* We searched for anything else that may be pertinent to the case, far as I can recall it, sir.
> *Duvall:* What, if anything, did you find?
> *Lt. Vick:* I don't recall, offhand, finding anything.
> *Duvall:* Is it your testimony, as I understood earlier, that you took the four expended cartridges into custody, grouped around that chair that you pointed out to the Jury and that's all?

Duvall seemed to have been misleading the jury. Lieutenant Vick corrected him.

> *Lt. Vick:* Yes, and one [cartridge] out of the kitchen.
> *Duvall:* One out of the kitchen?
> *Lt. Vick:* Yes sir.

Quickly Duvall shied away from the subject of the expended shell in the kitchen, and Goodman apparently took no notice of its potential significance. But he did spot another area the State hadn't explored, and he brought it up on recross.

> *Goodman:* And you were asked whether you examined or inspected the home and found certain things. Did you find the nude pictures in the father's desk?
> *Lt. Vick:* No sir.
> *Goodman:* Who did?
> *Lt. Vick:* I don't know.

Goodman might have been wise to establish through Vick just who had found the pornography and what it consisted of. Were there pictures of the Dresbachs in the nude? Had these photographs been taken in the home? Had the police made any effort to identify the people in the snapshots? But Goodman didn't pursue the issue.

The State's next witness was Dr. Charles S. Petty, the Assistant Medical Examiner from Baltimore who had performed autopsies on Pat and Shirley Dresbach. Under questioning from Osborne Duvall, Dr. Petty offered his opinion that Pat's death "was due to multiple gunshot wounds with hemorrhage into the chest cavities." He then described all the evidence of injury he had found in the victim, including "two . . . gunshot wounds [that] entered on the left part of the buttocks, in its upper portions, just as the buttocks joins the small of the back; and in both of these instances the bullets coursed upward in the body."

There would be subsequent indications that the significance of these two wounds was not lost on Osborne Duvall.

Remember that Lee testified he had not seen either of his parents shot. In fact, he swore he had not even seen Wayne with the rifle in his hands until after the shooting. And Wayne had left the impression—later he would swear to it—that he had done all his firing from his position in the living room. But the wounds in the small of Pat Dresbach's back could only have been made at much closer range. And because the bullets had coursed up through his body, it looked likely that they had been fired when Dresbach was lying on the floor. The expended cartridge found in

the kitchen provided added evidence that Wayne had come close
and shot his father again.

But Duvall and Goodman busied themselves trying to establish
the alcohol content of Dresbach's blood. After Dr. Petty testified
that there had been no trace present when he did the autopsy,
Goodman proved that the liquor Pat had consumed the previous
night would have been assimilated by morning. Since Dresbach's
alcoholism wasn't at issue, it is difficult to say what Goodman
gained in this debate.

After the assistant medical examiner left the stand, Osborne
Duvall announced that the State had presented its evidence, and
Judge Michaelson called a recess for lunch.

3

All morning Wayne had sat listening to the testimony against
him. Rather, he had let the tidal wave of words wash over him.
Some of the words had registered, some of them had struck him
as untrue, but this didn't anger or excite him, and during the
lunch break he said nothing to his lawyers. It wasn't just that he,
like many of the people in the gallery and perhaps on the jury,
had had a hard time following the disjointed testimony. He didn't
much care what was said. He didn't see that it would have any
effect on him. He remembered clearly what had happened that
morning in January, and while some witnesses had presented an
inaccurate picture of events, he knew that when his turn came to
testify, he would swear to an even more inaccurate version.

He didn't see that this would have any effect on him either. No
matter what he said now, he couldn't save himself. The one thing
he could do, he thought, was limit the damage—tell his story in
such a way that nobody else was hurt and nobody ever learned
enough to ask him questions which he found painful.

When they returned to the courtroom at 1:10, Albert Goodman recalled Lieutenant Ashley Vick to the stand. Having seen
frequent references in the psychiatric profiles to Wayne's "lack of
affect," Goodman apparently decided to seize upon this absence
of emotion as one proof of the boy's insanity. He asked Vick

what Wayne's mood had been when he made his confession, and the lieutenant said he had been "very calm, unemotional."

One can only conjecture how the jury reacted. Content to let people draw their own conclusions about a son who shows no emotion after murdering his parents, Osborne Duvall asked no questions.

Next Goodman called Lloyd Smith to the stand. This was the moment the Talberts and Father Dawson had been waiting for. They believed Wayne's lawyer would now weave together the threads of evidence he had previously left dangling; at last he would explore the Dresbachs' home life in depth.

After some preliminary questions about Smith's rank and position, Goodman directed his attention to January 7, shortly after Wayne had confessed.

> *Goodman:* Now, as a result of his apprehension, what investigation, if any, did you make for the State?
> *Lt. Smith:* Well, I went to the home to see, I had heard various things about the alleged, about the subject here, and I went to the home to try and get any evidence for or against the boy.
> *Goodman:* What did you find?
> *Lt. Smith:* Well, upon investigation of the parents, Mr. Dresbach and Mrs. Dresbach, through various pieces of evidence I obtained—
> *Duvall:* May it please the Court, I object, he says the investigation of the parents.
> *Goodman:* No, I mean for the investigation of the defendant, either for or against him. What did you discover and uncover?
> *Duvall:* That relates to the defendant now, sir?
> *Judge Michaelson:* Of course, the use of the words are carrying an import which presumes something. He says he was looking for something that could be used as evidence. He can't say whether it was evidence or not.
> *Goodman:* That's true, sir. I'm not directing his attention to evidence. [Then to Lt. Smith] But, you made an investigation as a result of this killing?
> *Lt. Smith:* Yes sir.

Although the State's attorney had not objected and Smith had not mentioned what he unearthed in the course of his investigation, Judge Michaelson abruptly told the jury to take a recess and sent them out of the courtroom. Then he asked Goodman:

Judge Michaelson: Court wants to know if this line of questioning relates to this pornographic semblance of various and sundry articles and pictures? Counsel is going to have to lay some foundation to show that it has some connection with the issues in this case. Simply to put it into the record just for what it may be worth, Court is not going to permit.

Goodman: I understand that, Your Honor. My purpose in asking this witness the question and developing the presence and the discovery of pornographic literature is to show the environment in which Wayne was reared, and to show that it would affect his attitude and his ability to act normal.

Judge Michaelson: Unless you have some basic evidence through others to come in, from somebody who is an expert to state as a positive fact that this had something to do with this killing, then the Court is going to rule it out. That's why it sent the jury out so it wouldn't be fiddle dee dee, fiddle dee dum here in front of the jury.

Goodman: We have no pinpointed evidence, other than the fact that the officer did discover, and we'd like to proffer through this witness, if Your Honor pleases.

Judge Michaelson: Well, you can take exception to what the Court's action is, put into the record, if you wanted to proffer, what you wanted to introduce through this witness, and the Court will rule on it. As indicated, it will sustain the objection to it. You may have your proffer in the record for whatever it may be worth. Dictate to the stenographer what you want to present by this witness and that will be that.

Goodman: We, first, except to the Court's refusal to allow us to question witness on the discovery of certain materials in the residence of the late [H.] Malone Dresbach. Now, we proffer that through this witness we would develop that his investigation and examination of the home uncovered a large quantity of pornographic literature, pictures of nude women and other obnoxious photographs, which would tend to create an atmosphere very detrimental to the proper rearing of a child 15 years of age in that home.

Judge Michaelson: All right. Anything else from this witness?

Goodman: Yes sir.

Judge Michaelson: Bring the jury in.

When the jury returned, Goodman resumed questioning Lieutenant Smith, taking a new tack in his effort to describe Wayne's home life and its disastrous consequences.

Goodman: Was there any time just prior to the shooting incident, which you had occasion to interview Wayne Dresbach, the defendant?

Lt. Smith: Yes sir.

Goodman: When was that?

Lt. Smith: I have had, I made several reports on Wayne—I have them here in my briefcase—where we received instances of him running away.

Duvall: Now, object to the witness. Answer is not responsive. Mr. Goodman asked him when he interviewed him, and the witness has taken off.

Goodman: Just answer, when did you have your interview, Lieutenant?

Lt. Smith: May I look at my records? (Witness looked at his records.) On October 11th, 1960.

Goodman: Where did you interview him?

Lt. Smith: At the Edgewater Sub-Station, second floor in the back room.

Goodman: What was the occasion?

Lt. Smith: Wayne had run away from home and he was staying with several other boys and they had gone back to the home—

Duvall: May it please the Court, before Lt. Smith proceeds I assume that his testimony is based *in toto* or in part on the report which he made and I think he should be questioned as to whether or not this report was not filed with the Juvenile Court, and if so, then we are confronted with the law which says that the proceedings in Juvenile Court cannot be made a matter of public record. And even though this may be, in fact, a copy of his report which he keeps in his file, if he uses this material in testifying in this case, aren't we violating that provision? Therefore, I believe his testimony should be excluded.

Judge Michaelson: Did you make any contact with the Juvenile Court in connection with that case?

Lt. Smith: Yes sir, I did.

Judge Michaelson: You made a record of it over there?

Lt. Smith: Yes sir, I have the original here.

Judge Michaelson: Sustain the objection.

Wayne had been bedeviled by dozens of Catch-22's, but this was one of the most maddening. Proceedings of the Juvenile Court are, indeed, supposed to be kept confidential to protect underaged offenders from publicity that might brand them as criminals and blight the rest of their lives. But in Wayne's case the damage had already been done. Newspapers all over the country had published summaries of his juvenile record.

A second reason for this rule of confidentiality is to prevent juvenile records, which often contain hearsay and gossip, from being used *against* a defendant who is on trial as an adult. But Goodman believed Wayne's juvenile record would help him, indicating that he had run away five times to flee parental abuse. It would also have shown that the Dresbachs had recklessly charged him with larceny and had left him in jail several days.

Yet Osborne Duvall, twisting the law's intent, insisted on excluding evidence which might have exculpated the boy or at least explained part of his motivation.

Goodman had to start over in his attempt to introduce material from Lieutenant Smith's investigation.

Goodman: Now, Lieutenant, how many times were you required to investigate the defendant because of his running away from home?

Lt. Smith: Actually, I only investigated this one time, but one of my officers investigated the other time and the case was closed, no prosecution.

Goodman: The other time there was an investigation. So what was that, just two times your office investigated Wayne?

Lt. Smith: Yes.

Goodman: And was his case ever referred to the psychiatrist for the Anne Arundel County Health Department?

Lt. Smith: Yes sir.

Duvall: Objection.

Judge Michaelson: Well, he can answer whether it was referred. That part is all right.

Duvall: Well, he wouldn't know except by hearsay, if that referral was by the Court.

Judge Michaelson: Well, if it's by hearsay, Court will sustain the objection. I presume he had definite knowledge of it.

Goodman: You made the referral?

Lt. Smith: No sir, Mr. Ogle made the referral after the father withdrew the charge against the boy in Juvenile Court.

Goodman: Was any further treatment given to the defendant as a result of that referral to the psychiatrist?

Lt. Smith: Yes.

Duvall: Objection.

Judge Michaelson: Is this your own knowledge, Lieutenant?

Lt. Smith: Yes sir. I have in my briefcase a report from Dr. Winiarz who called me on the referral and she sent me a copy of the report at my request, of the talk she had with Wayne and Wayne's mother and father and a brother.

Goodman: What was her recommendation?

Duvall: Objection.

Judge Michaelson: I don't think you can produce through this witness— The proper source to get it from is from the person who made the examination.

Michaelson seemed to be saying that Goodman should have called on Dr. Elizabeth Winiarz. Otherwise the judge would not admit into evidence her recommendation that Wayne should receive psychotherapy and be removed from his adoptive home and put into a boarding school away from a family which, in her opinion, needed "intensive case work."

But since Dr. Winiarz had made these recommendations on the basis of a Juvenile Court referral, Osborne Duvall would most likely have objected again to the introduction of confidential information concerning an underage offender. That is speculation, however, since Goodman appeared not to have been in a position to produce Dr. Winiarz—only her report.

> *Goodman:* We have the record of the Health Department summons to Court. We have someone who can produce it at this moment, the hospital record or the Health Department record. I'd like permission to receive that report now. They're the office reports. They're made in the ordinary course of business.
>
> *Judge Michaelson:* Well, aren't you getting your cart before the horse? I think the proper procedure, approach to this—I simply assume it all relates to your pleas in this case.
>
> *Goodman:* That's right, sir.

The judge then launched into one of his lectures which tended to be longwinded, but short on clarity and complete sentences.

> *Judge Michaelson:* You've got to get something first to establish as a definite proposition and then show what supports it. There's nobody yet that's indicated anything from an expert standpoint as to the mental capacity of this individual. And just simply to throw out these things here and there to indicate, well, maybe there's something wrong with this nature, and maybe there's something wrong with that nature, but all falling short of what the issue is in this case. Simply putting into the record something which at this point is not properly introducible procedure, as the Court sees it.
>
> *Goodman:* What is Your Honor's ruling then on the question I'd asked?
>
> *Judge Michaelson:* Either that you have, I presume, expert testimony which will support the plea. Then, having had established your contention you have a right to introduce what

mounts up [to] the conclusion going by the expert which establishes that which supports your contention.
Goodman: Very well, sir.

But the judge wasn't finished.

Judge Michaelson: Not simply start off first and pick up a few little things, like building a house, putting bricks together and going up to the top and then concluding. This situation is the other way around. You have claimed he's not guilty by reason of insanity. He was insane at the time he committed this act and insane now. From your side you should have somebody who says that that is the situation.
Goodman: Very well, sir. Thank you very much, Lieutenant.

Snapping shut his briefcase, Lieutenant Smith left the stand "mad as hell."

But Smith could not have been more frustrated and furious than Albert Goodman. Years later he would claim he had never forgiven Benjamin Michaelson for his refusal to let Lieutenant Smith testify. The judge had not only destroyed Goodman's strategy of putting the Dresbachs on trial, he had laid down an ultimatum: Either introduce an expert witness and have him swear to the boy's insanity, as defined by the M'Naghten Rule, or abandon your original pleas.

Still, Goodman delayed calling his psychiatrists. Instead he put Wayne on the stand, and the decision must have caused him considerable trepidation. After all the difficulty he had had communicating with his client, he had to have known that Wayne would be inarticulate and oblivious of his own interests. But perhaps he thought the boy's indifference to self-incrimination might convince the jury of his insanity.

Goodman: Are either of your parents living now?
Wayne: No sir.
Goodman: When did they die?
Wayne: January 7th.
Goodman: What year?
Wayne: 1961.

> *Goodman:* How did they die?
> *Wayne:* I shot them.
> *Goodman:* What prompted you to do that? Just why did you do it?
> *Wayne:* I don't know. Just went to bed that night and I started [to think] back over the years about all the things they did.

Of necessity, Goodman had to cover some old ground. As Wayne offered an understated account of his academic troubles, his father's drunkenness, and the times he was beaten or badgered in front of company, he could not have been an altogether unsympathetic witness, even for the most hardhearted juror. Neatly dressed in a navy-blue suit and white shirt, his wheat-colored hair in a crew cut, he looked like a little boy pretending to be grown up, and he sounded far out of his depth as he struggled to cope with subjects which had many adults in the room squirming.

> *Goodman:* Have you ever been to nudist camps with your father?
> *Wayne:* Yes sir.
> *Goodman:* Where?
> *Wayne:* Once when I was about 9 or 10.

The question had been "Where?" not "When?" But that was a minor misunderstanding. Far more important, Wayne had left the impression that he had not been to a nudist camp in the last five or six years, and that he had gone only once. But Goodman didn't stop to correct him.

> *Goodman:* What else did you think about [that] night? How did your father treat your mother?
> *Wayne:* He beat her all the time.
> *Duvall:* I'll object to leading. Mr. Goodman first asked him what else he thought about and then suggested an area for him to testify.
> *Goodman:* This is a little child, 15 years of age. I want the jury to get the background of his experiences at home. I think that's important.

Duvall: I realize that. I've been very liberal.

Judge Michaelson: I don't like to say this. You have a two way sword. He killed his mother. He didn't protect his mother. All the testimony about what the mother and father did, I don't think is relevant at all. If he favored one in preference to the other it might have some bearing on it.

Goodman: We'll get to that if Your Honor will permit us. (Then to Wayne) What happened when your mother went to Europe in 1959 or '60?

Wayne: Well, a little after she left, I ran away with another boy and his father came and got us back. When I came back, there was some woman there. And then after that, after she left, two more came.

Goodman: How long did they stay there?

Wayne: About a weekend. Never during the week. Just from Friday 'til Monday morning.

Goodman: Where did you and Lee sleep?

Wayne: We each had separate bedrooms upstairs, and there was one bedroom downstairs.

Goodman: Just one?

Wayne: Yes sir.

Goodman: How many bedrooms altogether upstairs?

Wayne: Two. Could have made four though.

Goodman: None of these women slept upstairs?

Wayne: No sir.

This was a sanitized way of saying that Shirley had left the boys for a long period with their drunken, promiscuous father who had brought women into the house and had sex with them, sometimes with two of them at once. After so many passages like this, one is left wondering whether the judge and the lawyers were any more capable than Wayne of discussing sexual matters with candor. And what did the jury make of all the euphemisms and evasions?

Goodman: Do you remember when it was that your mother returned from Europe?

Wayne: It was a couple days before we started school because school started September 5th, I think.

Judge Michaelson: 1960?

Wayne: '59.

Judge Michaelson: You see, that's all remote, the lapse of a year and a half.

Goodman: But, if Your Honor pleases, this young man says he started thinking about what experiences he had had with his father and mistreatment by his father through his life, and these are the things he reflected on the night before the shooting.

Judge Michaelson: Yes, but they're all incidents, things that happened but the question is, what bearing does it have on this issue in the case?

Goodman: They have a bearing on his mental attitude if Your Honor pleases, and they had something to do with his general approach to the sequence of events that occurred later on. I think we're entitled to show just what was in his mind.

Judge Michaelson: Court is willing to give you certain latitude, but we've got to keep this within bounds somewhere.

Perhaps more incisive questions from Goodman and more comprehensive answers from Wayne might have created a compelling narrative that Michaelson would have found acceptable. But as it was, Goodman never managed to get into the record Wayne's recollections of the battering his father had given his wife and the two boys the night Shirley returned from Europe.

Turning to the morning of January 7, 1961, Goodman tried to present a clear picture of the events leading up to the murders, but had trouble phrasing his questions.

Goodman: Where was the gun or whatever you call it? Is that a rifle or gun?

Wayne: Rifle.

Goodman: Very well. Then you got the gun and you say you went back into the living room. When did you put more pistols, not pistols, but bullets—see, I don't know anything about guns. When did you put any bullets in there, if you did?

Wayne: When I came down from the office and there was some shells in the kitchen cabinet.

Once he had the story straight to his satisfaction—and presumably to the jury's—Goodman double-checked the details against the confession Wayne had given Lieutenant Ashley Vick.

Goodman: Then you said this: "I went to the living room and stood behind the television so that I would not be seen easily." Did you tell Lt. Vick that?

Wayne: I told him I stood right where I showed the jury. Right there. (Pointing to one of Owen Dove's photographs) My arm was about like this, side of the television.

Goodman: Did you say that you stood behind the television so that you could not be seen easily?

Wayne: I didn't say "so I could not be seen easily."

Goodman: Well, did you say that you stood behind the television or beside?

Wayne: I said beside it, I think.

Goodman: You did? Well, then you weren't hiding from your father?

Wayne: No.

Goodman: Well, you were asked this question also: "Did he know what you were going to do?" speaking of Lee, and your answer was, "No." And this was what Lt. Vick asked you: "When did you first plan to shoot your mother and father?" and your answer was: "I had planned it before, but I never did it, then last night I made up my mind that I was going to do it." When was "the before" you were talking about?

Wayne: Well, that was last summer and I just thought of it, that's all. I didn't really plan it.

Goodman: And that was a thought for a second to shoot whom?

Wayne: My father.

Goodman: Lt. Vick asked you when you planned first to shoot your mother and father. Did you recognize the question as for both mother and father?

Wayne: I must not have.

This was by no means a full list of the conflicts and inac-
curacies, but it did suggest that Wayne's confession was flawed
and often misleading.

Then, although his client had just sworn that he had not
"planned" to shoot either parent last summer, Goodman asked:

> *Goodman:* Had you planned to shoot your mother last sum-
> mer too?
> *Wayne:* No sir.
> *Goodman:* How did you happen to shoot your mother this
> time?
> *Wayne:* I don't know, I just couldn't control myself.
> *Goodman:* When did you start shooting at your father?
> *Wayne:* When he came out of the bedroom.
> *Goodman:* And when did you stop?
> *Wayne:* I don't know. When he was in the kitchen.
> *Goodman:* And then what happened after your father went
> into the kitchen?
> *Wayne:* My mother came out.
> *Goodman:* And what did you do?
> *Wayne:* Just turned around and shot her.
> *Goodman:* What made you do that?
> *Wayne:* I don't know, I just couldn't control myself.
> *Goodman:* You had the automatic in your hand?
> *Wayne:* Yes sir.
> *Goodman:* Had you intended to kill your mother?
> *Wayne:* No sir. I love my mother.
> *Goodman:* How did you feel toward your father?
> *Wayne:* I didn't love him.
> *Goodman:* Why not?
> *Wayne:* Because all the things he did.

On cross-examination Osborne Duvall attempted to contradict
this testimony and reemphasize Wayne's premeditation.

> *Duvall:* Now, before January the 7th, and sometime since
> Christmas of 1960, had you ever indicated to your brother
> that you were thinking of killing your parents?
> *Wayne:* No sir, only one morning, only the morning I did it.

Duvall: No, I mean, on some other time since last Christmas, but before the day of the shooting, do you remember telling Lee that you were going to kill your parents?

Wayne: Not that I remember.

Duvall: You don't remember?

Wayne: No sir.

Duvall: Could you have and now forgot?

Wayne: I don't think so.

Like Goodman, Duvall asked Wayne for his version of the events of the morning of January 7. Sensing that the boy's story had cast an ambiguous light on his younger brother's testimony, the prosecutor needed to reiterate Lee's contention that he had not seen Wayne with the rifle until after the killings. So Duvall doggedly led Wayne back through the Dresbach house, double-checking his statement every step of the way.

Duvall: Then from the living room you went to the kitchen, did you not?

Wayne: Yes sir.

Duvall: Isn't that where you found Lee for the first time that morning?

Wayne: Yes sir, he was reading the paper.

Duvall: Reading the paper. And at that time, did you have any conversation with Lee or make any statement to him about what you intended to do?

Wayne: Yes, I told him when I came back down with the gun.

Duvall: Let me see if I understand you correctly. Didn't you see Lee in the kitchen reading the paper before you had the gun in your possession?

Wayne: Yes sir, I did.

Duvall: All right, now, that's the time I'm talking about. The first time that you saw Lee when you didn't have the gun with you, did you make any statement to him about what you intended to do?

Wayne: When I didn't have the gun?

Duvall: Yes.

Wayne: No, I didn't.

Duvall: You did not? Then you went out of the kitchen, up some steps to the office, is that correct?
Wayne: Yes sir.
Duvall: And took this .22 automatic rifle off the gun rack?
Wayne: Yes sir.

Duvall: When did you put the 4 additional bullets in the gun?
Wayne: When I came downstairs the second time and went in the kitchen.
Duvall: You went in the kitchen the second time and Lee was still there?
Wayne: Yes.

Duvall: Now, on this occasion where did you have to get the bullets that you put in the gun?
Wayne: They were in the cabinet right beside the door in the kitchen.
Duvall: In a cabinet in the kitchen?
Wayne: Yes sir.
Duvall: And did you load the gun in the kitchen?
Wayne: Yes sir.
Duvall: Was Lee present?
Wayne: Yes sir.
Duvall: Did you, at that time, tell Lee that you were going to kill your parents, or one parent?
Wayne: I told him I was going to kill my father.

Unable to shake Wayne from his story, Duvall posed several questions raised by Dr. Petty's autopsy report.

Duvall: . . . After you fired the first shot at your father, before you stopped shooting at him, did he at any time face you, turn toward you?
Wayne: I think he did, I'm not sure.
Duvall: Did you understand the doctor's testimony this morning, that he had, that is, your father had a bullet wound which entered from the front of the chest?
Wayne: Yes sir, I heard that.

Duvall: Do you now have a recollection as to whether your father ever turned face to you during the time you were shooting him?
Wayne: Well, I guess he did. He just proved it, the doctor did.
Duvall: Well, I'm asking you what your recollection is. Do you have a remembrance of your father turning, facing you?
Wayne: Not very clearly.
Duvall: Where was your father when you stopped shooting at him?
Wayne: He was in the kitchen.

Finally Duvall got to what appears to have been the point of his questions.

Duvall: Do you recall whether or not you fired any shots at your father while he was lying on the kitchen floor?
Wayne: No sir.

Here was a dramatic indication that the State's attorney understood that Wayne must have come close and shot his father while he was on the kitchen floor. But then, curiously, he did not cite Dr. Petty's autopsy report to prove the boy was lying. One can only speculate why he didn't press the issue. It is quite possible he had been planning to tell the jury that Wayne had cold-bloodedly continued to pump bullets into his father's prone body, when suddenly he realized this might harm the State's case more than it helped. While it would have made Wayne seem a merciless killer, it would also have shown that he had shot his father in front of his brother and, even if Wayne did not claim that Lee had prompted him to do this, it would have damaged Lee's credibility.

Shying away from this dangerous topic, Duvall questioned Wayne about his confession, stressing its validity, although never resolving its inconsistencies. Then he tried to suggest that in the months preceding his death, Pat Dresbach had been relatively benign, seldom beating his son or even punishing him. And finally he returned to what had become his favorite subject.

Duvall: Now, I'll ask you once again, Wayne, are you sure that sometime before Christmas or New Year's and the time of this shooting you had not made a statement to Lee that you intended to kill your father?

Goodman: Object to that, Your Honor. He's been over that several times.

Duvall: I think I've only been over that once before, sir. Possibly twice.

Judge Michaelson: What was that? Made a statement? What?

Duvall: To his brother, Lee, as to the time I specified, as to whether or not he was going to kill his father or his parents, however he expressed it.

Judge Michaelson: Objection to the question?

Goodman: I'm objecting because the State has asked the defendant that several times. He's gotten the same answers twice.

Judge Michaelson: It's already been asked. If he's answered it, there's no use to repeat it.

Although Osborne Duvall's cross-examination had opened some intriguing possibilities, Goodman chose not to take up any of them. Instead, perhaps preparing the way for the psychiatrists, he concentrated on Wayne's puzzling behavior after the shootings. The boy readily admitted he had driven off to a basketball game, picked up two friends, and gone to a gas station to buy orange soda pop and bubble gum.

It is worth wondering, however, whether the jury interpreted this as evidence of insanity or simple callousness.

4

For the rest of that hot, humid afternoon, debate about Wayne's mental competence dominated the trial, circling dizzily through the stale air of the courtroom. Much of it was prolix, repetitive, and, above all, confusing, since there were frequent interruptions by Osborne Duvall, then fragmented, stream-of-consciousness rulings by Judge Michaelson. One has to wonder how—or whether—the jury was able to follow the arabesques of testimony.

Duvall's strategy was simplicity itself. He objected to everything—the order in which Goodman called his witnesses, their qualifications, their opinions. Finally he appeared to object to the entire field of psychiatry. But then he changed his mind when he called on his psychiatrist as a rebuttal witness.

Goodman's first witness was Curtis Marshall, a specialist in electroencephalography, who had barely identified himself when Duvall jumped to his feet.

> *Duvall:* I rise, not to concede to the gentleman's qualifications, but I would like to make an objection; either at the bench or with the jury excused.
> *Judge Michaelson:* Suppose counsel come up here and tell the Court.
> *Duvall:* (At the bench) May it please the Court, I will object to Dr. Marshall's testimony, which I assume Mr. Goodman is going to develop regarding the electroencephalogram taken, which was read by him; also one that was taken at Clifton Perkins. I know Mr. Goodman has Dr. Ainsworth here, who is Guttmacher's psychologist. I will object on the same basis. I think we ought to have the air clarified at this time. Until Guttmacher gets on the stand and expresses an opinion that under the Maryland Rule this boy was insane at the time or now, I do not think this testimony is admissible. . . .

> *Goodman:* It's my understanding that with a plea of not guilty by reason of insanity at the time of the commission of the crime, or even at the time of the trial, the defendant is permitted to call experts to testify as to every examination, as a result of every examination made in an effort to determine what that state of mind was when the incident occurred. . . .
> *Judge Michaelson:* Court is inclined to have every one of them testify, then when you get to the essence of this,

whether or not, in his opinion, he was responsible, sane at
the time he committed the crime, then all this is surplusage,
doesn't mean anything.

But Duvall wasn't satisfied. He wanted to raise objections to
defenses which Goodman had never indicated he would offer.

Duvall: May I point out one thing further? I don't know, because of the choice of language Mr. Goodman used, I don't
know whether it was intentional, but this may bear on the intent of the defendant. The Court of Appeals in the last para-
graph of Judge Alver's opinion in the Spencer case partly
rejected that this medical testimony would come in to show
a lack of ability to premeditate the murder charge in that
case.

The judge then went the prosecutor one better in anticipating
unacceptable defenses.

Judge Michaelson: Not only that, you can't show the irresistible impulse phase of it either. He [Wayne] already said
he couldn't control himself, which means an irresistible impulse. It's not a defense, that's not a defense. If it points to
establish that there is a basis for the defendant to be ad-
judicated insane, and not simply to say that he had an examination, was given a brain wave test, showed some brain damage etc. etc. It doesn't all add up to whether or not these
experts can say, in their opinion, was he insane at the time of
the crime. They hedge on it and you don't have the proof. It
simply anticipates on cross examination, which is certainly
proper to ask the expert, whether or not in his opinion—and
that's the crux of the whole thing, is to dress it up here and
parade it around and you get nowhere. The crux of it is, on
cross examination he be asked whether or not he can say, as
an expert, this defendant was insane at the time he committed this crime, and is insane now.
Duvall: I think he has to say that on direct examination before he's subjected to cross examination.

As the conversation continued and Judge Michaelson's syntax slithered into an impenetrable thicket of garbled clauses, a ten-minute recess was called. But when the jury returned, Curtis Marshall was finally allowed to testify that Wayne had had two EEG examinations—one on January 11, the other on May 11.

> *Goodman:* . . . Now, will you tell us what your findings were upon examining and reading the two electroencephalographs?
> *Duvall:* I'll renew my objection.
> *Judge Michaelson:* Overruled.
> *Dr. Marshall:* . . . My notes on the particular time, this is the one of January the 11th, 1961. This is a grossly abnormal record showing both 14-6 and projected spikes in the dozing record. Thus this patient definitely falls into the convulsive disorder category. I would feel that it would be well worthwhile going into the history to see if it is possible to unearth episodes of bizarre sensations or activities to correlate with electrical findings, specifically autonomic patterns.

As for the results of the test done on May 11, 1961, Dr. Marshall added:

> . . . it is essentially the same type of tracing, but not quite as clear evidence [of] projected spikes as the previous tracing showed. Thus, even though the tracing does confirm and support the previous findings, it cannot be construed as in itself making a diagnosis of epilepsy. Such a diagnosis can only be made on clinical grounds.
> *Goodman:* Now, as a result of your interpretation of both of these electroencephalographs, did you arrive at a diagnosis of the condition you were examining?
> *Duvall:* I'll object here on the basis that this gentleman is not a psychologist, psychiatrist, an M.D. specializing in his chosen field.

Goodman tried to defend the credentials of his witness, but once again got caught off guard.

Goodman: You're a neurologist?

Dr. Marshall: I am not a neurologist.

Goodman: Well, I thought you headed the Department of Neurology at Johns Hopkins?

Dr. Marshall: I teach at Hopkins. I am part of the teaching staff of the neurosurgical department. I am not a neurosurgeon.

After further wrangling between the attorneys, Judge Michaelson ruled:

I think you can get at it—what was his findings as a result of those two tests.

Goodman: Thank you, sir. What were your findings as a result of your interpreting both of these electroencephalographs?

Duvall: Object to that.

Judge Michaelson: Overruled.

Dr. Marshall: My findings were that the electroencephalographs on this patient were the type which I see usually in patients who have some deep line brain damage.

During cross-examination Duvall established that Wayne had had no history of seizures, bizarre sensations, autonomic behavior, or any other symptoms associated with the tracings Dr. Marshall had described. Then he got Marshall to concede that, in the absence of clinical evidence, a 14–6 pattern did not necessarily indicate a mental disorder.

Goodman next called on Leonard H. Ainsworth, Chief Psychologist with the Medical Services of the Supreme Bench, City of Baltimore, who had administered a series of eight tests on April 14 and May 8. At Goodman's request, he described these tests and the purpose of each one.

Goodman: And as a result of your examinations and test[s], did you arrive at a finding?

Dr. Ainsworth: Yes sir, I did.

Goodman: What were your findings?

Dr. Ainsworth: Would you like me to read my report?

Duvall: No sir, I object.

Goodman: You just tell me your findings.

Dr. Ainsworth: As a result of my findings, I find that Wayne is a boy who tends to think very concretiscally—

Judge Michaelson: Thinks what?

Dr. Ainsworth: Concretiscally. Concrete is the word—concretiscally.

Judge Michaelson: Will you tell us please what that means?

Dr. Ainsworth: Yes, it's the type of person who can function fairly effectively as long as things are with realities of life, here and now situation, who . . . runs into serious difficulty whenever he's forced to deal with anything abstract. . . . Now, Wayne is the type of boy who has difficulty in anything outside of a concrete level. . . . And the fact that he . . . performed poorly in tests requiring effective visual-motor control function, that leads one to suspect the presence of organic brain damage. He's a boy who tends to project his own hostilities and his own aggression on to others, which is a defense mechanism. He's inclined to feel that there is only one way to do things, and that is his way. I think he [was] singularly lacking in the appropriate affect during the examination.

Goodman: What do you mean by that?

Dr. Ainsworth: The stimuli presented to him during this testing process frequently is of a type that would excite people or stir up their emotional life. This would be the relatively normal response of the average person. Wayne's affect remained unusually flat during the entire testing process. And this would add up . . . to suggest that he was suffering from a paranoid personality.

Duvall: Object, and move to strike out paranoid personality. As a psychologist I don't think Dr. Ainsworth is qualified to make that quotation. I think the psychiatrist can make a deduction on it, but I don't think a psychologist can or should.

Goodman: Is that in your field?

Judge Michaelson: Is that in your report?

Dr. *Ainsworth:* Yes sir, I do it every day in my work.
Judge Michaelson: Do you have that in your report?
Dr. *Ainsworth:* Yes sir, I do.
Judge Michaelson: All right, overruled.
Goodman: What were you saying?
Dr. *Ainsworth:* Diagnostic impression was that of a paranoid
personality, with presence of an organic deficit mark.

Osborne Duvall had to have felt the pressure now. Even though
the defendant had confessed, there was a chance that all Duvall's
efforts could be brushed aside by a successful insanity plea. The
State's attorney tried to regain the offensive by challenging Dr.
Ainsworth's methodology, but he didn't make any headway. In
fact, he unwittingly opened the subject of the severe maternal
deprivation Wayne had suffered and, perhaps fearing that this
would appeal to the jury's sympathies, Duvall cut short his cross-
examination.

Finally Goodman called on Dr. Manfred Guttmacher and
spent several minutes eliciting a litany of the man's qualifications.
Guttmacher was an author, an educator, an internationally re-
nowned forensic psychiatrist of thirty years' experience. He described the examinations he had given Wayne, then explained
that these were the same tests which, as Chief Medical Officer, he
had often administered for the Supreme Bench in Baltimore.

Goodman: Well, as a result of your examination and analysis
of the defendant, were you able to arrive at a medical diagnosis of his psychiatric condition [on] January the 7th, 1961,
at which time he's alleged to have shot his parents?
Dr. *Guttmacher:* I think so.
Goodman: What is that diagnosis?
Dr. *Guttmacher:* Well, I think that we're dealing with a
very disordered individual. I think that it's hard to pigeonhole the type of personality effect which he has. I think paranoid personality is as accurate a pigeonhole as one can find
for this very . . . complex and unusual picture that he presents. And I think that he is socially, certainly, very malad-
justed and [a] sick individual.

Goodman: What treatment have you suggested for him?
Duvall: Object to that.
Judge Michaelson: Sustained.

The prologues were over. The defense had fed the jury as much miscellaneous information as it could. Now Goodman had no choice but to ask the question, the rigid, formulaic inquiry, on which his case and Wayne's fate largely depended.

Goodman: Based on your examination of the defendant . . . do you have an opinion as to whether the defendant at the time he committed the acts charged was capable of distinguishing between right and wrong in respect to such act and to understand the nature and consequence of his act?
Duvall: I'll object to the form of the question. I think the last phrase has been omitted [from] the question.
Judge Michaelson: "As applied to him."
Goodman: Oh, "as applied to himself."
Dr. Guttmacher: Yes, I have an opinion.
Goodman: What is that opinion, Dr. Guttmacher?
Dr. Guttmacher: I think with a very strict interpretation of this law, as I understand it, I believe that the patient meets the test of responsibility. I don't think that he could be considered as technically insane, from a legal point of view, although, medically, I think he's a very disordered individual.

With the last leg apparently knocked off his defense, Goodman nevertheless labored to salvage something, since he knew it was still up to the jury to interpret this testimony.

Goodman: What significance did you give to his lack of emotion, as you described [it]?
Dr. Guttmacher: Well, I think this is one . . . of the most striking and one of the sickest characteristics of this boy. I think that I've examined perhaps 5,000 people involved in criminal behavior. I don't think I've ever seen anyone who shows less, what we call affect, less emotion. . . . I think that this is one reason that one feels they're justified in put-

ting him in the category of paranoid personality. As I think he feels right now that what he did was justified.

On cross-examination Osborne Duvall wasted no time. He went for the jugular vein and kept gnawing at it. Six times he asked essentially the same question.

Duvall: Now, let me ask you specifically . . . the same question Mr. Goodman asked you. In your opinion, on January the 7th, 1961, did Wayne Dresbach have the capacity and reason to enable him to distinguish between right and wrong, and understand the nature and consequences of his act, as applied to himself?
Dr. Guttmacher: Yes, I believe that he did.
Duvall: Today, June 30th, 1961, in your opinion, does Wayne Dresbach have the capacity and reason sufficient to enable him to distinguish between right and wrong and understand the nature and consequences of his act as applied to himself, and thereby assist his counsel in the trial of his case?
Dr. Guttmacher: Yes, I think he has.

Then, to hammer home his advantage, Duvall introduced Dr. Jacob Morgenstern, Superintendent of Clifton T. Perkins State Hospital, to testify as a rebuttal witness. After establishing Morgenstern's *bona fides*, Duvall asked the crucial questions and got the answers he wanted. In Dr. Morgenstern's opinion, Wayne could distinguish between right and wrong and he understood the nature and consequences of his act.

Duvall: Did you find evidence of a paranoid personality disturbance in this patient when you examined him at your hospital?
Dr. Morgenstern: . . . we did not feel that this patient's condition could be formulated as one specific classification. It is multi-basic type of behavior which this patient represents, it's a mixture of a number of things, it's not just one symptom. The boy, in our opinion, has features of a neurotic person, has the features of a passive dependent person. He shows anxiety, he shows a number of other features, he's inadequate

in his behavior. He reacts to things in a way which [is] not one which you would expect of him. He's easily frustrated; he shows that he's not mature enough even for his age; he is quite insecure; there is a lot of torment. The boy, even [though] he says it doesn't matter to him that he was an adopted child, inwardly there's no question that it hurt him. He felt abused and ill-treated by his father, and probably there is some justification for [this feeling] . . .

Duvall: I understand then, Doctor, that in your opinion, Wayne Dresbach consciously perceived a grievance against his father, and that his action was not taken because of unconscious impulses or thought processes, is that correct?

Dr. Morgenstern: I would say to the major extent there might be some unconscious motivation which I cannot delineate, but I have a feeling that most of his gripes against his father were conscious motivation.

Under cross-examination Dr. Morgenstern agreed Wayne needed psychiatric care and he admitted that some members of his staff had found evidence of schizophrenia. And finally, since those reports were available to Dr. Morgenstern, Goodman got it into the record that the Remedial Education Center and the Anne Arundel County Mental Hygiene Clinic had both recommended psychotherapy for Wayne before the killings. But after this he had nothing more to offer and the defense rested.

Judge Michaelson: Court would like to know, does counsel wish to abandon the plea of insanity now?

Goodman: Yes, Your Honor, we have no evidence to show that.

One among many great curiosities in this trial was the fact that Albert Goodman entered a plea of not guilty by reason of insanity when he knew in advance that Guttmacher would testify that Wayne was sane. Goodman's alternative was to try to find a psychiatrist who believed the boy was mentally incompetent. But when asked about this years later, Goodman explained that he had confidence in Guttmacher's expertise and doubted he could have found anyone to declare Wayne insane under the

M'Naghten Rule. He had decided to go ahead with his plea, however, hoping that detailed testimony about Wayne's emotional problems would still sway the jury.

It was after 5 P.M. The temperature had fallen and an evening breeze, laced with the scent of brine, blew along the streets leading from the harbor. Elsewhere in the courthouse, employees were locking their offices and leaving for the weekend. Everybody —everyone except Wayne, that is—must have been thinking about a shower, a drink, and dinner. The jury seemed eager to finish.

> *Judge Michaelson:* Gentlemen of the Jury, do you want to go through with this case, or have a recess and have something to eat and then carry on?
> *Foreman:* We'll go through with it.

Like their opening statements, the attorneys' closing arguments were not included in the transcript. But a rather melodramatic synopsis, the only record of these arguments, appeared the next day in a local newspaper.

Having had his star witness, Lieutenant Smith, thrown off the stand, then having been forced to abandon his plea of insanity, Albert Goodman scrambled to gather up the few remaining shards of his case. Still, according to the newspaper, he:

> presented a touching and magnificent defense of the child-killer. He had the sympathy of everyone in the courtroom, the Judge, the jury, the prosecutor. He dwelt upon the boy's crises under the intolerant ambitions of a father refusing to accept a son's natural limitations and failures; he begged for understanding and leniency for the "explosion" which resulted in the killing—the boy's frantic need for escape, the torment of an overbearing adult mind.
>
> "The lad was insane when he shot his father," said Mr. Goodman. "What actually happened was murder in the second degree by a mind rendered incapable of realizing the enormity of his act."
>
> Mr. Goodman did not take the extreme stand for acquittal; he did not plead for murder in the third degree. True to the

precepts of the law, he marshalled his facts and presented them in their entirety to the jury. With no verbosity, with quiet eloquence, he defended a young criminal whose act, by the writing of the law, merited death.

Then Osborne Duvall, the State's Attorney, did what he had to do. He asked for a verdict of first degree murder for the youth. He too made a touching and magnificent address to the jury on behalf of justice. He called for the ultimate verdict for the deliberate, premeditated, planned murder of a father by his son—a murder committed not in self-defense or sudden, overwhelming impulse, but with careful consideration and "malice aforethought." In a voice charged with sympathy and understanding, the State's Attorney pointed out that harsh parental discipline is no excuse for murder. He promised as much help and psychiatric care as the State could give the youth, but whatever the boy's personality disturbance might be as diagnosed by the testifying of psychiatrists, they declared Wayne Dresbach was legally sane when he killed his father Jan. 7th, 1961, and legally sane at his trial that day, June 30, 1961. And in the killing, there was not one missing factor of murder in the first degree.

Yet after these arguments, as Judge Michaelson emphasized, it was up to the members of the jury to reach their own decision. Even his instructions to them and his explanation of the law were, he said, "advisory only, and you may accept or reject them as you finally determine the result." For Maryland is the only state where the jury decides not just a defendant's guilt or innocence, but interprets the law as well. A jury may return a verdict which is the result of its own assessment of the facts and perceptions of justice, regardless of what the law supposedly requires. In effect, because their deliberations are secret, juries in other states also have this power, but Maryland is the one state where juries are instructed of their prerogative.

Even though the indictment was for murder in the first degree, the jurors could reach a verdict of guilty of second degree murder, guilty of manslaughter, or not guilty. And although the State's attorney had not asked for capital punishment, they could deliver an unqualified verdict of guilty which would allow the judge to impose the death sentence at his discretion.

At 6:02 P.M., as the jury retired for its deliberations, Father Dawson and the Talberts agreed that those twelve men had a great deal to ponder. Throughout the day Wayne's friends had grown increasingly upset at the tenor and direction of the trial. It had struck them as sloppy and fast, as if it were some cursory proceeding in which the conclusion was foregone. But now, after the judge's instructions, they were filled with renewed hope. Regardless of Michaelson's refusal to permit much testimony about the Dresbachs, regardless of the opinion of the psychiatrists, the jury could declare Wayne innocent. Or it could find him guilty of a less serious charge. As the Talberts and Father Dawson saw it, when you considered Wayne's age, his wretched home life, and his emotional instability, leniency was reasonable.

Father Dawson was about to suggest that they go eat dinner. The jury had seven hours of testimony to wade through; it might well take them that long just to rehash the evidence about Wayne's ability to premeditate a murder. Father Dawson had read of many cases where deliberations had lasted for days. And in Maryland, where the jury had so much more responsibility, wouldn't that make for longer deliberations?

But before he could speak, there was some commotion at the front of the courtroom. The jury was coming back. Father Dawson thought it had to be for additional instructions. They hadn't been gone more than a few minutes.

But Judge Michaelson called the court to order and asked the foreman whether they had reached a verdict. The foreman said they had.

The judge told Wayne to stand and face the jury, and Father Dawson was stunned. Things were moving too fast again and he was overwhelmed with confusion. A moment later the entire room was confused.

"How do you find the defendant?" Judge Michaelson asked.

After consulting a scrap of paper in his hand, the foreman announced a verdict of insanity.

The courtroom erupted. That wasn't a verdict.

The clamor from the other jurors was almost as great as that from Osborne Duvall. Quickly they straightened things out, and the foreman corrected himself. The verdict was guilty of murder in the first degree. Following Duvall's suggestion, they had not recommended the death penalty.

It took a bit longer, however, to explain why the foreman had botched his announcement. Finally the man admitted he couldn't read. For hours an illiterate had listened to the complex testimony of lawyers, doctors, psychologists, and psychiatrists. Then he and the other jurors had deliberated a total of twelve minutes before declaring a fifteen-year-old boy guilty of first-degree murder. As far as anyone could recall, it was the quickest verdict in a murder trial in Maryland history.

Sentencing was postponed until the following week. But the penalty was virtually automatic. Life in prison.

5

The Dunns didn't have a radio in their car, so as they drove to Franklin Manor that evening, they had no way of knowing the trial was over. For the most part they remained silent, praying that Wayne would be released. It reminded Mary Helen of that ride to the beach six months ago, when they had heard about the Dresbach murders and sped down, hoping against hope that it wasn't true.

As they pulled into the driveway, however, a neighbor rushed over and told them the news. Without bothering to unpack, the Dunns piled back into their Buick and headed for Annapolis.

"Now it reminded me of racing off to Edgewater the morning he was arrested," Mary Helen remembers. "Karen was crying, and I was about to break into tears. It just didn't seem possible they'd put a boy in jail for life. Not after what he'd already been through.

"I really can't say why we went to Annapolis that night. What could we do for him now? Halfway there I thought they probably wouldn't even let us see him. But I wanted to let him know we had tried, and so we drove on. And when we got there, the police surprised me and said, yes, we could talk to him. I think they were as shocked by the verdict as we were.

"Ever since his escape, they wouldn't let us go upstairs. We went to that visiting room—the hallway lined with barred windows—and while I waited for them to bring him down, I was afraid it was going to be one of those terrible times when nobody could find anything to say and Wayne just stood there, looking blank.

"But then when he came down, he didn't look blank. He looked just like any little kid who's terrified and hurt and about to cry. That's exactly what he did. He stepped up to the window and started bawling. He didn't wait for me to make the first move. He reached through those bars and hugged me and kept on crying. It was the first time I'd ever seen him show any emotion.

"We told him not to worry. It wasn't over yet. We wouldn't let this case drop, and we weren't about to abandon him. Without giving it any thought, I said there would be an appeal. I just naturally assumed there would be one.

"As usual, Wayne didn't have much to say. That was the most frustrating thing. He kept everything bottled up inside. Sometimes it nearly drove me nuts. I wanted to grab him and shake him and shout at him to tell people exactly what had happened.

"I used to think if only he hadn't killed his mother, then she could have defended him and explained to the police why he shot his father. But the more I learned about her, the more I began to wonder. She didn't do such a great job of defending him back when his worst crime was running away from home. So I'm not sure she would have stuck up for him. I'm just not sure about anything where Shirley Dresbach's concerned."

Afterward, the Dunns drove back to Franklin Manor, and Mary Helen hurried down to the Talberts'.

"Father Dawson was there and they were all sitting on the front porch. That summer we spent a lot of evenings on that porch, discussing the trial and trying to decide what to do next. The thing we couldn't get over was how quick it went. They said it didn't seem like Wayne had a chance. Nobody wanted to go off half-cocked and make accusations, but it looked like the deck had been stacked against him. Not a single character witness got to testify in his favor and none of the Dresbachs' friends were put on the stand and forced to tell all they knew. Then Lieutenant Smith was thrown off the stand. The impression we got was that somebody very high up had pulled strings, and Wayne was being railroaded.

"But of course none of us knew a damn thing about the law. That's what strikes me now—how naïve and ignorant we were. And poor! Since then I've read plenty of books about cases like Wayne's. But the big difference between them and his is that some smart lawyer or group of influential citizens always decided to step in and take up for the kid. I mean, look at the case of that boy up in Connecticut. [The Peter Reilly case, which became the basis for a best-selling book, *Death in Canaan,* then a TV movie.] The townspeople backed him up right away. Then a journalist started digging to uncover the true story. And a lot of famous writers and movie directors donated thousands of dollars to finance an appeal.

"Well, Wayne had nothing like that. There were relatives and family friends—wealthy, powerful people—who could have helped him, but they didn't do a damn thing. It was left up to us —Father Dawson, the Talberts, Bob and Evelyn McCracken, and us. Each family kicked in a hundred bucks, then a distant relative of the Dresbachs—just one, mind you—sent a check for a hundred, and with five hundred dollars in the bank we decided to appeal and carry it all the way to the Supreme Court, if we had to." Mary Helen smiles, shaking her head. "Maybe we're lucky we didn't know any better. Otherwise we'd have given up at the start."

Most people already had given up on Wayne. From time to time somebody new would stop by the Talberts' in the evening to sit on the porch and drink lemonade, listen to the discussions, then offer an opinion. But not one of them made a donation. Maybe they assumed it wasn't their place. If the Dresbach family wasn't helping to finance an appeal, why should they?

In the minds of some people, there was another reason not to get involved. Wayne *had* killed his parents. Whatever his motives, whatever the mitigating factors, he never denied that. And, as one friend of Pat and Shirley said, "Nothing they did to him was a capital offense. How can you justify defending a confessed double murderer?"

No one was more keenly aware of this question and the moral dilemma it raised than Father Paul Dawson. But he had concluded that if what the boy had done was horrifying, then surely the behavior of the Dresbachs, which had driven Wayne to murder, was more horrifying yet and had to be exposed during an appeal.

The young priest also believed it was important to examine Lee's place in the scheme of things. To what extent had he been adversely influenced by his home life? What were his feelings about his mother and father? Did he, like his brother, need help?

Where Lee was concerned, Father Dawson found it difficult to say anything with assurance. While he was more talkative than Wayne—at times he could be quite voluble—he wasn't necessarily more communicative, and Father Dawson's dealings with him had made him pause and consider all the possibilities. As his pastor, he had tried to get through to the younger brother just as he had with Wayne. But the boy struck him as remote and detached. There had been a lot said about Wayne's "lack of affect," but Lee seemed no more willing to express his feelings. His behavior at the funeral parlor—his failure to look at his father —and at the requiem mass—his willingness to receive communion when he wasn't an Episcopalian—had always puzzled Father Dawson. Now having heard uncontradicted testimony that Lee had known in advance what Wayne meant to do and had done nothing to discourage him, the priest was deeply troubled.

He had no desire to blame Lee. Who could say what pressures or fears had influenced this fourteen-year-old boy? Still, he thought that in the name of fairness and accuracy, Lee's actions before and after the killings should have been discussed fully during the trial. If nothing else, that might have provided more insight into the turmoil of the Dresbach family.

As Father Dawson saw it, then, an appeal would be a way of reassessing all the evidence, exploring every avenue of inquiry. He didn't believe that Wayne should be set free. The boy needed care and counseling. But having watched Benjamin Michaelson in the courtroom, he no longer had any illusion that the judge would place Wayne in a special school. He would have to go to jail. But Father Dawson could not bear the thought that Wayne would be there for the rest of his life, with all hope of rehabilitation and redemption lost.

Even if the appeal failed, Father Dawson felt it was well worth the time and money. For months now, he had watched as Wayne was ignored by his own relatives and processed through the legal system by doctors who seemed interested in him solely as a specimen. After this, and after his lifelong mistreatment at the hands of the Dresbachs, Wayne "needed a strong demonstration that he was of value as a human being. Frankly," Father Dawson said, "the feeling I got up to this point was that he was a non-person. He was that cold, ruthless psychopath. Maybe even more despicable than that—a brain-damaged kid who committed this murder and now let's get him out of sight and forget about him. Part of our motivation came from the knowledge that if we fought for him, it would prove to him somebody cared. It would prove to other people he was worth caring about."

And so Father Dawson found a lawyer from Baltimore—Marshall Levin, later a Maryland circuit court judge—who agreed to take the case to the Court of Appeals. First, however, they had to resolve a ticklish problem.

As Levin pointed out, since Wayne already had a lawyer, as well as a guardian, Father Dawson and his group lacked the authority to hire the boy a new attorney without C. J. Pettit's permission. While Levin understood the tenseness of the situation—everybody feared that Pettit, at the insistence of the Dresbach family, would refuse to let them mount an appeal—he could not proceed until he had Pettit's approval and Goodman's agreement to withdraw.

There was another reason to contact Pettit. As executor of the will, he held the purse strings to the Dresbach estate. Perhaps he could allocate some funds for Wayne's appeal. After all, the boy had not been convicted of his mother's death—he would never be brought to trial on this charge—and might therefore have the legal right to inherit from her. Furthermore, Pettit and his counselor, Nathaniel Blaustein, might make a contribution.

Father Dawson explained the situation to Wayne and asked him to notify C. J. Pettit that he wished to appeal his conviction, with Marshall Levin representing him. Then Levin wrote Nathaniel Blaustein, introducing himself:

> I might add that my fee will be derived through the efforts of Father Dawson. . . . Due to the nature of the referral, I had kept the figure of [the] fee at a low amount. Under normal circumstances the amount of my fee would certainly not

be less than $2,500. Therefore, if Dresbach is entitled to share in the estate of his mother, I would like to state, at the outset, that Mr. Pettit should ultimately consider a request for fee on my part in order to make up the difference.

Three weeks later Nathaniel Blaustein replied that Mr. Charles J. Pettit was not opposed to an appeal. On the contrary, he wanted Wayne to have every advantage under the law. Unfortunately, however, Pettit couldn't commit any money from the Dresbach estates for Wayne "by reason of the circumstances under which his parents met their death."

But, as far as he was concerned, anyone desiring to proceed with an appeal could feel free to do so. "Since it is questionable whether Wayne will inherit from his parents' estates, there would appear to be no reason why a pauper's oath could not be filed in his behalf. . . ."

The letter contained no indication that Pettit or Blaustein might want to help and, in fact, neither man ever did make a donation. In this respect they were no different from other friends of the family, none of whom responded to the pleas for funds which Father Dawson and his group ran in newspapers and on radio in Washington, Baltimore, and Annapolis.

There was also no mention in the letter of any stocks, securities, or personal possessions which Wayne owned outright and which might have been made available to him. Five years later, he discovered he had money coming to him for some Studebaker stock which was in his name. His cornet, his clock radio, ice skates, fishing rods and tackle, bicycle, and his half share of the boat and outboard motor Lee and he owned in common were all sold at auction, along with other items from the Dresbach house. But Wayne never learned where the money went.

Finally, Levin had no choice but to follow Blaustein's suggestion and petition the court that the adopted son of one of the most prominent families in Anne Arundel County be declared a pauper.

To Wayne, it seemed he had come full circle. Born in poverty, he had been adopted by a wealthy couple. But what should have been a fairy tale had turned into a nightmare. Now he was as poor and helpless as he had been as an infant.

6

On July 7, 1961, a hearing on sentencing was held in Annapolis and Judge Benjamin Michaelson ordered Wayne "confined to the Maryland Penitentiary for the period of your natural life." The same day, C. J. Pettit and Albert Goodman filed a petition that he be sent to Patuxent Institute to determine whether he was a "defective delinquent."

Before the transfer, however, Wayne had to be processed at the Maryland Penitentiary in Baltimore, a grim, crowded, and dangerous place. Fortunately, the day after he arrived, he came down with a respiratory infection, a relapse of the bronchitis he had suffered last winter when he fell into Chesapeake Bay while duck hunting with his father. "Fortunate" is the word everyone used to characterize this ailment since it put Wayne in the infirmary for three weeks, segregated from the rest of the prison population. Otherwise, his indoctrination to the state pen would probably have included beatings and rape.

Patuxent Institute would be much better, everybody assured Wayne. They made it sound more like a hospital or vocational school than a prison. Small cellblocks, close supervision, and single cells reduced the threat of violence, especially sexual attacks, and there were said to be relatively enlightened programs of psychotherapy, and varied educational and recreational facilities. But what Wayne liked best was the opportunity, as he understood it, for an early release. Unlike the penitentiary, where he would have had to serve eleven years before being eligible for a parole hearing, Patuxent would review his case every year. And the criteria for release were two simple questions: Is the inmate dangerous to society now? Has he been rehabilitated? Since Wayne didn't believe he had ever been a danger to society and he thought there was nothing wrong with him to start with, he was convinced he would be out soon.

Yet although it was in many ways a progressive prison, unique in Maryland and seldom matched anywhere in America, Patuxent had a bad reputation in 1961 and, among inmates, it was the most dreaded penal institution in the state. For one thing, it got the dregs—the people with "the lousiest treatment potential in

the world," according to its current associate director, Arthur
Kandel. "They would be rejected by most private practices."
Under Maryland's strict definition, the inmates were all sane, but
they had severe psychiatric problems or low I.Q.s, a history of
sociopathic behavior, and convictions for rape, murder, or repeated
serious offenses.

What prisoners most despised, however, was the sentencing
policy. Once a man was found to be a defective delinquent, he
received an indeterminate sentence. While this meant that Wayne
might get out earlier than expected, it also meant that someone
convicted of a far less serious crime might remain at Patuxent
long beyond his original sentence. In theory, if a prisoner did not
respond to therapy or could not convince the review board it was
reasonably safe for society to terminate his confinement and
treatment, he could be imprisoned there for the rest of his life.

In the late 60s, Patuxent inmate William McDonough wrote a
series of desperate letters to *Playboy*, bringing the blatant inequi-
ties of this system to the attention of civil libertarians. As
McDonough described the situation, and as Wayne would soon
discover, prisoners who had been found competent to stand trial
were later declared mentally defective and incarcerated in an
institution which would not release them until they proved they
were as fit to be free as they were to be convicted. This had all
the earmarks of another Catch-22 or a parable by Franz Kafka,
especially since the Maryland insanity test was absurdly re-
ductive—could the defendant distinguish between right and
wrong?—while Patuxent Institute's parole standards proved to be
subtle and complex. During his trial, a defendant's sociopathic
tendencies or paranoid symptoms didn't in any way diminish
his responsibility. But after his conviction, these same symptoms
could keep him in Patuxent Institute indefinitely.

Finally, in 1977, the Maryland General Assembly enacted legis-
lation to end this injustice. Today the state cannot label men
defective delinquents, then confine them with indeterminate sentences. Instead, a convict must apply for admission to Patuxent
and if he is deemed eligible—less than half the applicants are accepted—he retains the right to drop out at any time, and under
no circumstances can he be incarcerated beyond the period of his

original sentence. But, like a lot of things in his life, this law came too late to help Wayne.

Patuxent Institute stands on acres of flat, manicured lawn just off Route 75 in Jessup, Maryland. Although the grass, the trees, and flower beds might give it the appearance of a college campus, a double fence, bristling with barbed wire, encloses the grounds, and strategically located towers offer the guards open fields of fire in every direction. Inside the squat red-brick building, iron grates and metal doors leave no doubt that this is a prison.

But when Wayne arrived one sweltering afternoon in August, Patuxent reminded him more of Clifton T. Perkins Hospital. The feel of the place, the look of the other inmates, just wasn't like jail. He thought it was much worse.

Locked in the quarantine wing, where he would remain until he had undergone thorough evaluation, Wayne found himself among men who paced the cellblock, never saying a word. Others sat rigidly still, but wouldn't stop babbling. Still others never left their cells. Limp from the heat, from drugs or depression, they lay on their bunks night and day, looking in their ill-fitting gray uniforms like rumpled sacks of dirty laundry.

One fellow stood in a window facing another cellblock and shouted, "Hey, look at this, hey, look at this." His fly was down, his penis in his hand. Over and over, he masturbated, letting his sperm shoot between the bars.

One night an older man set his penis on fire, burning it down to a charred stump. The guards carried him away, and Wayne never saw him again. Nobody had any idea why he had done it.

Frightened and depressed by this place, Wayne felt wasted. He had not had a full night's sleep in over six months now, not since the morning he shot his parents. He couldn't relax; he had to stay on guard. Everyone had warned him—sometimes in a friendly fashion, other times with scarcely veiled threats—what would happen if he didn't.

Another thing that unnerved him was that while he knew nobody here, they all appeared to recognize him. His case had received so much publicity everybody in the institution had heard about this pretty, baby-faced killer, and many of them wanted to see what he was like, to test him for weaknesses, to take advantage if they could.

One day in the shower room, a man stepped close to Wayne. "Hey, baby-cakes, how about slipping on back here? I got a friend wants to fuck you."

"That wasn't the first time somebody came on to me that way," Wayne recalls. "I knew he was just trying to get me mad. Nobody would say anything if he really meant to crack on you. But I was plenty pissed, I guess because I was tired and still tense from the trial and being transferred into this zoo full of freaks. So I went over to a gang of this guy's friends. Everybody was watching. There I was, a hot sixteen years old and a hundred forty pounds, naked and soaking wet, and ready to take them all on.

"I turned around and stuck out my ass. 'Here it is. You like it? Nice, isn't it? Come and get it.' Then I spun back around and started screaming, 'Just try. Because the first motherfucker that touches me is dead. I'll kill you, I'll kill every one of you.'

"At first a few of them thought it was funny. But when I went on screaming, they stopped laughing and the looks on their faces changed. This one black dude said, 'Hey, the little bastard's crazy.' One by one they got the hell out of that shower room—which was great, I thought.

"But then when I was back in my cell, I realized what I had said. I was already convicted of two murders, and here I was threatening to ice somebody else. It sounded sick, and I wondered if all those psychiatrists weren't right.

"The worst thing, though, the way I figured it, I didn't have any choice. Little as I was, I had to play crazy if I hoped to survive. I had to come on like a stone-cold killer to keep people from climbing on me. I saw myself going on like that for the rest of my life—half the time trying to convince the shrinks I was sane, and the other half working to show the cons I was crazy, I was nobody to fuck with."

Then, at last, Wayne saw a friendly, familiar face.

"Don't you remember me?" the inmate asked. "I knew you a long time ago. Back in Lanham."

Suddenly the name returned to Wayne. We'll call the boy

Ronnie. He had lived not far from the Dresbachs and occasionally came over to their corral and rode the horses. Because
he was a few years older, they had never been close friends. But
Wayne was glad to see him now. Ronnie seemed glad, too.

"When I read you were here, I was hoping I'd get a chance to
say hello before I leave," Ronnie said.

"You getting out?"

"Well," he said, grinning, "you never know."

Wayne didn't ask what Ronnie was in for. At Patuxent that
question was taboo. If it slipped out in group therapy or in the
course of a conversation, fine. But you never fished for information. Wayne did say, however, that he hoped he and Ronnie
would end up on the same tier.

"Yeah, we might just end up the same place."

The next day in the yard, Ronnie ran to the fence and climbed
up to the strands of barbed wire. A guard with a bullhorn ordered
him down, but Ronnie slipped gingerly through the wire and
dropped to the ground on the other side. When he ran for the
woods, the guard's voice changed. It sounded as if he were beg-
ging him to stop. Then there was a shot from one of the towers,
and Ronnie fell in a sprawl, a small neat hole in his back, a big
ragged one in his chest where the shell had ripped through. That
evening he died in the infirmary at the Maryland Penitentiary.

When he heard the news of Ronnie's death, Wayne stayed in
his cell, lying there listening to the inmates in the hall.

"All I know is I've seen just two men get out of here. One
burned his cock off. The other was shot dead. So don't go telling
me this ain't no fucking jail. And don't go jiving me you're going
to talk your way out of here."

Wayne no longer had any illusions that he would soon be
released. The way he was going, he'd be lucky to stay alive. And
lucky for what, he wondered. To last another day, another
month, another year? For what? To watch that same fellow stand
in the window stroking his meat? To spend every waking hour
worried that he was about to be jumped? To lie awake every
night, thinking?

Not long before dark, the dealer, an older con, rapped on his
door, just as he did every night, and asked if Wayne needed any-

thing: cigarettes, beat-off books, dope, whiskey, pills? But all Wayne wanted was sleep.

"Gimme something that'll put me out," he said.

"Sure, baby. Feeling a little low? Try one of these yellow pills, and it'll pick you up."

"I don't want to be up. I want to sleep."

"Well, I got nine of these red birds. How many you need?"

"All of them."

For an instant, the man hesitated. "One or two'll do you."

"Are you selling or not?"

"Sure, baby. Just space them out. I'll get you some more next week."

When the man left, Wayne dropped the nine pills into his cup, filled it with water at the sink, and drank them all down. Then he lay back on his bunk. Although he had no idea what the pills were, he figured nine of them should do it. He would sleep the night through. And, if he got lucky, he'd never wake up.

Autumn 1978

1

The summer Wayne was convicted, my stepfather, Tommy Dunn, had to work nights. My mother had finally admitted her vision was blurring, and she frequently asked me to drive her down to Franklin Manor for meetings with the small group which was financing the appeal.

From the start, their discussions struck me as aimless and naïve. Sitting there silently, feeling smugly superior as one can only when he is eighteen and about to go off to college with the blind conviction that he already knows it all, I thought the talking should stop and the action should start. Or, if they insisted on talking, I wished they could be more incisive. Why couldn't they come out and say what the Dresbachs had been doing? There were words to describe it.

The legal system also struck me as longwinded and unreliable. All its labels seemed cut to fit somebody—anybody—other than Wayne. I remember listening to Marshall Levin, who wore white linen suits and spoke in a quiet urbane voice, as he emphasized the necessity of unearthing some technical error, some reason, for requesting a new trial. When I expressed the vehement opinion that the suppression of evidence about the Dresbachs was the error Levin should explore, he listened politely, but said little.

I found his attitude enigmatic, not realizing then that law itself is the enigma. Like my parents, I yearned for some dramatic revelation which would grant Wayne a new trial and guarantee that he would be acquitted—or, at least, get a lighter sentence. To us, this meant finding witnesses who knew the Dresbachs well, had seen what went on in the house, and were willing to testify.

For several months, then, my parents did some amateur sleuthing. They pumped Wayne and Lee for the names of family friends, but learned that the boys usually knew first names or nicknames. When at last they had a few names they could trace, they discovered they lacked the experience—much less the authority—to cross-examine people.

"There always came this awful moment," my mother remembers, "after they admitted they had been close to the Dresbachs and visited their home a lot, when the next question had to be, 'Did you know about the nudism and the wife-swapping and the orgies?' But I just couldn't ask it. I didn't believe they'd tell me the truth anyway. So I'd ask if they were willing to serve as character witnesses for Wayne in the second trial. I figured I'd turn a list of their names over to the lawyer and he could question them."

In the fall of 1978, I drew up a list which couldn't have differed much from the one my parents had compiled. And at first it wasn't any more productive than theirs had been. Some of the people I wanted to interview had died. A few had left the area and couldn't be located. Others refused to talk once they learned about the book I planned to write.

But then I telephoned a woman who sounded as if she had been expecting my call for the last seventeen years. Not that she was eager or excited; it was more as if she had been carrying around a heavy burden and was relieved to have someone to share it with her.

For reasons that will become obvious, she demanded anonymity. We'll call her Tina Commers. She is married and lives with her husband and children in one of those Washington suburbs where rolling farmland has been bulldozed of vegetation, then subdivided, and where the houses are bland and huge, and appear blander and bigger still because they are surrounded by newly planted shrubs which look perpetually stunted.

On a warm autumn afternoon, when her husband was at work and her children in school, Tina and I sat on her sundeck which looked out on a neighborhood of identical sundecks. Tall and blond, she might once have been beautiful, but time and children and work had coarsened her features and thickened her waist. Still, her green eyes hadn't faded, and she gazed out, unflinching, as if at the spot where she knew my questions were leading. At times, in her impatience to get there, she jumped ahead of me. I had to ease her back and take her step by step through the rumors and accusations I had heard about the Dresbachs.

First I wanted to know how she had met them.

"Pat handled a divorce for me a long, long time ago," Tina said. "He was very friendly and told me he wanted me to meet his wife. He thought we'd be good friends. He was right. I liked Shirley. When he was sober, I liked Pat, too. He was smart and lively and knew a lot of people. I met all kinds at his parties." She went on to mention several well-known Washington names.

"For me it started out as a good time. I was single again and didn't have any kids, and it all seemed very exciting, very glamorous. It wasn't till later that I learned how sick it was."

"Sick in what way?" I asked.

"Oh, Pat and Shirley had a lot of problems."

"What kind of problems?"

"If you've talked to anybody, you must have heard."

"I heard he drank, and they had fights," I said, deciding not to raise any questions about sex until I knew more about Tina.

"Yeah, they fought. Sometimes he acted like he hated her for the kind of family she came from. He said she thought she was too good for everybody. I never saw him do it, but Shirley claimed he'd knock her around when he got drunk.

"Another problem was money. He made a lot, but never as much as he liked people to think. That's why Shirley had to do income-tax work.

"But I guess the biggest thing was the kids. I don't know what caused more trouble; the kids they adopted or the ones they couldn't have. Pat used to say he'd pay any amount of money to have a child of his own. He'd say it right in front of Shirley. You can imagine how that hurt her. One time she screamed, 'You knew all along I couldn't have babies. Why the hell did you marry me?' Then she ran out of the house, and Pat said she was probably going off to try to commit suicide again. Maybe this time she'd make it."

"So he actually said that," I mumbled, struck by how closely her story agreed with what I had heard from others.

"Yeah, Pat could be one cruel bastard. And not just with his mouth, either. I remember the first time I saw how bad he could be. They had company at their place in Lanham, and a couple of kids were climbing in and out of a car. Then one of them slammed the car door on his hand, and the kid's fingers were crushed. It was obvious he had to go to the hospital.

"But Pat said, 'Hell no!' He didn't want to break up the party just because some kid was crying. He said you couldn't let children run your life. They were always whining about something. What he suggested was, wash the boy's hand and stick it in a bucket of ice, forget him and go on with the fun.

"It was like Pat didn't care about anyone else's pain. Of course, the kid's parents didn't listen to him. They rushed the boy to the emergency room. But I wanted to ask Shirley, 'Is Pat a sadist, or what?' Then, when I had sex with him, I found out."

Noticing some reaction on my part, Tina paused. "You knew about Pat and me, didn't you?"

Concerned that she might be testing me, I admitted I didn't. I said I had heard rumors about the Dresbachs' affairs, but nothing about her.

"I thought somebody must have told you," Tina said. "It's no big deal. Pat ran around a lot. He kept a little apartment downtown where he took women during the day."

"Is that where you went?"

"No, it was always at his house. I'd come for the weekend."

"While Shirley was away in Europe?"

"No, she was there. That was the screwy part. She was always there. The three of us were in their living room the first night Pat asked me to have sex with him. I thought he was joking. But Shirley told me to go ahead. She didn't mind. She seemed to like the idea. While she was cheering me on, Pat took off his clothes.

"He wanted to do it right there on the floor. I asked about the boys. But Shirley said they were upstairs asleep; they had strict instructions not to come down when there was company. So I did it. I don't know why. Partly I was scared, partly I was excited, really excited. And the two of them were so insistent.

"Like I say, that's when I learned just what a sadist Pat was. He didn't waste any time. He bit me and scratched me and slapped me on the breasts and in the face. I started crying and begged him to stop. Stop everything. But he kept on until he was finished, and I was nearly hysterical."

"What was Shirley doing?"

"Sitting there watching."

"Do you think she liked it? The rough stuff, I mean?"

"I don't know. I don't see how anybody could. But she didn't stop him. Never said a word. Afterward, I was still sobbing and said I was leaving. But suddenly Pat got very tender, like seeing me in pain turned him on. He said if he'd known I didn't like it, he wouldn't have done it. From now on things would be different."

"Were they?"

"Most of the time. Oh, some things were the same. Shirley was always there."

"Just watching?"

"No, sometimes she came down on the floor with us. The three of us became very close. It was almost a family thing, and there were these little rituals we went through. Pat liked to take bubble baths, and he wanted us to sniff him and say he smelled like perfume or flowers. And he was a little guy, you know, but he thought he was very well equipped, so you had to notice that and say something flattering."

"After that first time he never beat you?"

"No, but I saw him do it to other women. At parties he'd go wild. He'd throw down this white rug in front of the fireplace, grab a girl, and start things off. Pretty soon everybody would be down there with them.

"Not me, though. I never went for group sex, no matter how much Pat tried to drag me in. The three of us was my limit. He used to show me these pictures he took of daisy chains. He said they once had thirteen couples linked up that way and there was always room for one more. But I wouldn't do it. I didn't like it and I didn't like all Pat's pictures and movies. That was never a turn-on for me."

"Did he have a lot of pornography?"

"God, yes. He had everything you can imagine. There were people who traveled to his place from all over to see the stuff."

"Did he sell it?"

"I don't know. I was never in the market myself."

"You say you didn't like the pornography or the group sex or his sadism. Why'd you keep coming back?"

"I don't know anymore. I guess because it was exciting, it was different. And I was young and alone, and they showed me a lot of attention. You know," she said irritably, "no matter what people have told you about them, the Dresbachs weren't monsters."

I didn't reply, and a few moments later when Tina resumed speaking, the edge of defiance had died from her voice.

"I actually liked Shirley and the boys better than Pat. Sometimes I'd go to their house for the weekend, and we'd party Friday and Saturday night. But the best time was Sunday morning. I'd get up early and fix breakfast for Wayne and Lee. Then, before long, Shirley would wake up and we'd all sit around the table and talk. It was nice."

"Were you still involved with them when they were killed?"

"No. We were in touch. We talked on the telephone. But that was about all. It had got to be too much for me. Pat wouldn't quit pushing. He pushed other people and he pushed himself. I don't know what he was after. Maybe just whatever he hadn't done before. I couldn't go the whole distance with him. I don't know who could put up with all the tricks he pulled."

"What tricks?"

"Well, after a while, when I thought we were pretty close, he started setting me up with other men. Or trying to, anyway. He'd have a friend or business associate in town and he'd ask me to date the guy. The first thing the guy would do after dinner is grab for me. I told Pat damn quick, I'm no call girl, no whore. I'm not going to ball somebody just because he's in business with you.

"He pulled the same stunt with other women, I learned. Then one time he tried to marry me off to this old man, this retired Army general. He said the guy was rich and would take good care of me. He must have been seventy-five. Maybe he had offered Pat money to find him a woman. I don't know. I told him I didn't want to hear anything more about it.

"Then Pat made me a proposal himself. Not for marriage. He asked me to have a baby with him. He said he had done it twice before. He claimed Wayne and Lee were his sons and he had paid some woman $3,000 to have them. That's what he offered me."

"Wait a minute," I said. "Are you sure about that? About Dresbach being their father?"

"That's what he told me. I didn't know whether to believe him, though, because later on, when Wayne was causing him a lot of trouble, he changed his story. He still said he was Lee's father, but not Wayne's. Me, I always thought both boys looked like him."

As I tried to digest this news, I stared at Tina and realized that she, too, bore some resemblance to Lee and Wayne. "Are you their mother?"

She laughed.

"I mean it. There are ways I can check this out," I said with far more certainty than I felt.

"Look, that's crazy. Their mother doesn't look anything like me."

"How do you know?"

"I've met her. I saw her a few times at Pat and Shirley's."

"Doing what?"

"She was there for a party and when she left, Pat told me who she was."

"And you believed him?"

"Why would he lie about something like that?"

"He told other people a different story. He said she never knew who had adopted the boys."

"Oh, she knew all right. I heard her asking about Wayne and Lee."

I was anxious for more information about this woman—her name, her age, appearance—but Tina claimed she didn't remember. After several minutes of futile probing, I asked why she thought Dresbach wanted to have a baby by her.

"I don't know. I just know he kept harping on the subject."

"But he never said why he wanted more children?"

"No. I wondered about that myself, and I had a few suspicions."

"What suspicions?"

"Well, whenever he saw a girl ten or eleven years old, he'd make a filthy remark. He told friends who had kids that it wouldn't be long before they could bring them to his parties. Then one weekend a couple showed up with their son. I don't know how old he was. Maybe seventeen or eighteen. He was tall and gawky, the way some boys are at that age, and he kept hanging around, not saying anything, just watching the women.

"I was wondering—worried, really—whether his parents were going to let him stay until Pat threw down the white rug and got it on with somebody. But the boy's mother didn't wait for that. She stripped and called the boy down on the floor with her and . . . they did it. Oral sex. You know, sixty-nine. And everybody, including the father, stood around watching."

"What did you do?" I asked.

"I got the hell out of there. That was too kinky for me. I went upstairs. After an hour or so, I left the bedroom to go to the bathroom and that boy broke in on me and said he wanted to fuck. When I told him no, he backed me into a corner, got me by the throat, and started choking. I think he might have raped me or killed me if Pat and his father hadn't heard me struggling and pulled him away.

"After that, I'd had it. I saw Pat and Shirley every once in a while, but I didn't want to get involved again. I knew sooner or later something horrible was going to happen, and I was worried about Wayne and Lee. What I worried was whether Pat planned to drag them in on his parties the way that crazy couple did their boy. You know, he had already taken them to nudist camps. Maybe he wanted to have more kids and do the same thing with them.

"Well, who knows what he had in mind? He was a strange man, Pat. But I was right about one thing, wasn't I? Something horrible did happen. When I heard the news I can't say I was surprised."

"Did you ever contact anybody and tell them what you knew about the Dresbachs?"

She gave me a sidelong glance, then shook her head.

"And no one contacted you?"

"Yeah, somebody called and asked if I'd be a character witness for Wayne. But I never heard from them again."

"Would you have testified?"

"I suppose if they had put me up on the stand under oath, I'd have had to talk. But I wasn't about to volunteer. You see, by that time, I was remarried and had a baby and I didn't want to ruin my life. You can understand that, can't you? I wasn't sure my testimony would have helped anyway. What do you think?"

2

The obvious people to answer Tina's question were the State's attorney, the attorneys for the defense, and the judge. In separate interviews with each man, I asked whether an eyewitness account of the Dresbachs' behavior, with particular emphasis on Pat's sadism, his dealings in pornography and procurement, and Shirley's acquiescence in all this, would have made a difference at Wayne's trial.

Although he still has offices on a side street across from the courthouse in Annapolis, Albert Goodman has more or less retired. He has left the bulk of his practice to Theodore Bloom and confines himself to a few cases he handles for people he knows well. But after reviewing his files, he agreed to make a special trip to the office to talk with me. That morning in September he wore a beige leisure suit, a string tie, and a bolo made of silver and a chunk of turquoise—a flamboyant outfit for the aging, sunburnt little man.

One impression emerged clearly from Goodman's remarks; he had a sense that he had been treated shabbily. When the case fell into his lap, he pointed out, Wayne had been in jail two months without legal representation and had repeatedly confessed his guilt. Goodman and Bloom had had to fight a rear-guard action, gathering whatever evidence might support a plea of insanity.

Under the circumstances, Goodman felt he had done all that was possible, and it angered him to hear that anybody believed he had bungled the trial, or that there might have been a conspiracy against Wayne. He reiterated that he barely knew Harold Malone Dresbach, had had only the most formal contacts with Nathaniel Blaustein, and had never met C. J. Pettit or any other friends or associates of Pat and Shirley. How could anyone imagine there had been a cover-up when he had worked so hard to introduce evidence against the Dresbachs?

Goodman also said he had been irritated and insulted when he wasn't allowed to carry through with an appeal and wasn't consulted by Father Dawson and his group before they replaced him with Marshall Levin. Considering all the effort he had expended, he didn't feel he had been adequately appreciated. "Afterward I never heard from Wayne. Never even got a thank-you note or anything."

When the discussion turned to the Dresbachs, and I told him what Tina Commers had revealed, he was appalled. Apparently, even Lieutenant Smith's investigation had not produced such sordid details. Goodman said that anybody privy to this information should have come forward and helped defend Wayne. He felt they were under moral and ethical obligation to do so.

But as for whether this would have made a difference at the trial, that was a difficult question. Or, to be precise, the difficulty was to predict whether the judge would have ruled it admissible. Given the temper of the times in 1961 and the conservative character of the county, Goodman had no doubt that information so unfavorable to the Dresbachs would have helped Wayne. The jury might well have reached a verdict of second-degree murder or manslaughter. But, once again, the critical question was whether Judge Michaelson would have permitted him to explore the matter in any depth. After all, he had refused to let Lieutenant Smith testify, and Albert Goodman feared that this new evidence would also have been stricken.

Since Osborne Duvall was dead—at age fifty-seven he discovered he had cancer and moved back in with his wife and sons to die at home—I called John Blondell, who had been an assistant State's attorney in 1961. Now in private practice, Blondell laughingly described himself as having been "a young punk absolutely in awe of Ozzie Duvall and Albert Goodman." Yet, although he stressed that Duvall had run the case, he recalled the issues and quickly summed them up.

Since Wayne never denied killing his parents, the only question was whether it had been self-defense—which no one claimed —or whether the defendant was legally insane—which none of the psychiatrists said he was. Thus evidence about the Dresbachs' private lives, no matter how lurid, was irrelevant, and Blondell believed that the State's attorney would have objected—and objected strenuously—to any defense strategy which attempted to put the parents, not the boy, on trial. Despite Wayne's age and the Dresbachs' squalid personal lives, Duvall had done what he saw as the duty of his office. He had an indictment for first-degree murder, a strong case, and he wanted to win it.

Theodore Bloom, who played an active role assisting Goodman during the trial, is a cheerful extroverted man, quick with a joke, quick with a grin. Yet behind the good humor, behind horn-rimmed glasses, he has the sly, clever eyes of a raccoon. Nothing seems to slip by him. He said he always felt a great deal of sympathy for Wayne and continued to do *pro bono* work for him while he was in Patuxent Institute. But his assessment of the situation corroborated John Blondell's.

"On a human level, what happened at home affected the boy. It shaped him in some way. It upset him and angered him. But in legal terms the question is strictly whether that drove him insane —insane as described by the M'Naghten Rule, where he didn't have the ability to distinguish between right and wrong and couldn't assist in his own defense. Well, you've read the transcript. Psychiatrists on both sides swore he wasn't insane. And that was that."

Anything else, Bloom patiently explained, was beside the point. In his opinion it didn't matter what the Dresbachs did at home. It didn't much matter what was in Lieutenant Smith's report. It would have been pointless to introduce character witnesses for Wayne. "What could they have said?" Bloom asked. "That he was a killer with good character? What we needed was someone to say he was insane."

The morning I arrived for my meeting with Benjamin Michaelson, he had forgotten it and was still in bed. While I waited in the living room of his large, well-appointed home in Severna Park, his wife awakened him and, fifteen minutes later, the judge lumbered downstairs, scowling through his glasses.

Once I explained who I was, his memory improved, but he was apt to have clearer recollections of distant events than of what had happened yesterday. He staunchly maintained that he had never known the Dresbachs and he did not believe he had spoken to Wayne that evening in 1961 when the boy had been brought to his house in shackles. Or, if he had said something, it wasn't anything that should have disqualified him from the case.

Then, ruminating in a general fashion about the trial, he characterized it as "tragic," but said he had had no choice except to sentence Wayne to life in prison. In his opinion, nothing I told him excused the killings and he would never have allowed the defense to introduce a lot of "irrelevant hearsay information." Maybe if Pat and Shirley had forced the boys to participate in their sexual activities, maybe then there would have been some grounds for self-defense or a reduced charge.

But short of that . . . well, it was "tragic. A boy like that from a good home sent to jail for life." Even the transfer to Patuxent Institute hadn't made things much better since, as Michaelson admitted, in those days, Patuxent wasn't all it should have been. But what could he do? His hands were tied. Society just couldn't condone that sort of thing, no matter how badly the boy "thought" he had been mistreated.

3

Bewildered by these interviews, I drove to my parents' house in suburban Washington, thinking it was not possible that in the period of a few days I had discovered what seemed to be significant information, only to learn then that it was inadmissible, legally useless. As I repeated to my mother what I had heard, I realized that, in spelling things out for her, I was actually trying to assimilate them myself.

I told her that despite our years of suspicion, despite the whispers and innuendos from so many sources, there might not have been a cover-up. In all likelihood, the police and lawyers had not done more digging into the Dresbachs' private affairs because they believed that was irrelevant.

"What do you mean? What about the things that Commers woman told you?" my mother asked. "Those parties and the pornography and—"

"They don't matter."

"Don't matter?" she demanded. "How could they not matter? Think of all the awful things he was exposed to. And what about the things his father did to him? The beatings and punishments. He was a battered child. Look at these battered wives you read about who shoot their husbands. They get to introduce evidence about the physical and emotional abuse they've been through. Why wouldn't that be just as valid—more valid—for a child?"

I shook my head. "I don't know. Maybe I asked the wrong people. Maybe I shouldn't have gone back to the lawyers and the judge who tried the case. I might have gotten a different answer from somebody else."

"Why, that's outrageous," she said. "Why should you have to go comparison shopping to get justice?"

"Well, attitudes change. Interpretations of the law change. Different lawyers have different styles, different abilities."

She didn't want to hear it. She fell silent, and her nostrils flared and her face hardened into an expression of anger I had feared as a child. Although now over sixty, she is still no one to cross. Physically she may have yielded some ground over the years, but the intensity of her emotions can be daunting.

When she spoke again, her voice was calm at first, then gradually gained heat. "I suppose after all this time I should feel relieved. I should think, well, at least I know now he got a fair trial and it didn't matter that those people who were buddies with the Dresbachs didn't come forward and help. But I feel worse. I don't care what those lawyers and the judge said. How can anybody claim Wayne got a fair deal?

"I'll tell you, I'd rather believe there was a conspiracy than think our system of justice could do something like this to a fifteen-year-old boy. What they're saying is that a child doesn't have any real rights, doesn't have any way to protect himself. His parents can do any damn thing to him, and he has to take it. You call that fair? That's legal? Okay, then I'm a criminal because I'm still on Wayne's side!"

After

1

Nine red birds were not enough. For two days Wayne drifted in a semi-conscious state, dreamless and incoherent. Then he woke with a thundering headache and an enormous hunger.

He never attempted suicide again. To this day, he cannot explain why. Ultimately, under desperate circumstances, perhaps the decision not to kill oneself is as inexplicable as the decision to do so. But whatever his reasons, Wayne remained alive through ordeals and disappointments that might have unhinged older, presumably stronger men.

Immediately after making up his mind not to commit suicide, he had to decide whether to "get married." He had had proposals. And threats. A few inmates had offered cigarettes and companionship. Bigger ones had promised protection and warned him he'd never survive alone. But Wayne went his own way and started lifting weights, hoping that muscle, along with his reputation as a killer, would keep him safe. Although he would never grow taller than 5′7″, he gained forty pounds, most of it packed onto his shoulders, biceps, and chest, and eventually resembled a miniature Arnold Schwarzenegger.

With the same numbing, metronomical rhythm as he pumped iron, he began "doing time"—an expression that can have little meaning to anyone who hasn't been in prison, serving an indeterminate sentence. The public documents—the graphs and reports in his files—may appear to chart a course or indicate progress. But to Wayne they seemed random, pointless, repetitious. Like the exercises—tens of thousands of curls, reverse curls, dead lifts, and bench presses—that filled out his body, the tests, therapy sessions, and academic and vocational courses were at first only excuses for filling up his days. He didn't believe they were leading anywhere. For someone with his sentence, where could they lead? He was just killing time before it killed him.

Meanwhile, Marshall Levin filed an appeal, basing it on the
question of whether Judge Benjamin Michaelson had committed
a reversible error when he remarked:

> I don't like to say this. You have a two way sword. He killed
> his mother. He didn't protect his mother. All the testimony
> about what the mother and father did I don't think is
> relevant at all. If he favored one in preference to the other it
> might have some bearing on it.

Levin argued that this statement had prejudiced the jury, particularly since Wayne wasn't on trial for his mother's death.

But on April 27, 1962, the Court of Appeals of Maryland ruled
that, since no objection had been raised at the time of Michaelson's remark, "the question is not properly before us for review."
Then it added: "Even if the matter was properly before us a
different result would not follow" since the record disclosed that
Michaelson's comment had occurred after Wayne's confession
had been admitted into evidence and after he had acknowledged
that he had killed both parents. Thus the judge had not revealed
to the jury anything they did not know.

Deeply disappointed, Father Dawson had the ordeal of driving
to Patuxent Institute and telling Wayne the bad news. There
could be no more false encouragement now, no more optimism
that the boy would be out of jail soon. Since they had failed in
their efforts to finance this appeal through donations, Father
Dawson knew better than to promise they would carry it to a
higher court. It seemed to him their last chance was lost; yet he
tried to hold his own emotions in check so he wouldn't upset
Wayne any more than was inevitable.

They met in the visiting room, and Father Dawson wanted to
be affectionate with him, to comfort him as he would any child
whose hopes had been dashed.

"I said, 'Wayne, I'm sorry it didn't go through. But I hope
you'll understand how much all of us care for you and love you.
We're still with you.'"

As a priest, Father Dawson had had a lot of practice offering
condolences, but he thought that no matter what was said, it

sounded inadequate. For a moment he shared Wayne's frustration at not being able to convey the full depth of his feelings.

But then, through his own stinging eyes, he saw Wayne's pupils blur and two perfect tears trickle down the boy's cheeks. Hastily he blotted them; more tears followed.

"I thought he was crying because the appeal had failed, and I didn't blame him. But as he went on sobbing, I realized it was because of what I had said, because he understood we all loved him and weren't about to abandon him. After that, our relationship changed. It wasn't so hard to get through to him.

"I'm not saying things turned around overnight. There had been too many years when his parents discouraged him from showing emotion. But down deep Wayne had always been a feeling person. Even on his worst days, the times when he looked so lost and shut into himself, I could sense his yearning. He might not have been able to express it, but I knew he appreciated what people were doing for him.

"And no matter what those psychiatrists said about his lack of affect, he was very warm. I think the thing that set him apart from the Dresbachs and explains why they were so cruel to him was that he was emotional. For people like them, sentiment was a weakness, an encumbrance. I really believe they hated and tormented him for that as much as anything, and it left him ravenous for contact with people.

"I encouraged him to discuss his feelings. I urged him to keep a personal journal. That never worked out. But I got him to write letters. He was very faithful about it. They weren't masterpieces. In fact, they were sad enough to make you cry when you knew what he had been through. Look at this. It's like he had to bleed out each word." He produced one of Wayne's letters, written several weeks after the appeal failed.

Father Dawson,

Just came in from watching television and thought I'd write.

I got a visit yesterday from Mr. and Mrs. Dunn and Karen.

I'm reading a real good book right now, it is "The War of the Worlds" by H. G. Wells.

I don't like to leave [a] so-called letter this short, but I honestly cannot think of anything else to write. I'll try better next time, okay?

Your friend,
Wayne

2

Stratified into four tiers, Patuxent Institute runs generally according to behaviorist theory, with reinforcements given for good conduct and the appropriate response to treatment. As an inmate advances from one tier to another, he enjoys more freedom and better facilities until finally, on the fourth tier, the prisoners virtually govern their own lives. They spend less time locked in, and are allowed to decorate their cells with plants, pictures, and personal belongings which are forbidden on lower levels. There is also a game room where inmates entertain visitors and throw an annual Christmas party. During the summer months, inmates on the fourth tier are permitted to go out onto the front lawn every Sunday and picnic with their families and friends. Patuxent Institute even provides tables and brightly colored umbrellas. But each man's case is reviewed every six months, and his privileges can be revoked for infractions of the rules or a failure to make progress in therapy.

For Wayne, the problem was getting started. He began working in the kitchen and taking courses toward his high school equivalency certificate. But in group therapy he could not bring himself to speak. It wasn't just that he didn't care to discuss his crime or the darker secrets of his childhood. He didn't want to reveal anything at all about himself. Already the other inmates knew too much about him, and he felt they used it against him.

Because of the way he spoke, because of his relatively privileged background, many of them accused him of being a snob. "I remember one guy in group therapy saying, 'You little asshole, you had it made. You had a good family and money and a nice house. And you blew it. You just fucking blew it!' How could I convince the guy, who probably came from a slum somewhere, that those things don't matter, that I hadn't had it any better than him?

"There was no way I could win. Whenever I talked in therapy, they accused me of sounding like a stuck-up bastard. And if I kept quiet, they asked, 'What's the matter? You too good to talk to us?' Before long I got the message. They were going to keep jumping on my case until I dropped everything I had picked up at home and school and in the neighborhood. Well, one thing I learned, I'm adaptable. You can turn into a goddamn chameleon if it's a question of surviving."

In addition to continuing his weight training, he took on protective coloration in the form of more jailhouse tattoos—two blue dots, like snake eyes, on the soft pad of flesh between his thumb and first finger, five dots on his wrist, and a wicked-looking dagger on his left forearm with "Life" at the hilt and "Death" at the tip.

Then his teeth started going bad. Perhaps it was the prison diet or inadequate dental care. Wayne never knew for sure. But by the time he was twenty he had nothing left except a mouthful of black, aching stumps, and he looked like any other low-rent con in the joint.

He talked like them, too. Good grammar deserted him, his slang was now of the slammer, not the schoolyard, and he peppered every sentence with obscenities. "The thing is, you don't want to be different. You don't want to stand out and become a target."

Soon he pretended to share all the assumptions of the other prisoners. Blacks were "niggers," people to hate, avoid, or fight, if necessary. He mastered the subtleties of sexual discrimination. "Real queers," he was taught, should be treated with contempt, unlike "real men" who could have sex together as long as they understood it was only because there were no women.

But personally he thought better of the "real queers" than he did of some "real men" who would yoke you around the neck and rape you. And although he professed to feel contempt for child molesters, he tells of a poignant incident at Patuxent.

"The guy had been there about a year. Everybody liked him, but nobody really knew him well. He kept to himself. The way he talked, he must have been heavy upstairs. A college man maybe.

And he could play every musical instrument from a goddamn zither to a saxophone. What he did best, he played the guitar and once he started, it was—nice college word—*mesmerizing!* The television went off and everybody sat down and damn well listened.

"The funny thing was, he couldn't sing. He just played. Strange. All the different kinds of music he made, but he couldn't carry a tune singing.

"Well then, a new guy came on the tier, somebody who knew this guitar player and knew he was in for child molesting, and the new guy right away kicked the story around the joint, and that finished it. One day the guitar player was everybody's favorite; the next day he was shit.

"After that he stayed in his cell. You'd hear him in there alone picking and playing, but people pretended not to listen. They liked that music, but they wanted no part of him. A shame. I sort of felt sorry for him sometimes when I thought about it."

3

In fall of 1963, Wayne was released from Patuxent Institute for an afternoon. He spent it in court, "being sued by Lee, Pettit, and Blaustein," he says. Actually, it was a hearing to determine his right to inherit from the Dresbach estate. But since his brother, his guardian, and the counsel for his guardian sat on one side of the room while Wayne and his court-appointed lawyer, Theodore Bloom, were on the other side, he saw it as an adversary proceeding. Perhaps if somebody had explained the legal necessity of this hearing, Wayne would not have felt so hurt and ill-used. But it struck him as another betrayal and a final severing of his ties to those who had been close to the Dresbachs.

After Judge Matthew Evans decreed that he should "not inherit from, or in any way participate in the distribution of the estates of his deceased parents," Wayne never again saw C. J. Pettit, although for years the man continued to be listed as his guardian and theoretically was still the protector of his "interests" and "person."

Nathaniel Blaustein, he recalls, visited once more. In the late 60s Lee dropped out of college, joined the Air Force, and was stationed in Vietnam. But before he shipped out, he showed up at Patuxent with Blaustein. "They said they'd made out some kind of legal document," Wayne remembers, "a tentative will or something, and in the event Lee was killed over there, if I was still in jail, I'd get five dollars a month. There wasn't any provision I remember for my getting anything if I was out and Lee died. It was only if I was incarcerated.

"Five dollars a month! I said, 'I don't need that shit.' It hurt me, matter of fact. I knew what kind of money Lee inherited, and it was a chunk. I could *bum* five dollars a month! There were guys in the joint that would give me that much."

Perhaps it was inevitable that the two brothers would grow apart and that the course of their lives could be plotted on a graph that charted the divergent influences of heredity and environment, nature and nurture. While one boy groped through adolescence in prison, the other attended a private high school, then a series of colleges. While Wayne forced himself to join the discussions in group therapy, continued pumping iron, and kept an eye open for the junkies, rapists or psychopaths who might attack him, Lee joined a fraternity, took up golf and tennis, and worked summers as a water-ski instructor. His huge upper torso a mural of tattoos, his mouth full of rotten teeth, Wayne no longer looked much like his brother. Yet he felt Lee should have made a greater effort to stay in touch.

After all, each boy was the other's only known blood relative, and despite their present differences, they shared early childhood secrets and a close common bond with the Dunn family. Lee had left the McCrackens in 1963 and was now living with Mary Helen and Tommy and their children.

But Wayne maintains that although the Dunns visited him every Sunday, Lee seldom was with them. "It seemed he was always busy. Total times he came to see me all the years I was in jail I could count on both hands. And then he never stayed till the end of the hour. I used to time him. Once he stayed eleven minutes. The record, though, was seven minutes. He had to go play golf.

"There was only once he spent any real time with me and that was the first year I was on fourth tier and he came up for the

Christmas party. He was never concerned about me. Like if I needed money, he'd never ask. Christ knows I needed it, but I couldn't count on him for anything. Look at the records—it's all in my files—how often he visited and what he gave me."

The Equity files at the Annapolis Courthouse reveal some interesting figures about the disbursements from the Dresbach estate.

From April 1963 until April 1966, Lee owned a Fiat convertible, then an Austin-Healy roadster, then a Ford sedan, which was destroyed in an accident. Afterward, he bought a new Volkswagen Beetle, but weeks later, it, too, was wrecked. So Lee purchased yet another new Volkswagen, and a year later had another accident. In that three-year period, he spent over $5,000 on cars, while giving Wayne gifts totaling $63.03.

"Don't ask me to explain it," Mary Helen Dunn says. "I never understood the way Lee and Wayne got along. Or didn't get along. I have three sons and I'd hate to think of them treating each other like that. What am I saying, three sons? I had five sons! Lee and Wayne were like my own. That's why it hurt to see trouble between them. Lee told me that as soon as he turned twenty-one, he was going to share his inheritance with Wayne. But he never did.

"I don't like to criticize. It must have been hell to survive a childhood like his. I mean, if their home life was bad enough to drive Wayne to murder, then I guess it's understandable that Lee would rather forget it all, forget even his own brother. I know the whole time he was with us he used to have horrible nightmares and we'd find him sleepwalking all over the house. Sometimes he'd be wandering around with his pillow and blanket, like he was searching for a place to rest.

"Still, I didn't see why he couldn't do more to help his brother. Or to help us, for that matter. Helping Wayne would have helped us.

"You know, we had four kids, all going through high school and college, and I had to work full time and Tommy had two jobs. Over the years, looking out for Wayne got to be harder and harder, and it was a hell of a strain on our nerves and what little savings we had.

"Almost every Sunday we drove up to visit him and it was a round trip of fifty miles and we always tried to take him something. At Christmas he'd send us a list of things he needed. It was just what you'd buy for a kid going off to college: towels and face cloths and toiletries and cigarettes and snack foods. During the summer, we'd fix picnic lunches for him and, I guarantee you, when Wayne was lifting weights, he ate more than my whole family put together. I've seen him polish off a dozen pieces of chicken. Or he'd ask us to bring six of those roast beef sandwiches from Arby's and he'd eat them along with a big bowl of potato salad. Then he started calling over his friends who didn't have families; before long, I felt like we were feeding the whole prison.

"It added up, believe me. And that's when it was hard to accept Lee's attitude. Here we were doing all we could for Wayne. Father Dawson visited and sent gifts, and so did the Talberts and the McCrackens. But his own brother and his guardian, both of them loaded with dough, were doing next to nothing. It ate at me more and more, and Lee and I started fighting about that and a lot of other things I don't want to go into. Finally he left and went to live in his fraternity house."

For the Dunns, the years since the Dresbachs' murders have been marked by setbacks, hardships, and losses about which they seldom speak and never complain. Mary Helen went virtually blind in her left eye, retaining only peripheral vision, and the family had to give up the cottage. As Mary Helen explains, it had become too difficult and expensive to look after two houses. "I won't kid you. I miss the beach. Losing the cottage was about as bad as losing my eye. But after I learned what the Dresbachs were like, and after all the bad memories, I couldn't bring myself to go down there anymore anyway."

Then Tommy had to take an early disability retirement. From countless days of walking the damp concrete floors of the laundry, and almost as many nights of standing on sore feet behind the bar at Bachelor Officers' Quarters, he developed chronic, painful back problems which forced him to resign.

Still, the Dunns prefer to talk about better times, pleasanter subjects. Their home is decorated with photographs of their children and grandchildren. As they sift through family memorabilia, they proudly show snapshots of Wayne. In Mary Helen's favorite, he is seven years old and smiling broadly as he sits on his pure white horse, Snowflake.

Tommy points to the program for "Graduation Ceremonies at Patuxent Institute." On August 20, 1965, Wayne received his certificate of high school equivalence.

"After all those years," Mary Helen says, "it wasn't just Wayne who was like one of our family. We got to know the guards and the doctors, and when we came up for picnics, half the time they didn't bother to check what we had in our baskets. One day we brought a watermelon for dessert, and when Wayne and his friends were ready to eat it, I reached into my purse and pulled out this huge butcher knife. All around me I heard these inmates kind of sigh or groan like they'd been hit in the belly. Wayne went completely white and whispered, 'Mom, put that back in your purse. Right now!' He was petrified they'd think I was smuggling the knife in to him. He forgot all about the watermelon. So did his friends. They drifted away damn quick. We left and I tried to act very casual, but I was scared stiff and couldn't imagine how I'd explain it if they found that knife. Fortunately, they didn't check us."

Then Mary Helen leafs through all the cards and letters Wayne sent her. "He never forgot my birthday. He never let Mother's Day or Valentine's Day go by without writing."

Like Father Dawson, she admits that his first efforts were cramped and short, as if he couldn't choke out what he meant to say. Sometimes he compensated by including a poem he had clipped from the newspaper, underlining the parts that most appealed to him.

Things That Count

The laughter shared with loved ones . . . the soft eyes
dimmed by tears . . . these things you will remember . . .
throughout the fading years . . . the times when nothing
mattered save for the fun at hand . . . these are the tender
moments . . . all hearts can understand . . . the happy hours
of childhood . . . are high upon the list . . . shining like a

beacon light . . . through time's hazy mist . . . *and last of all is mother's love . . . forever paramount* . . . these are life's priceless treasures . . . the things that really count . . .

Eventually, however, Wayne got better at expressing his feelings and his letters became longer, more introspective, and unabashedly sentimental—even though he knew each one would be read by a prison censor. June 12, 1966, he wrote to Mary Helen.

Dearest Mom,

I don't quite know what to write, to tell you the truth, Mom. It was truly a wonderful visit. I've never known such a feeling of togetherness with anyone as I knew yesterday with you all. More than any other time, I had the feeling of being a part of something—it gave me a sense of closeness, a family feeling. There's so much more I could say, Mom, but I just can't explain it on paper. You know me well enough to know what I mean, though, don't you?

I was watching Pat and Ellen [Mary Helen's oldest son and his wife] and they looked so happy. They make a good couple. They seemed to go together so well. I know they'll be very happy. I wonder how I'll feel when I'm about to get married? Oh well, it's not going to be for quite a few years, I know that much. That statement sounds like I can't face the responsibilities of marriage, doesn't it? That's right though, partly—not now anyway; but I will be when I decide to get married, I know that.

I almost burned up last night after I came in from the visit. The sun fried me like I was an egg. My face, arms, and the back of my neck—I could hardly sleep last night. The burn was worth it, though—such a great visit, I just can't get over it. I felt as though we were all one, you know what I mean? A real family feeling.

Well, I guess I'll have a cup of coffee. I just wish I could be sitting with you drinking coffee. We will though, someday.

That's about all for now, okay? Thanks for such a wonderful day, Mom! I love you!!!

4

The day when Wayne would sit down with Mary Helen and drink a cup of coffee began to seem as distant and unimaginable as the morning he had killed his adoptive parents. After his initial resistance, he had made rapid progress in therapy and reached the fourth tier in less than four years. The next step should have been work release, then parole, but although everyone agreed he was a model prisoner, a hard worker with high morale, nobody was willing to take the risk of releasing him.

Each year as the authorities at Patuxent went through the motions of reviewing his case, a social worker arrived at the Dunns' house to count bedrooms and measure the floor space and inquire whether they were still willing to let Wayne live with them. They always swore they were, and then they waited for the inevitable phone call—the one which Wayne was allowed to make as a kind of consolation prize. Hiding his disappointment, never expressing any anger, he would call and say that he had been denied parole again.

Ten times he was turned down. Five years he was stuck in the same place, on the fourth tier, like a blunt needle thudding along in the same groove. The Talbert, Dunn, and McCracken children finished school, left home, got married. The 60s unspooled like some frenetic film run at three times normal speed. John Kennedy was assassinated. Johnson beat Goldwater and bombed North Vietnam. At night, when Wayne plugged in his earphones, he thought he had tuned in another planet. All the rock stars were British, the language had changed. The newspapers and TV carried pictures of men with hair to their shoulders and women with dresses a foot above the knee. The war took over television and people threatened to bring it home. Martin Luther King was killed; then Robert Kennedy; then people stopped counting. Lee went off to Vietnam in 1968 and came back a year later. But Wayne was still in jail, killing time.

Speaking of those years at Patuxent, he displays surprisingly little bitterness. "I got a good education—school-wise and otherwise. I got my high school diploma. I know I read a book a day the whole time I was on fourth tier—from westerns to science fiction to the classics. We had a Great Books club and I read Socrates, Plato, the works. I studied radio and TV repair. My job was to keep all the TV's and radios in the joint going. I painted. I learned to play the guitar and drive a car. Every vehicle they had at Patuxent, I knew how to drive.

"I learned from the whole thing. I like to think I turned out halfway decent. Christ knows what would have happened if I had done hard time at the Maryland pen. Probably I'd have ended up getting raped or killed, or I'd have had to kill somebody. When I look at it like that, I realize I was damn lucky. I was in a place where I could make it day to day. There were people in the joint who I cared about and who cared about me. And I had people on the outside supporting me. Just knowing they were there and I could write them and talk to them every once in a while was enough to get me through.

"I ain't saying it was easy. Jail's jail. It isn't meant to be easy. And there wasn't a day that passed that I didn't think about what I done. First thing in the morning, last thing at night, there it was right in front of me. I know what kind of people my parents were, but what I did . . . well, that was the worst thing anybody can do. Sometimes it seemed to me it didn't matter how much time I served, it wasn't enough. Nothing would ever be enough.

"I had a lot of empty hours to chew on that thought. For years after I killed them, I never slept through the night—not unless I was bombed on red birds or something. What my normal pattern was, I'd go to bed at eleven or twelve, then at five of three—exactly five of three every morning—my eyes would pop open and I'd be wide awake. Don't ask me why; I just couldn't get back to sleep. So I'd get up in the dark and put some instant coffee in my cup, then turn on the water in the sink as hot as it would go and try to fix a cup of coffee. Then I'd just stand and stare out at the fucking window and maybe cry in my coffee. Many's the time they'd come around to wake us up for breakfast and I'd still be standing there, thinking.

"That time of night there isn't much else to do except think. After all the clanging and banging and screaming during the day, it was eerie. You see, there wouldn't be a sound anywhere in jail. It was like I was locked up there all alone. But from my cell I could look out to the road—Route 175—and I'd see cars speeding by and you couldn't help but play these little games in your head. Wondering about the people in the cars and where they were going and whether they were happy and why you couldn't be out there on the road with them. That's all I wanted—to be going someplace. If I couldn't sleep, if I couldn't forget what I done, I at least wanted to be moving."

Wayne might never have gone anywhere if it hadn't been for Dr. John Murry, the psychologist whose therapy group he got into after he had been at Patuxent several years. Wayne said he felt comfortable with Dr. Murry and no longer had any reluctance to talk.

Meeting John Murry, one understands why. A short, stout man with a shock of dark brown hair, Dr. Murry doesn't conform to any preconceived notions one might harbor about psychologists or prison personnel. Easygoing and jocular, he avoids the jargon of his profession, speaks with pragmatic directness, and, most important, he makes up his own mind.

Having reviewed Wayne's files, he had read the buzz words—"brain-damaged," "passive-aggressive," "paranoid personality," "14–6 EEG with spiking," "psychopath"—and he had seen a photograph taken when Wayne first arrived at Patuxent. The boy's face had been puffy, slack, and vacant. His eyes resembled B-Bs embedded in dough, his hair was a nest of loose wires. "Just looking at that," Dr. Murry says, "you could believe almost anything about him—anything except that he had a high-average I.Q. As for the other stuff, I never saw any clinical evidence of brain damage, 14–6, or psychopathic tendencies. A lot of doctors may have been basing their opinions on his crime or his appearance. Now look at this."

Dr. Murry produces another prison photo, this one from 1969. It does not appear to be the same person. It isn't simply that Wayne is older or that his hair is longer and carefully combed. His bone structure, the shape of his nose, lips, and eyes, all seem to have changed, as if a plastic surgeon had sliced away dead tissue and remodeled his features. Although the expression still is not happy—it is, after all, a mug shot—the eyes are focused, the jaw is set. With his mouth shut and his bad teeth hidden, the Wayne in this picture is a healthy, handsome young man.

That was the Wayne Dr. Murry had come to know in therapy —a thoughtful, even-tempered fellow who, in spite of all his muscles, was neither threatening nor aggressive. That was the Wayne who was denied parole every year.

"Something had to give; somebody had to show confidence in him," Dr. Murry says. "Otherwise he'd stay on fourth level the rest of his life. Or maybe lose hope and start sliding backward. He had done everything we asked of him. If we wanted him to keep improving, we had to offer him some incentive. So I finally persuaded the institute to let me take him to my house for 'day leaves.' You know, for somebody who's been behind bars ten years, just getting out of the joint for a few hours is a thrill.

"We went to my place and my wife cooked a pot of spaghetti, and the three of us and the kids ate dinner and watched TV. It was nothing earthshaking. I just wanted to prove to everybody that Wayne could handle it."

When asked whether his wife didn't feel some uneasiness about his bringing home a double murderer, Dr. Murry laughs. "She's used to it. Believe me, we've had a lot worse guys than Wayne over for dinner. I was never worried about him. If you look at the nature of his offense, you'll understand why.

"There were some doctors who seemed to think that to do what he did, he had to be a sociopath. But when you examine the facts and learn about his family, you discover he never struck out blindly against society or against some imagined enemy. He wasn't like those two losers in *In Cold Blood* who killed a family of absolute strangers—who transferred a lifetime of resentments and hostilities away from the people they really hated and laid it on somebody they'd never seen before. With Wayne there was no random violence at all. Two people—his parents—were mistreating him, and when he couldn't cope with it anymore, he killed them. After that, it was over.

"In here, he was never pushy. He didn't pick fights or try to prove he was macho. In my opinion, he had done what he thought he had to do to save himself, and afterward there was a great sense of relief. That's what surprised people. They expected him to show a lot of emotional torment and anguish. But what he had done with the murders was take steps to end his anguish and torment."

Most of Wayne's torment may have ended, but he was still doing time. For nearly a year he took "day leaves" with Dr. Murry. Then on November 19, 1970, the Board of Review granted him work-release status and Wayne was hired as an electrician's apprentice in a local union and began working in and around Baltimore during the day and checking back into Patuxent Institute at night. It was a period of enormous exhilaration for him, but also of enormous pressure. Although Wayne was almost twenty-six, he sometimes felt like a child. The world outside the fence seemed huge, disorderly, and frightening. There was so much that he had never done, so much that he knew nothing about.

For one thing, he was still a virgin. He had never dated a woman, much less had sex with one. Almost immediately, a few friends who had been released before him insisted on fixing him up with a girl. "I did all right," he says. "They kidded me a lot, but I did just fine."

Yet in some ways he was still a virgin and he was secretly grateful that he could retreat to his cell at night and stand in the window, staring through the bars, struggling to comprehend what had happened during the day. He knew now why some guys never wanted to leave the slam, why they always did something— violated parole, committed a petty crime—that would send them back for another stretch.

But not me, Wayne thought. He was determined to get out and stay out.

5

Happy endings, some people say, are all the same. But happiness itself is as varied as the human race; what pleases one man might sadden or embitter another. For Wayne Dresbach, the happy ending was a new beginning. On February 18, 1971, more than ten years after his arrest, he was granted parole.

Of course, it wasn't a clean start. With his record, after his childhood, how could it be? Although he worked steadily, and often held two or three part-time jobs, he couldn't find one that paid well and was permanent. For a while he was a house painter, but after another bout of acute bronchitis, a doctor told him he should try a different line of work before he ruined his already weakened lungs. Interestingly, considering his reputation for being unemotional, he then developed an ulcer, and when he applied for a chauffeur's license, he learned that his old problems with his right eye made that legally impossible. Because he was a felon, he couldn't get into most unions; and because of his bad teeth, he felt shy about any position where he had to deal with the public.

So Wayne bounced from job to job, switching every five or six months, working in pizza parlors and fast-food restaurants, doing day labor at construction sites and installing car radios. Once he was a bouncer in a nightclub; another time, another place, he was a bartender. For the last few years, he's been driving a truck in Baltimore, and he says he likes it.

Generally, he says he likes most things. He displays little or no resentment, even though he has had predictable difficulties with people who have learned about his past. While women don't appear reluctant to date him, he realizes that some of them prefer not to tell their parents or friends. So he stays with people who know him well and "accept me for what I am."

Once out on parole, Wayne tried to reestablish contact with Lee, who had returned to Washington, D.C. after his tour of duty in the Air Force. "I thought enough time had passed and things had changed to where we could have some kind of relationship. I took it on myself to drive down to Washington a few times. He didn't have much to say, but I expected that, at least in the beginning, and I thought we could work through it if we stayed in touch.

"Then one day I went down with a date, and Lee had a girl, too, and after sitting around his place for an hour not saying much, just letting the girls do most of the talking, we decided, what the hell, we'd go to the zoo. The crazy thing was, at that time Lee had become a D.C. cop. Doesn't it just figure—I'd end up a murderer and he'd be a cop?

"Well anyway, we went to the zoo, and Lee parked right in the middle of a crosswalk. Which is ticket time for anybody. So I told him, 'Lee, you're in the crosswalk.' But he said, 'I'm not worried about it,' and he takes his ticket pad and puts it up on the dashboard so any cop that comes along'll see he's a policeman and know not to ticket him.

"No sooner were we on the sidewalk when some guy with his wife and kids stops and says, 'Hey, buddy, you're in the crosswalk. You might get a ticket.' And he said it very nice too. But Lee says, 'Fuck it. I'm not worried about it.' I got pissed off at Lee and told him, 'That's a hell of a way to talk to somebody trying to help you.'

"After that, there wasn't a chance of having fun. Lee and me didn't say another word. Finally my girl, I guess she couldn't stand the tension. She said she wasn't feeling good, so I told Lee we were going to head on back to Baltimore. Suddenly he brings out this camera and asks to take my picture. But I said, 'Not me. I don't like to have my picture taken.' That ripped it. Now everybody was mad. We left before it got worse.

"On the way back, my girl started asking questions. You see, she didn't really know anything about what I done. So she was carrying on, asking why Lee treated me like that and saying, 'What the hell kind of brother is he?' What could I tell her? Finally, I just broke down and cried all the way to Baltimore. She must have thought I was nuts.

"Every once in a while I still went down to visit Lee, but it was always the same. I tried to talk, I tried to make conversation, but he never met me halfway. He'd let his girl do all the talking. I'm sure she knew what was going on. She was very nice and personable. But what could she do? That's a hell of a thing, if you ask me, when a man makes his girl take up the slack for him.

"He didn't even invite me to his wedding. I showed up one day and found out he had married the girl. He was kind of embarrassed and handed me this bullshit about wanting to ask me, but not knowing where I was, not knowing how to get in touch with me. But Mom, she had my address and phone number. He could have asked her."

After that Wayne decided not to force himself on Lee. He had a more urgent problem. His teeth were causing him serious trouble; the pain was constant now, and after every meal he had to spit out chips of enamel. Finally a dentist told him he had to have them all pulled and replaced by upper and lower plates. The bill, he estimated, would be a thousand dollars.

Since Wayne had neither the cash nor the credit rating to borrow money, he postponed the operation and tried to live with the pain. But before long he couldn't sleep and couldn't work. The dentist said if he didn't do something soon, there would be severe damage to his gums, and the bill would mount.

"So I swallowed my pride," Wayne says, "and drove down to try to borrow the money from Lee. He had a townhouse over in Virginia, and I knocked on the door and a stranger answered it. That's how I learned Lee and his wife had moved. He'd resigned from the police force and moved somewhere to the Midwest to take a job as a tennis pro at a country club. There was no forwarding address, no phone number. I don't know where he went. I never heard from him again. To this day I have no idea where he is."

Autumn 1978

With considerable difficulty, after half a dozen long-distance telephone calls, I located Lee in the town where he and his wife had opened a tennis shop. Although I had not seen him in years and although several people warned me he would be upset if I raised the subject of his parents' deaths, I expected to have little trouble talking to him. After all, we had lived in the same house as brothers and, despite the difference in our ages, I felt we had been close—in some ways closer than I had ever been with my real brothers, Pat and Kris.

As I've said, I also shared a deep sense of kinship with Wayne. But there was always something slightly abstract and, on my part, literary about our relationship. Visiting him in prison a few hours every month, I'm afraid I often viewed him more as a symbol than as a person, more as an extension of some secret part of myself than as himself. He seemed to me an "archetypal character"; he was that "marginal man, that alienated figure," whom my literature professors described as moving inexorably through the bleak landscape of the twentieth century. Once, in an excess of sophomoric existentialism, I went so far as to send Wayne a Christmas card with a bizarre season's greeting. Paraphrasing Camus, I wrote that all men are prisoners, and life is merely a matter of deciding what to do in the limited space and time which fate has allotted to us. Fortunately he was too kind to point out what an ass I was.

Lee certainly wouldn't have let me get away with that. We let each other get away with damn little, and there were no literary allusions in our conversations. Like many adolescents, we communicated with wisecracks, belittling remarks, personal digs, pitiless mockery. This was the way I dealt with all my closest friends; as I remember it, this constant razzing, this playful nipping at the flanks, was the way most boys expressed affection. When they were angry, they went for the jugular vein.

With Lee and me it never came to that. We never really

fought, never really had a serious conversation. We played basketball, we waterskied; in the parlance of that day, we "goofed off"
together, going to ballgames and movies, doing a running,
irreverent commentary whenever we watched television. Since I
didn't have a car, he usually subjected me to a charade of
grumpiness and hours of teasing, then loaned me his. For a while
we worked in the same Safeway grocery store, he as a bag boy, I
as a cashier, he to make spending money, I to pay my college
tuition.

After he had been living in our house awhile, he converted to
Catholicism, and on Sundays we went to Mass together. When
he transferred to Dematha, my high school alma mater, I gave
him my most prized possession—the red, white, and blue jacket I
had been awarded for sitting on the bench while my teammates
won the Catholic League basketball championship.

When I think of Lee now, I imagine him in his most characteristic pose. No, not a pose. In my memory he is never static. He
is on water skis and he is moving full speed, his compact, perpetually tan body coiled, his sunbleached hair slicked back by the
wind, his eyes narrowed against the salt spray. He is swinging
wide at the end of a yellow nylon tow rope, gathering speed, leaning sideways at an acute angle. Then he reverses directions,
swings back, and is suddenly airborne, leaping the wake in a sup-
ple explosion of muscle in which grace and aggression are mixed.

So when I found Lee at last and called him long-distance, I anticipated no problems which I couldn't overcome if I explained
things carefully and talked to him openly. Already I had had
some interviews and come into possession of information which
seriously troubled me, and I intended to give Lee every opportunity to tell his side.

But the moment I mentioned I was doing a book, he turned
irritable, uncooperative, insulting. He wanted to know why I was
stirring things up after all these years. Was it money? How much
was I being paid? How much was Wayne getting? Did I think
it was right that he should profit by his crime? He reminded me
Wayne had murdered two people and had also ruined a lot of
lives. Shirley's father, Arthur Shaffer, had still not recovered.

"You mean he's alive?" I asked. "He must be nearly a hundred."

Lee said Shaffer was in his late nineties and begged me not to go to Kansas and bother him. He warned that any questions about Shirley and the murders were liable to kill his grandfather.

I was more than willing to be reasonable. I didn't want to hurt anyone, especially not an old and infirm man. But I intended to finish what I had started. Nothing could dissuade me from that.

Lee flatly refused to be a part of any book about his brother.

Trying to calm him, I explained that he would be a part of it whether he cooperated with me or not. He had given a police deposition, he had talked to newspaper reporters, he had testified against his brother at the trial, his name and his testimony were contained in dozens of public documents. I could not very well re-create the case and leave him out.

Why did I have to re-create the case? he hotly demanded.

I told him that for Wayne's sake it was time the full story, the whole truth, came out. I asked him to think it over, discuss it with his wife, and talk to a lawyer. I was sure that if he did, he would agree that he should present his point of view. Though he swore he wouldn't change his mind, I said I'd call him back.

The call was delayed more than a month. I cannot say what Lee was doing during that time, but I did what I had urged him to do. I thought things over. Returning to the most rudimentary questions, I tried to reassess my motives. I knew money wasn't at the root of my interest; having taken an unpaid leave of absence from teaching, I was living on a small advance which I had shared with Wayne so he could pay his bills.

Although some people had warned me that a book might hurt Wayne, I finally had to accept what he said; he was the best judge of his interests and he wanted the story told. But in my eagerness to set the public record straight, in my willingness to help him voice his most secret memories and emotions, would I hurt someone else?

All that fall I discussed the question with my wife, my editor, my agent, several lawyers, a priest, then a psychologist. I considered backing out altogether; there were other books, easier books, I could write. Then I considered doing the book, but eliminating Lee, just leaving a blank where he should have been. But this, I thought, was another cowardly evasion. I was reverting to fiction, further from the truth than the trial had been; I was erecting a barrier every bit as impenetrable as the one the Dresbachs had raised around their private lives; I was becoming as cautious and circumspect as all those people I had criticized for not stepping forward to save Wayne; in effect, I was saying I would leave him a prisoner of his stunted and tongue-tied life rather than cause anyone, especially myself, any discomfort. This I would not do.

At last, I called Lee again. This time, it wasn't long-distance. I had traveled a thousand miles, found his business, and debated whether to barge in on him. But since I had always liked Lee and still did, and since I knew that what I had to ask him should not be said in front of his wife, much less his customers, I wanted to set up an appointment.

We never got that far. On the phone he was more adamant than ever. He said he knew I could use public documents and his trial testimony, but he threatened to sue me if I went beyond that.

Patiently, and with as much urgency as I could muster, I stressed that he was doing himself a disservice. Sometimes the public record didn't put him in a very flattering light. It would be to his advantage, I said, to clarify his past statements, correct what might be mis-impressions, and respond to the comments some people had made. But Lee refused to talk.

Still, I tried. I told him I believed it was as important to him as it was to Wayne to fill in the blank spots and discuss the events which had led up to the morning of January 7, 1961.

"It's nobody's business," Lee said.

"It's Wayne's business. He's already suffered from all the rumors and gossip. He thinks it's time to tell the story straight."

"Look, he shit in his bed. Now let him lie in it."

"Is that how you want me to quote you?" I asked.

"Go ahead. I don't care. I'll just deny I said it."

We stayed on the line a few minutes longer, but I realized the connection had been cut and I could not have felt much worse if a blood relative of mine had died.

After

Unable to find Lee, Wayne appealed to Father Dawson, who had frequently helped out with loans and gifts. Together they went to a finance office and, with Father Dawson co-signing, they managed to borrow enough money to pay for Wayne's false teeth.

"How could I refuse him?" Father Dawson asks. "Especially after his own brother let him down. I think one of the most heartbreaking things is that Wayne stayed so loyal to Lee all those years. You know, when he was at Patuxent he had to submit a list of ten people—that was the limit—who could visit and write him. And even though he rarely saw, or heard from, Lee, he kept his name on that list the whole time. He wouldn't drop him and he never criticized or blamed him the way he might have.

"Well, that's Wayne for you." Sitting in the office of his large, comfortable house on the outskirts of Baltimore, Father Dawson leans back in the chair. He has put on weight and wears glasses now. As he readily acknowledges, an inheritance from his wife's family has "allowed us to change our life-style." But far from being complacent, he is still a man of powerful commitments, particularly where Wayne is concerned. "He's a remarkable person. He's been through awful things all his life, and yet his spirits are high and he never despairs. When you realize the kind of childhood he had, you have to wonder where his goodness and decency come from. Most kids take their key from their parents. Good or bad, they follow the example set for them. But Wayne's character seems to have formed as a direct reaction against the Dresbachs. That's one of the things I admire most about him. He refused to live the way they did.

"Now, there's no denying what he did was hideous. But in light of what I found out later, his actions made sense. He had tried to escape many times and was always dragged back to his parents. What recourse did he have? He could have lost his mind and slipped into psychosis. He could have committed suicide. Or he could destroy the people who were destroying him. When you look at it like that, there was a logic to what he did. He made the best choice possible under terrible circumstances."

Fully aware of what he was saying—he had virtually justified murder—and reminded of how heretical this might sound coming from an Episcopalian priest, Father Dawson adds, "I hope I'm not misunderstood. You see, I recognized myself in Wayne. I felt as though the whole thing had happened to me personally and I couldn't let it drop. He was a soul—no, not just a soul—a human being in need, and I had to reach out to him."

In retrospect, however, Father Dawson acknowledges that it was never a one-way relationship. Much as he helped Wayne, he believes Wayne may have helped him even more by the example of his endurance and courage. In the end, the boy opened for the priest depths of experience he would never have had otherwise; and whatever Wayne might have lacked in formal education or social graces, he made up for with an elemental kindness and common sense.

"At first I thought his values might be a pretense," Father Dawson says, "a means of impressing the psychologists at Patuxent Institute and getting an early release. But over the years I saw he was consistent. He held to what he believed. He was never a Christian in any formal sense. He still hasn't been baptized, but he's a decent man.

"I hesitate to say this. I've always disliked the current fascination with antiheroes; I feel they're a poor role model for young people. But there's no getting around it. There was something heroic about Wayne. Heroic in light of the alternatives."

Literary comparisons occur to Father Dawson. Wayne might have been a character from a Dostoevsky novel. But unlike Raskolnikov, who in *Crime and Punishment* committed a gratuitous murder for theoretical reasons, Wayne committed a crime that was necessary to save himself.

"I don't mean to imply that there isn't a lot of unfinished business," Father Dawson says. "Wayne still hasn't found his place yet. The most troubling thing is he doesn't have a very good image of himself or of his own uniqueness and value. What I long for is some way for him to share his experience with other people. He's had a profoundly moving pilgrimage, and he deserves respect for the great distance he has covered."

Now

Like most of us, Wayne does not see himself as others do. Certainly he would never regard himself as a hero or a pilgrim. He's a working man, one who has a hard time sleeping. It is rare for him to enjoy a full night's rest, and most mornings he wakes long before daybreak, troubled by dreams that he is back in jail. As if to prove he's not, he immediately starts moving. He gets up, dresses hurriedly, and goes out to an all-night diner where he drinks coffee and reads the newspaper until it's time for work.

Staying busy, trying not to dwell on the past, has become for him an around-the-clock occupation, and fortunately he is blessed with a phenomenal constitution and a ravenous curiosity. Recently he taught himself to read Braille and is now attempting to devise a new method of teaching it to children. After work he helps coach a Little League baseball team and on the weekend he often visits the Dunns or Father Dawson. One of these days, he promises, he is going to buy a new car and drive to every state in the Union. But for now he spends most of his time driving a truck, working sixty hours a week to make ends meet.

Physically, he appears to have undergone another metamorphosis. Since his parole, he has lost more than twenty pounds, and his muscles lack the sharp definition they once had. Because of his job, he doesn't have a chance to work out every day and, ironically, he can't afford to eat as much, or as well, as he ate in prison.

His face has changed, too. He's older, his wheat-colored hair has thinned, and his false teeth have reshaped his mouth. He is never reluctant to smile now, and it's not just because of the new teeth. As he explains, he has a lot more reason to be happy than ever before.

As for his successful adjustment to life on the outside, he makes no great claims. "I didn't aspire to be a star or anything. But I'm not back in the joint, am I? That's all I care about."

Like many Americans, Wayne has strong opinions about capital punishment. "After ten years in jail, if they had come to me before I was released and said, 'Well, Wayne, sorry, son. They changed the law and you gotta hop in the chair and get the big shot,' I'd have said, 'Okay. Lead me to it.' I can relate to a guy like Gary Gilmore. Because I still think what I done was so bad that I should have to pay more. I don't think ten years is enough. Not for me, anyway.

"But now, seven years later, seventeen years after I did it, I know I'm still paying. Like I said, I never go to bed without remembering what I done, and there's never a day I wake up that it's not there waiting for me. Everybody pays one way or the other if they have a conscience. And I believe everybody has a conscience, small as it may be.

"Capital punishment," he repeats, shaking his head. "I don't know; I suppose if I had a wife and somebody raped or killed her, the first thought I'd have is they should die in the electric chair. But then you think about it for a while and you think wait a minute, I was in the position where I could have gotten it and I didn't. How do you decide who gets it and who doesn't? If you give it to one, how can you spare anybody? Or if you decide one killer doesn't deserve it, how can you turn around and say somebody else does? You can't do that. At least, I couldn't do the condemning. I'm just glad I didn't get it—although there were times when it seemed that might have been better than what I had to live with.

"I thought about killing myself, you know. I thought about it a lot. But I decided, what good would it do? It wouldn't change what I done.

"It reminds me of the question every psychiatrist asked in therapy. 'If you had it to do all over again, what would you do?' I used to say I'd have made a better effort to get along with my parents. Or I'd have run away and stayed away. I mean really hide. Or I'd have told somebody what was happening at home. But after a while I realized that's a stupid question, because to get back to what they call reality, you can't do anything over again.

"The psychiatrists used to say, 'Yeah, Wayne, but what we want to know is what you'll do the next time.' But you can't change things. There is no next time. How could there ever be a

time like the one I had with my parents? I'm a man now, not a
scared little kid. Nobody could do to me what they did back
then. And if anybody tried, I wouldn't have to kill them. I'd just
walk away.

"No, there's never going to be a next time for me. This is it,
right here. I did what I did. I'm not going to get to relive my
childhood a different way. I just have to go on living and, like I
say, I pay every day."